Library of
Davidson College

THE DEFENCE OF WHITE POWER

The Defence of White Power

South African Foreign Policy under Pressure

Robert Scott Jaster

Foreword by Helen Kitchen

St. Martin's Press   New York

© International Institute for Strategic Studies, 1989

All rights reserved. For information, write:
Scholarly and Reference Division,
St. Martin's Press, Inc., 175 Fifth Avenue, New York, N.Y. 10010

First published in the United States of America in 1989

Printed in the United Kingdom

ISBN 0-312-02829-6

Library of Congress Cataloging-in-Publication Data
Jaster, Robert S.
The defence of white power: South Africa's foreign policy under pressure/Robert Scott Jaster.
p. cm.
Bibliography: p.
Includes index.
ISBN 0-312-02829-6: $39.95 (est.)
1. South Africa—Foreign relations—1978– I. Title.
DT779.952.J37 1989
327.68—dc19   88-31413
                                                           CIP

To the memory of Jonathan Alford,
valued friend and colleague

Contents

Foreword by Helen Kitchen ix
Acknowledgements xii
Introduction: South African Foreign Policy in Context xiii
Map of Southern Africa xvii

PART I PERSPECTIVES

1 The Imprint of Afrikaner Experience 3

2 Perceptions of South Africa's International Role 8
  A Bridge to Black Africa 9
  A Military Ally 12

PART II THE MAKING OF FOREIGN POLICY

3 Decision-Making and the Foreign Policy Process 19
  The Policy Environment 19
  Parliament and the NP 21
  Contrasting Leaders: Vorster and Botha 24
  Competing Bureaucracies 31
  The State Security Council (SSC) 35
  Critique of the Process 39

4 Foreign Policy in Defence of Apartheid 42
  Apartheid under Attack 42
  Apartheid and National Security 44

PART III SHIFTING FOREIGN POLICY STRATEGIES

5 Deteriorating Security and Policy Reappraisal (1974–8) 51
  Détente and Vorster's Rhodesian Initiative 51
  Seeking a Settlement in Namibia 59
  Intervention in Angola, 1975–6 68

6 Growing Militancy and Isolation under P. W. Botha since 1978 79
  The Ascendancy of a Hawk 79
  The 'Constellation' Initiative and the Fall of Rhodesia 82
  Genesis of the New Militancy 88

Contents

7	**Namibia Policy and the War in Angola**	**92**
	The Shifting War Strategy	92
	Results of the War Strategy	101
	Botha's UN Diplomacy	104
	The Stalled Game-Plan inside Namibia	108
	The Reagan Factor	111
	Seeking Alternative Solutions	115
8	**Regional Destabilization**	**119**
	SADF Raids in Neighbouring States	119
	Renamo and other Proxy Forces	124
	Railway Diplomacy	132
	SADF Misadventures	135
	Assessing Destabilization	138

PART IV DETERIORATING RELATIONS WITH THE WEST

9	**Foreign Policy Responses to the West**	**143**
	Fading Hopes for Closer Ties	143
	Diplomacy under Pressure	146
	Seeking Allies Elsewhere	154
10	**Pretoria's Nuclear Diplomacy**	**159**
	Perspective	159
	The Kalahari Contretemps	161
	Growing Nuclear Capability	164
	The Question of Nuclear Targets	168
	Assessing South Africa's Nuclear Diplomacy	171

Epilogue	**173**
A Regime under Siege	173
Foreign Policy Imperatives and Constraints	174
The Changing Foreign Policy Environment	177
Alternative Scenarios	179

Notes and References	183
Index	198

Foreword

The immediately visible actions resulting from South African foreign policy decisions (the on-again-off-again declarations of willingness to negotiate on Namibia's future, raids against alleged external ANC bases, overt or covert support of 'contra' military operations in the region, periodic disciplinary slowdowns on transport routes vital to landlocked neighbours, support or blockage of a coup d'état attempt here and there, moves in the area of nuclear diplomacy) receive regular but generally disjunctive coverage in the international media. The reader is informed of such specifics as the target of a raid, the conflicting casualty counts, the text of a communiqué, and perhaps the identity of a captured South African commando. But seldom do news accounts, or even more structured academic analyses, view Pretoria's foreign policy initiatives or reactions in a broad historical, cultural, political and regional context.

Robert Jaster's book is of lasting importance because of the contribution it makes toward filling this contextual void. Drawing on dozens of interviews with South African and regional actors at all levels, as well as many other sources, he traces the evolution of Afrikaner political culture and the effect on leadership choices and foreign policy; the complex and contradictory elements of South Africa's economic interests in the region; Pretoria's love–hate relationship with the West; the extent of military/civilian/bureaucracy rivalries within the government and the relationship of these rivalries to the sometimes baffling contradictions in foreign policy developments; and the effect on South African foreign policy of failures to understand and sort out the political anomalies in neighbouring states.

In addition to providing an overview, Jaster also fills in some crucial gaps in the historical record. He details, for example, the often-rumoured but never fully reported sabotage by a senior South African intelligence official of a planned SADF operation in Mozambique in the mid-1970s. In tracing the incremental and uncoordinated steps by which South Africa entered the Angolan conflict in 1975–6 (including SADF decision-making details usually only available to insiders), he provides the reader with essential background for analysing Pretoria's current (1987–8) operations in Angola.

The book was completed as signals of some possibly significant changes in South African relations (or, at least, communications) with the Soviet Union began to emerge in early 1988. Tucked away in various sections are details on some historical antecedents for such a development. One example is the analysis of South Africa's growing frustration with perceived Western betrayal (e.g. the US decision to backpedal out of Angola in 1975). The author also calls our attention to unresolved differences within the white community over the country's basic identity – whether it is and always will be a 'part of the West', is a unique but nevertheless genuine 'part of Africa', or should focus instead on a posture of 'South Africa for itself'.

Whether as a result of strategic planning or coincidence, the publication of this cogent examination of the various dimensions of South African foreign policy could not be better timed. Various initiatives based on differing assumptions – the 'contact group' marathon, the Reagan Administration's 'constructive engagement' policy, the Commonwealth Eminent Persons Group exercise, the Comprehensive Anti-Apartheid Act enacted by the US Congress in 1986, the Free South Africa Movement's disinvestment campaign – have failed to move the government of P. W. Botha closer to the negotiating table at home or toward serious reconsideration of its 'Pax Pretoriana' regional posture. Although the situation within South Africa appears to be one of stalemate for the foreseeable future, the government's regional policy will necessarily be up for review if Gorbachev's interest in seeking political solutions to military conflicts in other parts of the world extends to southern Africa. Even now, governments (or at least individuals within governments) in the region are re-evaluating both domestic and external policies. And with a new President due to take over the reins of government in the USA in 1989, yet another assessment of US policy options in relation to South Africa and the region is just over the horizon.

Perhaps the two major basic truths that come through all the complexities dissected in this book are that (1) the key to improving South Africa's foreign relations is not nimble diplomacy but a sea-change in the international community's perception of this divided nation's domestic policies, and (2) southern Africa's conflicts are not externally generated offshoots of larger conflicts elsewhere, but are rooted in problems that are national and regional. With these guidelines, and the many others provided in Jaster's research, the reader will not only have a fuller sense of what has been going on in southern Africa in recent decades but will be better prepared to understand tomorrow's headlines.

HELEN KITCHEN
Director of African Studies
Center for Strategic and International Studies
Washington, DC

Acknowledgements

I am indebted to the International Institute for Strategic Studies (IISS) and a grant from the Rockefeller Foundation for making possible the research and interviews that culminated in this study. I am also indebted to the civil and military officials, past and present, in South Africa, the Front Line states, the US and the UN for their time, their trust and their candour in discussing various aspects of South African foreign policy with me. Since all but a few of those discussions were conducted on a non-attributable basis, the sources have necessarily been identified only in general terms.

Helen Kitchen of the Center for Strategic and International Studies (CSIS) has been generous in responding to my requests for information. She and Frank Pabian of Lawrence Livermore National Laboratory also provided insightful comments on parts of the manuscript. The IISS librarians have been diligent in acquiring hard-to-find books and documents.

I am particularly indebted to my wife, Shirley, for her understanding and support, and for insulating me from many of the obligations and demands of the outside world during these past months of intensive writing.

ROBERT S. JASTER

Introduction: South African Foreign Policy in Context

South Africa is a third-rank power with little influence in world affairs and only a negligible role in great power politics. Neither the US nor the USSR considers South Africa to be of vital strategic significance.

South Africa's population is in the order of 30 million, about the same as Argentina's. Its 1986 GDP of $64 billion was on a par with those of Argentina and Austria; but its per capita GNP of around $2000 places South Africa among the poorer half of the world's countries, along with Argentina ($2000), and well below the more industrialized countries like Austria ($9000).

As befits a small state on the periphery of global events, South Africa has conducted a foreign policy that is essentially reactive and defensive. Growing world condemnation of its domestic race policies and of its administration of Namibia over the past 40 years has led successive South African governments to seek the protection of a Western defence alliance, and to try to avoid being isolated internationally. Within the region South Africa has used its superior economic and military power to force neighbouring states to curtail guerrilla activities aimed at the Republic of South Africa (RSA), and to agree to *de facto* or *de jure* mutual security arrangements with Pretoria.

Given South Africa's remoteness from the regions and issues of major strategic concern, why should its foreign policy be of significance to the outside world? First, its foreign policy is a major pillar supporting the system of white minority rule. Indeed, the defence of apartheid has been the single, overarching function of South African foreign policy. As the armed struggle between the regime and its opponents has intensified, nearby states have increasingly been drawn into that conflict and have suffered from its military and economic spill-over. The growing challenge to white minority rule is also having an impact in the West, where popular feeling against the Pretoria regime has forced national governments to face some difficult policy decisions on South Africa which they were able to avoid or postpone in the past.

Furthermore, South Africa is by far the single dominant power in southern Africa, both economically and militarily. Its actions therefore have a profound effect on the rest of the sub-region, which comprises eight states spread in a broad band from Angola on the Atlantic to Mozambique on the Indian Ocean (Angola, Botswana, Lesotho, Malawi, Mozambique, Swaziland, Zambia and Zimbabwe). Six of these states are members of the Commonwealth, and the other two have extensive political and military links with communist states. Thus South African military and economic moves against neighbouring countries have caused problems for the Western powers, and have helped ensure that the USSR and Cuba exert a continuing military presence in the region. Indeed some of the region's sputtering little wars, in which South Africa plays the dominant role, have at least the potential to flare into larger conflicts involving confrontation between the superpowers.

South Africa's leaders are well aware of these risks. At some point they may judge it to their advantage to try to provoke just such a confrontation. Far from accepting South Africa's position as a peripheral, third-rate power, successive South African administrations have made their own assessments of global strategic trends, and have tried to chart a foreign policy course that would be compatible with their current global assessment. Foreign and defence policies are thus formulated in response to local events and to the leadership's world view at the time, flawed though that might be. Within that general framework foreign policy has been perceived as an issue of ultimate survival: survival of the regime, and of white minority rule, in a hostile and increasingly threatening environment at home and abroad.

Indeed, South Africa's foreign policy has been essentially a search – a futile and often misdirected search – for security. Most notable has been the continuing search for allies and clients: powerful Western allies who might be persuaded to place South Africa under the Western nuclear umbrella; fellow isolated states, particularly those like Israel and Taiwan, which could provide needed military hardware and technology; and docile and dependent neighbours who might be pressured into accepting Pretoria's definition of the threat to regional security and joining South Africa in regional defence arrangements. Pretoria's leaders have been willing to welcome as an ally any state which would support their struggle against an alleged Moscow-directed external threat, and which would accept, or at least not challenge, their system of white minority rule.

This study analyses South African foreign policy as primarily the political leadership's response to domestic political imperatives and to the officially perceived threat of a 'total onslaught' – a threat which has been elevated into an ideology of survival. In South Africa, where a preponderance of political power as well as the broad trust of the electorate are vested in the leader of the ruling National Party (NP) as State President (formerly Prime Minister), his views and personality have a decisive impact on the conduct of foreign policy. This has been particularly marked in the administration of P. W. Botha, a dominant personality who has strong views on foreign policy and who, as State President, exercises considerably more formal power than previous South African prime ministers. Yet foreign policy under Botha, as under the preceding Vorster government, has been subject to intense bureaucratic conflict which has sometimes left the policy in serious disarray. Growing pressures on the regime from within and without have raised the foreign policy stakes and intensified the bureaucratic infighting.

Other than as the aftermath of military defeat or violent revolution, or of a sudden and unexpected shift in the external political environment, a country's foreign policy seldom undergoes abrupt, dramatic change. Even then the realities of geography, economics and national history usually reassert themselves. A nation's foreign policy thus tends to be marked more by continuity than change; therefore to single out any particular year as a turning-point in its foreign policy is necessarily subjective and somewhat arbitrary.

There are none the less valid reasons for selecting the year 1975 as a major watershed in South African foreign policy. Most important, of course, was the Portuguese withdrawal from Angola and Mozambique and the profound shift it brought in the regional balance of power. In June 1975 Mozambique gained its independence under the guerrilla leader, Samora Machel, a self-declared Marxist who immediately allowed Rhodesian guerrillas sanctuary from which they could open the fateful second front against the Smith regime. The Portuguese withdrawal from Angola in 1975 led to open warfare among the three guerrilla movements contending for power there, each with the backing of one or more outside states. By mid-1975 ripples from the chaos and civil war in Angola had spread to the border of Namibia. Alarmed by the events in Angola, and seeing an opportunity to influence political developments there, South Africa's military chiefs prevailed on the Vorster government to let them intervene. By November South African forces and their guerrilla allies had penetrated deep into Angola in a major campaign to prevent a victory by the Soviet- and Cuban-backed MPLA.

The decision to invade Angola is important on two major counts. It brought an abrupt end to Vorster's much-heralded *détente* initiative in the region, and it marked the start of the military's ascendancy in foreign policy. South Africa's Angolan venture was a débâcle, both politically and militarily. But its failure was blamed not on the military or the then Defence Minister, P. W. Botha, who had urged intervention on Vorster; rather it was charged to political indecision and the collapse of US and African support.

In sum 1975 saw a dramatic change in the long-standing power-balance in the region, and the beginning of a major shift in South African foreign policy, largely – but not entirely – in response to the new regional reality. Events of the next several years helped give final shape to the new policy, which emerged fully under the Botha Administration. The new policy has been one of blatant belligerency and aggression towards neighbouring states, particularly those suspected of harbouring guerrillas operating against South Africa. It has also been a policy of defiance towards the West, and subordination of diplomacy to the twin imperatives of domestic politics and white minority rule. Finally, the policy has achieved enough success to vindicate it in the eyes of the leaders, even though its long-term effects will pose problems for the West, and may be disastrous for South Africa as well as the region.

The analytical focus of this study is the rapidly changing external environment faced by South Africa's leaders after 1974, and their foreign policy responses to it.

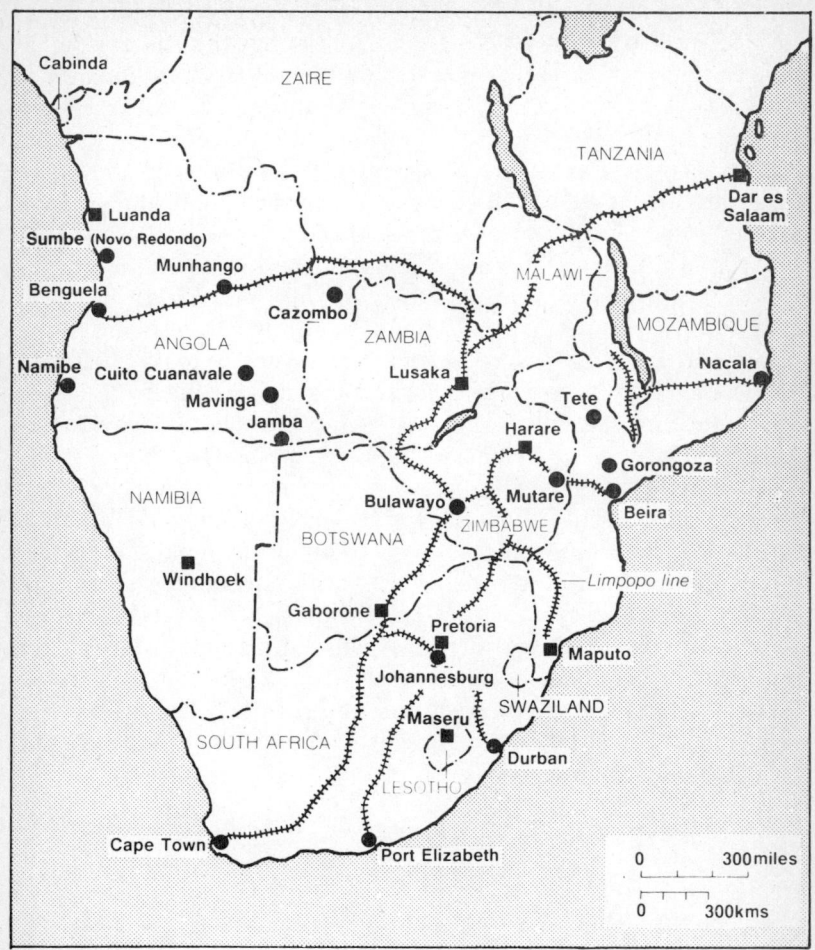

Southern Africa

Part I
Perspectives

1 The Imprint of Afrikaner Experience

When Afrikaner nationalists came to power with the electoral victory of the National Party (NP) in 1948, the new national leaders brought with them a unique background: a background of shared historical and cultural experience, a strong ethnic identity and a shared ignorance of the outside world.

This is not surprising. The settlers from Europe who emigrated to the Cape Colony during the seventeenth and eighteenth centuries were white, Protestant, North European and mostly Dutch, which was the common language in the Colony. Their geographic isolation during the next 200 years was accompanied by cultural insulation from the European mainstream:

> In the course of the eighteenth century, while the rest of the Western world was profoundly affected by the secular and universalistic ethos of the Enlightenment, swept by the rising liberal and democratic tide of the 'Atlantic Revolution', and finally transformed by the vast social changes attendant on the Industrial Revolution, Trekboer society took shape in the vast open spaces of the Cape interior quite removed from all these influences.[1]

Indeed, by the time Britain seized control of the Cape Colony at the end of the eighteenth century, the Trekboers – young landless settlers with no economic prospects in the settled Cape Town community – had fanned out across the Cape and established isolated farmsteads as far as 500 miles from Cape Town; by then the settlers recognized themselves as members of a distinct ethnic group, and referred to themselves as 'Afrikaners'.[2]

In their isolation the Afrikaners developed the qualities needed for survival on a remote and harsh frontier. High among these were independence, self-sufficiency and resistance to outside interference. The farther the Afrikaners penetrated into the interior and distanced themselves from colonial administration and protection, the more important these qualities became, particularly as the trekkers came into armed conflict with various African peoples over land, water and cattle. To prevail over hostile tribes – some of which fielded impressive armies – and an often hostile physical environment, the

Afrikaners chose strong, authoritarian leaders. The settlers soon dominated many local black groups, from among whom they acquired slaves and farm-labourers.[3] Although racial segregation was *not* a feature of frontier life, the settlers assumed and insisted upon white supremacy from the beginning.[4]

The British conquest of the Cape, and its subsequent abolition of both slavery and the legal distinctions between races in the 1830s, led to a second Afrikaner migration: the famous Great Trek out of the Colony to areas beyond the reach of British administration.[5] The British takeover thus reinforced Afrikaner frontier attitudes and added another: xenophobia. Although the Afrikaners established independent Boer republics in Natal, the Transvaal and the Orange Free State, their independence was brief.

By the 1880s the recent discovery of gold was bringing a flood of new immigrants to South Africa, and the Afrikaners' hopes of pursuing their own life-style and their own 'native' policy were dashed. Conflicts between Britain and the Afrikaner republics over native policy, Anglicization of the administrative service, British territorial annexations and political rights for the new, mostly English-speaking, immigrants erupted into open warfare, culminating in the Anglo-Boer War (1899–1902). The war brought not only military defeat, but the social and economic collapse of the Afrikaner people.

That war, and the continued political and economic subjugation of the Boers in its aftermath, led to a great surge of Afrikaner nationalism. Over the next 40 years, leaders of the Afrikaner people created a network of interlocking organizations through which the *volk* were mobilized in a far-reaching national revival. Political parties and an array of economic self-help programmes devoted their energies to the practical aspects of Afrikaner recovery. Afrikaner intellectuals began drawing on the past to create myths of the Afrikaners' unique ethnic attributes which had enabled them to survive as a people. Hannah Arendt describes this sort of 'tribal nationalism' as one which:

> always insists that its own people is surrounded by 'a world of enemies', 'one against all'; that a fundamental difference exists between this people and all others. It claims its people to be unique, individual, incompatible with all others, and denies theoretically the very possibility of a common mankind long before it is used to destroy the humanity of man.[6]

The Afrikaner myth-makers did, in fact, emphasize Afrikaner unity and exclusivism: only by banding together as a *volk* and making no concessions to foreign pressures or to the barbarians, it was argued, had they been able to prevail over the forces of evil arrayed against them.

By the 1940s Afrikaner political leaders had gone even further, ascribing to the *volk* a unique and divinely-inspired civilizing mission:

> It is through the will of God that the Afrikaner people exists at all. In His wisdom He determined that on the southern point of Africa, the dark continent, a People should be born who would be the bearer of Christian culture and civilization. . . . God at the same time prevented the swamping of the young Afrikaner People in the sea of barbarianism.[7]

It was a short step from crediting the Afrikaner people with the divine mission of preserving white Christian civilization to claiming that the NP and its policy of apartheid were the best way to assure the future survival of the *volk*.

During the early years of national revival Afrikaner political leaders identified a danger to the *volk* from a new source: communism. A major revolt by Afrikaner miners in 1922 threatened to split the Afrikaans community along class lines. This, in itself, put the fragile Afrikaner national movement in serious jeopardy. Adding to its leaders' alarm was the involvement of a small group of militant communists, who for a time played a minor but vocal leadership role in the strike. The Smuts government chose to portray the white miners' revolt as 'a foreign-led aberration, rather than the product of genuine indigenous tensions'.[8] There was also concern because the South African Communist Party (SACP), which had been founded only the year before the strike, soon attempted to organize black trade unions and worker education courses, though with scant success.[9]

In the 1950s the emerging black resistance to apartheid found South African communists prominent among its white supporters. Particularly alarming to the *volk* was the communists' unequivocal advocacy of racial equality, 'a thrust at the very heart of [the Afrikaner's] ethnic existence'.[10] Successive NP governments since 1948 have tapped this deep vein of fear among the *volk* to persuade the Afrikaner electorate that South Africa's racial troubles and pariah status are due not to the policy of apartheid but rather to a Moscow-orchestrated campaign designed to destroy the existing social and political structure, and to place the country's riches under communist control. This notion has, of course, been easier to sell since the accession of self-declared Marxist regimes in Angola and Mozambique, and their use as sanctuary by guerrillas operating against South Africa and Namibia. Indeed, as will be discussed later, the myth of a communist 'total onslaught' is one which South Africa's leaders themselves have accepted and upon which defence policy has been based.

These, then, are the major historical and cultural experiences that have informed the Afrikaner community and shaped the world views and political style of its leaders. The actual impact of these experiences on South African foreign policy will be brought out in subsequent chapters. It is possible, of course, to lay too much stress on 'the Afrikaner character' as a determinant of policy actions, and to ignore the constraints and imperatives that would have affected the foreign policy of *any* white South African rulers, whether Afrikaans or English-speaking. Yet no country's foreign policy can be understood outside the context of its ruling group and that group's particular values and attitudes. This is more the case in South Africa, where the Afrikaners have held political dominance for 40 years, with close to a two-thirds parliamentary majority most of that time; where the ruling party has been infused by an ideology of ethnic survival and has, until recently, dedicated itself to carrying out an extreme and unique programme of racial subjugation in nominal pursuit of that ideological goal.

Indeed, Afrikaner political leaders frequently have cited the lessons of their tribal experience as a basis for particular policy positions. Thus the Afrikaners have survived, it is asserted, not through accommodation and concession in the face of outside pressure, but by being defiant and unyielding. That this is a shared value among Afrikaners is shown by their selection of strong-willed, authoritarian individuals as their national leaders. While these leaders have evoked reassuring images of toughness and strength, the other side of such personalities is often an inability to see, let alone internalize, opposing points of view. Discussion, particularly with an outsider, is perceived not as a dialogue leading to better mutual understanding, but as an occasion to enlighten the other person, to set him straight. This same quality has contributed to South African disappointment and frustration in foreign relations when other governments have failed to react as expected by Pretoria, or have failed to appreciate or understand a particular South African move.

The totality of the Afrikaner experience has led to distinctive Afrikaner views of South Africa's regional and global roles. It has sometimes led to distorted notions of how other states perceive South Africa. This, in turn, has resulted in a number of failed and costly foreign policy initiatives.

2 Perceptions of South Africa's International Role

There is an inherent ambivalence in the term 'Afrikaner': a European who springs from the soil of Africa. This same ambivalence is evident in the Afrikaner leaders' split image of South Africa's national identity. Their perception of South Africa as uniquely both European and African has exerted a strong influence on foreign policy initiatives over the past 40 years.

As one aspect of that split image the leaders see South Africa as an outpost of European Christian civilization, an integral part of the modern industrial West, a natural ally of the West against what they perceive to be the advance of barbarism, radicalism, incompetence and irresponsibility in the rest of Africa. They have long believed that South Africa should be acknowledged and valued as such by the Western democracies. They say it is clearly in the West's interest to support South Africa's aspired role as defender of NATO's southernmost flank against Soviet expansionism. This European aspect of the split image thus suggests the *separateness* of the Republic from the rest of Africa, and implies a deep cultural and political gulf between them.

The other side of the image is a perception of South Africa as an integral part of Africa. This aspect is based on the RSA's superior economic, technical and military power; its leaders' African heritage; and their long and intimate experience in dealing with South Africa's own African peoples. Because of all this, they claim that South Africa should be accepted by the other regional states as the leading regional power, the major spokesman for the region, the guarantor of regional security and the country best able to assist the region's economic and technical development.

Implicit in both images is the centrality of the West in South African foreign policy. Indeed, at least until the advent of the Botha Administration, South Africa's leaders viewed an improvement in relations with Africa primarily as the key to achieving better relations with the West. Recently, however, deteriorating relations with the West led South Africa to announce new initiatives to forge closer bonds with Africa, particularly with neighbouring states. Yet such moves seem to have been more rhetorical than substantive, and prompted by a desire to defy the West rather than by any real change in the leaders' perception of Africa's strategic importance to South Africa.

As successive NP governments faced growing external criticism and hostility over apartheid, they have consistently tried to convince the West of South Africa's vital strategic importance. It is in the West's own interest, the argument goes, to ignore or accept South Africa's domestic race policies and to support the white minority government since it alone can offer stable, anti-communist rule over a country which stands astride the Cape Route and which is the major Free World source of several strategic minerals.

Further, South African leaders have aspired to fulfil a dual role in Western strategy: a bridge from the West to black Africa, and a southern arm of NATO. Time and again South African leaders have shown their belief in South Africa's ability to play these roles effectively, and a conviction that the Western powers would come to share that perception. Time and again they have been puzzled, disappointed and angered when the West declined to accept apartheid South Africa as a strategic ally, and when African governments rebuffed their attempts at bridge-building. Yet South Africa has continued to pursue each of these roles.

A BRIDGE TO BLACK AFRICA

The bridging idea emerged in the mid-1950s as South Africa's new NP leaders saw that the European powers, particularly Britain, were preparing to relinquish their colonial hold in Africa. Until that time Pretoria's Africa policy had meant no more than the maintenance of close collaboration with southern Africa's white-ruled territories. By the late 1950s, however, South Africa's foreign minister was declaring his government's 'vocation' in Africa, where 'it must play its full part as an African power' and as a bridge between Africa and the West, because South Africa was 'the West's most reliable ally in the struggle against Communist penetration in Africa'.[1] At that time South Africa had no intention of dealing with the emerging black African states as equal and sovereign entities; when South Africa's foreign minister, Eric Louw, proposed in 1959 that he pay an official visit to the new black-ruled states, the entire Cabinet was against him.[2] What the

South Africans sought was some kind of South African suzerainty or patronage arrangement to supplant British authority as Britain withdrew from its southern African territories.

Of particular concern to South Africa were the three British High Commission Territories, now the independent states of Botswana, Lesotho and Swaziland (BLS). Were they to remain British protectorates, a liberal British 'native policy' on the doorstep of apartheid South Africa would become a source of friction in Pretoria's domestic race relations. As independent entities, on the other hand, they might become bases for subversion against South Africa. Soon after the NP took office in 1948 D.F. Malan, the Prime Minister, declared that South Africa's defence could not be effectively organized without control of these territories. Like his predecessors, Malan demanded *and fully expected* that Britain would hand over the three territories for incorporation into South Africa. Asserting his country's claim, Malan said:

> South Africa also has the right, by virtue of its position as a white man's country and its experience during the course of years in connection with the native problem and the coloured problem, to aspire to leadership in this matter and to act as adviser to the peoples of the Northern territories.[3]

South Africa's claim was based on the South Africa Act of 1909, which provided for the transfer of these Territories to South Africa, subject to a number of safeguards for African rights. As elaborated in British parliamentary debates at the time, however, the British government stated that no change would take place without Parliament's approval, *after* consulting the peoples of the territories. By 1950, when Malan demanded their transfer without such prior consultation, strong African opposition to incorporation into apartheid South Africa had already emerged, and no British government could have won the support of a British Parliament for the transfer.

H.F. Verwoerd was the first South African prime minister to recognize that incorporation simply was not on, and that Britain was grooming the Territories for independence. Moreover, in his eyes, incorporation into South Africa (which had become an independent republic in 1961) would have posed a danger to white rule in the Republic. Instead Verwoerd proposed another solution, equally unlikely to win British approval: gradual independence of the Territories under South African guardianship and tutelage along the lines of Verwoerd's domestic Bantustan system.[4] Neither Britain nor the Territories showed any interest in that proposal. Whitehall continued to move the three towards independence, which was granted to Botswana and Lesotho in 1966 and to Swaziland two years later.

By then South Africa had a new Prime Minister, J.B. Vorster, who initiated a policy of broad rapprochement not only towards the new BLS states, but with other black-ruled countries as well. His 'Outward Policy', based explicitly on the proposition that South Africa's future 'lay in Africa and nowhere else', included economic aid offers and low-key diplomatic overtures.[5] Vorster's policy had a dual objective: to win the support of conservative African leaders in a continent that was becoming increasingly hostile to South Africa in the UN, OAU and other such organizations; and in so doing to pave the way for better relations with the West.

The Outward Policy scored some initial successes. Among them were Vorster's state visits to the Ivory Coast and Liberia, and the first opening of diplomatic relations with an African state, Malawi. But Vorster failed to achieve his larger objective of winning broad African acceptance and recognition of the apartheid regime. Although all the neighbouring states found it economically advantageous to engage in various technical and economic arrangements with South Africa, only Malawi extended diplomatic recognition.

The outward policy of the late 1960s ran out of steam following a series of inconclusive discussions between Zambian and South African officials. But Vorster's interest in playing an active role in regional affairs was given new urgency by the Portuguese coup in 1974 and the accession of the Frelimo government in Mozambique. This led to Vorster's *détente* initiative in which, for the first time, a South African leader engaged in a joint effort with a black African leader, Zambia's President Kaunda, to resolve a local conflict: the Rhodesian war. The collapse of their effort, followed by South Africa's invasion of Angola in 1975, brought an early end to *détente* (for an analysis of the *détente* exercise, see Chapter 5).

South Africa's next African initiative occurred early in 1979, less than a year after P.W. Botha became prime minister. He and his foreign minister proposed a 'constellation' of southern African states with South Africa at its centre. Unlike Pretoria's previous regional *démarches* the constellation proposals were not directed at improving its relations with the West. Indeed they represented an explicit rejection of Western-led peace efforts in Namibia and Rhodesia, and an outright move to seize the initiative from the West in resolving regional conflicts. In this formulation of South Africa's role in Africa, the notion of a bridge to the West was supplanted by the idea of a wall around southern Africa: the RSA and its neighbours would join together voluntarily to work out solutions to the region's political, economic and security problems independently of the West. No independent black states showed any interest in the proposal, however. (The 'constellation' initiative, and African responses to it, are analysed in Chapter 6.)

By 1979–80 immediate security issues had become the driving force behind Botha's Africa policy. With the rise in guerrilla attacks against South Africa and Namibia from neighbouring sanctuaries, the government turned to coercion – economic pressures and armed attacks against neighbours – to extract the sort of security cooperation that diplomacy had failed to achieve. The period 1980–8 was marked by a worsening security situation along the borders and inside South Africa, as well as a deterioration in Pretoria's relations with the West. The search for a bridge-to-Africa had been supplanted, for a time at least, by Botha's destabilization policy (which is analysed in Chapter 8).

It must be said that only the insensitivity of South Africa's NP leaders to the strength of anti-apartheid feelings in Africa and the West can explain their long efforts, doomed from the start, to win acceptance as a bridge between the two.

A MILITARY ALLY

For 30 years South African leaders have nurtured hopes that South Africa would be accepted by the Western powers as a southern arm of NATO, or at least that some sort of military alliance could be established committing the West to the defence of South Africa. They came closest to achieving that goal during the Cold War period of the 1950s. South Africa provided air support for the West's Berlin airlift and Korean campaign. Those gestures were meant to demonstrate South Africa's commitment to the war against communism, and to involve South Africa in military planning and operations with the West. Moreover, an important element in South African strategy at that time was to engage the perceived communist enemy as far from South Africa as possible.

In 1951 the Malan government promoted the idea of an African defence organization: an alliance between South Africa and the colonial powers in Africa which was to have links with NATO.[6] During the next few years the South Africans took part in several conferences on African defence sponsored by the colonial powers, and accepted a British invitation to join the abortive Middle East Defence Organization; but they failed to win support for an African defence organization.

Finally, in 1955, South Africa and Britain signed the Simonstown Accord, under which Britain turned over its naval base at Simonstown, near Cape Town, to South Africa. The signatories agreed, in extremely general terms, to contribute forces for the defence of southern Africa against external aggression. The UK was granted the right to use the base during hostilities in which South Africa was not involved, thereby jeopardizing South African neutrality; but that was a small price to pay for the formal linking of British defence interests to its own, particularly since neutrality was not a South African objective at that time. During the first few years of the Accord the British and South African navies conducted joint exercises, and the UK supplied South Africa with frigates, helicopters, and long-range aircraft to reinforce South African Defence Force (SADF) capabilities to patrol the seas around the Cape.[7]

By the early 1970s the real prospects for South African accession to a Western defence alliance had grown increasingly dim. The Cold War had ended, the nuclear stalemate dominated superpower strategy, and the effective cruising-range of Western navies and aircraft had been greatly extended. The strategic importance of the Simonstown base, and indeed of the Cape Route itself, was thereby diminished. These factors, together with the growing antipathy to apartheid in the West, virtually ruled out any chance for a peacetime alliance between Western governments and South Africa. The US had already declared an arms embargo against South Africa in 1963. In 1975 Britain terminated the Simonstown agreement, and two years later the UN Security Council (UNSC) adopted a mandatory arms embargo against the RSA.

The South African government none the less continued to hope for, and to plan for, expanded and more formal military ties with the West. Even as British use of Simonstown was tapering off, South Africa in 1972 announced plans for a vast expansion of the base, which would eventually be capable of handling 50 warships, including nuclear submarines: a capacity far beyond the future requirements of the South African navy.[8] As part of this initiative South Africa made office space and dormitory facilities available for Western military personnel at Silvermine (its computerized, bomb-resistant complex for monitoring ship movements in the waters around the Cape).

In May 1978, when the Western powers intervened militarily in Zaire following a guerrilla attack on Zaire's Shaba Province, Vorster appealed to the West to reconsider its NATO strategy. He commended President Carter and the Western powers for planning to strengthen NATO, but warned that the 'total onslaught of the Marxists' demanded that the West should do more than strengthen the North Atlantic area:

> if you only strengthen the North Atlantic area you leave your flank wide open. *You also have to look at the South Atlantic region and even further, to the Indian Ocean . . . You must look at the Cape Sea Route . . .* taking into account that the NATO defence has to be improved, *why do you withhold arms from the one stable country in this part of the world?*[9] (italics added)

Even as late as 1981 Prime Minister Botha said that the Simonstown facilities were 'flexible enough to support ships of other countries interested in the growth and stability of South Africa'.[10] By then, however, Botha appeared to have few illusions about the prospects for any *fundamental* shift in Western policy, in spite of the friendlier tone of statements emanating from the new Reagan Administration (see Chapter 9 for an analysis of Pretoria's relations with the West during this period). With the exception of clandestine American collaboration with South Africa during the Angolan civil war, military links since the mid-1970s have been limited to the exchange of intelligence information and of low-key official visits, and to some official laxity in Western compliance with the UN arms embargo.[11] The maintenance even of these links has depended more on the attitude of particular Western administrations than on any continuing and recognized Western military need. For example, US 'gray area' exports to South Africa, as well as intelligence exchanges with Pretoria, were sharply curtailed by the Carter Administration but resumed under President Reagan.

Thus, in spite of growing Western concern over Soviet and Cuban military intervention in southern Africa after 1975, the West made no moves to recognize or call upon South Africa as a military ally in the region. In fact, South African military actions against its neighbours in the 1980s led several Western governments to provide weapons and military training to Zimbabwe and Mozambique (this development is analysed in Chapter 8).

Part II
The Making of Foreign Policy

3 Decision-Making and the Foreign Policy Process

THE POLICY ENVIRONMENT

The foreign policy milieu in South Africa is not like that in the Western democracies, where there is broad public interest in foreign affairs and where various constituencies are able to exert influence on foreign policy through lobbying, public relations campaigns and other forms of pressure brought to bear on the legislative and executive branches of government. In South Africa the foreign policy environment is more like that in a communist or typical Third World country where there is no tradition of a continuing foreign policy dialogue between government and the public, and where policy decisions are taken by a small group of senior Party and government leaders with little or no participation by anyone outside the ruling circle.

This is not to say that South Africa has no active foreign policy community. Academic think-tanks, business associations and other groups systematically engage in the study of foreign affairs and the dissemination of publications on foreign policy issues. The government itself draws on several think-tanks for special studies and research in foreign affairs. On several occasions President Botha has met representatives of major business groups concerned with the overseas impact of government policy.

Neither can the leadership afford to be insensitive to the impact of foreign developments on the South African public at large. In order to sustain white morale and confidence in the government the leaders must demonstrate that they can cope effectively with external threats and pressures. They must also try to convince the restive black majority of the regime's staying-power and of its ability to counter any armed attacks from within or without.

Yet, for several reasons having to do with South Africa's unique political system, the leadership is to a large extent insulated from the pressures of outside interest groups, and conducts foreign policy with little need to be accountable to its constituents, to Parliament or the public at large.

First, the National Party is responsible to a narrow white constituency of some 2 000 000 registered NP voters: less than 7 per cent of South Africa's total population of around 30 million. And the NP's white, mostly Afrikaner constituents tend not to challenge the leadership. As one NP parliamentarian told an interviewer, 'In South Africa the people are overwhelmingly uncritical of the leadership. We politicians subscribe to the maxim: act, then talk. We first proceed, and then we explain.'[1] This is particularly true of foreign policy issues, in which NP supporters are neither particularly interested nor broadly well-informed. They generally defer to their leaders' knowledge and experience in these matters, and accept the official views expressed by the leadership.

Moreover, on such major policy issues as Namibia, the neighbouring states and the West there are large areas of consensus among whites. Various opinion polls have shown that the great majority of whites share the official perception of the threat to South Africa as set forth in statements by government leaders and reiterated by the South African Broadcasting Corporation (SABC) and other government media. In a 1982 poll of whites, for example, 80 per cent disagreed with the statement that the government was exaggerating the communist threat to South Africa. Among NP supporters the figure was over 93 per cent. More than 80 per cent of those polled approved of cross-border strikes against African National Congress (ANC) sanctuaries, and over 70 per cent agreed with the statement, 'The government of Zimbabwe constitutes a real threat to South Africa's safety'.[2]

A third major factor allowing the leadership a high degree of independence in policy formulation is of course the Party's long-standing and overwhelming parliamentary majority. As of mid-1988 the NP held 123 out of the House of Assembly's 166 directly elected seats: a 74 per cent majority. Given the strict Party discipline demanded of its MPs, the NP can usually count on their complete support. The Party's numerical dominance in Parliament thus means that there has been no need for the government to bargain with opposition parties to win their support, or even to explain or defend its policies to the Opposition.

The Botha Administration, in particular, has used its parliamentary majority to increase the power of the executive *vis-à-vis* Parliament, and to concentrate executive power in the hands of the state president. How it has gone about this, and what its effects have been on foreign policy, will be analysed later in this chapter. The Botha government's majority has also enabled it to enact several pieces of Draconian security legislation so broad as to deter newsmen and the public from inquiring closely into government affairs, and so severe as to inhibit leaks by government officials.

This, then, is the peculiar environment in which South African foreign policy is made. The key actors are the state president and those in his immediate circle, together with senior members of the security and foreign policy bureaucracies. The roles of Parliament and the NP caucus are also of interest, largely because of the contrast between their foreign policy input and those of Western parliaments.

PARLIAMENT AND THE NP

For more than 30 years the ruling National Party has enjoyed a parliamentary majority ranging from around two-thirds to three-quarters. That, together with its success in terminating the right of the judiciary to invalidate Acts of Parliament, has given successive NP administrations a virtual *carte blanche* to enact whatever legislation they decided on. Thus Parliament has been 'little more than a convenient mechanism for giving legislative effect to the will of the Prime Minister and cabinet.'[3]

Until 1982 parliamentary opposition was confined to parties representing political liberals, mainly from South Africa's English-speaking community. Their MPs consistently attacked the government's apartheid policies. They rejected a bipartisan foreign policy because of apartheid's negative impact on South Africa's foreign relations.[4] They used the annual no-confidence debate and those on defence and foreign policy to challenge government ministers and call public attention to particular aspects of foreign policy; particularly the growing international isolation of South Africa because of apartheid. Government leaders frequently choose not to argue the substance of the Opposition's criticism, but instead suggest that public airing of sensitive foreign policy issues will only play into the hands of South Africa's enemies. Often national security is cited as the reason for ministers' refusal to be drawn out in foreign policy debate. Sometimes government spokesmen have challenged the patriotism of Opposition MPs.

While government leaders have frequently consulted Opposition leaders on specific issues, they have not considered this a regular or necessary parliamentary practice. Following the débâcle of South

Africa's 1975 invasion of Angola, Vorster disclosed that he had occasionally informed Graaff, leader of the United Party, about Angolan developments although the chief of the Progressive Federal Party (PFP), Eglin, was kept entirely in the dark because Vorster did not trust him.[5]

During parliamentary debate on the Angolan episode Vorster again showed his contempt for the Opposition by refusing to engage in serious debate: this despite widespread white criticism of the government for keeping secret its involvement in a war in which young national servicemen were sent to fight without authorization. Although casualties were light – 43 killed and around a hundred wounded by official count – they came as a shock to South African whites, who had been told nothing of the invasion. Yet when Vorster was later challenged to explain South Africa's involvement, he treated it almost light-heartedly. Noting that the Defence Force was sent in initially to 'chase Cuba [sic] and the MPLA away from the [Calueque] dam' near the border, he told his parliamentary opponent, 'It is rather difficult, Sir, when you chase a man to decide when to stop.'[6]

The new constitution that took effect in September 1984 increased the power of the ruling party *vis-à-vis* its parliamentary opponents. Although two new chambers of Parliament were established, one for Asians and the other for Coloureds, the majority party in the white chamber, the House of Assembly, controls the entire system. In particular it controls the electoral college which elects the all-powerful state president. He in turn appoints his Cabinet, can dissolve any or all chambers of Parliament, decides which pieces of legislation to put before each House, and has sole responsibility for African (that is, black) affairs. The majority white party also dominates the President's Council, which decides issues in dispute among the three chambers, and controls appointments to parliamentary committees. Under this system Opposition parties in the white Parliament are likely to be given only token representation on the President's Council and parliamentary committees and to be excluded from debating issues that the state president defines as exclusively relating to black, Asian or Coloured affairs.[7]

There is no reason, however, to believe that the NP leadership will be able indefinitely to ignore and disdain Opposition parties' views on foreign policy. Since 1982, when the Party's right wing broke away to form the Conservative Party (CP) under Treurnicht, the government has for the first time faced a parliamentary Opposition on the right numbering some 20 MPs. In October 1985 the far-right

Herstigte Nasionale Party (HNP) won its first parliamentary seat. So far these parties have posed no real threat to the National Party's solid parliamentary majority. The results of several by-elections in 1988, however, showed a sharp rise in support for the CP, so much so that a swing of 10 per cent to the CP in the next election could change the balance of power in Parliament. Should the NP's parliamentary majority begin seriously to erode, the leadership could find it necessary to make substantial concessions on foreign policy or other issues in exchange for opposition support on major pieces of race reform legislation.

Indeed, something like this occurred during a brief parliamentary crisis in September 1986, after the government had called an extended session of Parliament to consider race reform legislation which it then failed to introduce. This provoked an angry revolt by all the opposition parties, who accused the government of contempt of Parliament. President Botha personally intervened to regain their parliamentary cooperation; but he was forced to agree to a number of concessions, including a demand by the PFP that a select committee be appointed to evaluate sanctions and the steps needed to counter them.[8]

On a number of specific foreign policy issues, however, the opposition parties and the government have been in accord. All oppose Western sanctions, for example, even though the PFP charged that Botha's failure to move decisively on fundamental race reform made sanctions inevitable. The PFP supported Botha's idea for a constellation of regional states, and joined the government in criticizing Western actions in Namibia. The PFP also noted that it was being kept better informed by the government since Botha had come to power.[9] The Conservative Party, too, has supported the Namibia policy but has continued to voice suspicions that Botha was planning to 'sell out' the Territory's 70 000 whites.

Even within the Party the leadership faces little challenge on foreign policy. This was not always the case. In fact, foreign policy was the major cause of the traumatic split in the Party in 1967, when opposition to Vorster's plans for opening diplomatic relations with black-ruled states led a group of NP delegates to bolt the Party and form the HNP.

The NP, however, like the Afrikaner community itself, shows a high degree of consensus on foreign policy matters and serious disagreements are rare. This consensus reflects more than simply an identity of outlook, however. Party members, including MPs, are by and large not much interested in foreign affairs and not well informed about them. Their experience of other societies is remarkably limited. According to a 1980 survey,[10] some 70 per cent of the Party's MPs did not read a foreign newspaper regularly (that is, once a week), and almost none read foreign academic journals. While more than 75 per cent had travelled abroad, most of those had visited Western Europe and/or the US; only a quarter of the Party's MPs had ever visited an African country.

Moreover, Party discipline is strict – far more so than in the UK – and the penalties for breaching discipline are severe. When Parliament is in session the NP caucus (that is, NP members of parliament) meets weekly on the day after the Cabinet meets. Cabinet ministers explain and defend their programmes to the caucus in what is said to be frank and open discussion.[11] Policy differences in the Cabinet are often reflected in the caucus. Once a Cabinet decision has been approved by the caucus, however, it is binding on all the Party's MPs.

In foreign policy matters the caucus 'is little more than a forum for the [State President] and Minister of Foreign Affairs to explain government policies and actions and to mobilize support, if necessary'. Communication on foreign affairs is said to be 'essentially a one-way flow', with statements by the State President and Minister of Foreign Affairs often being provided *ex post facto*.[12]

In short there is little inclination or incentive for NP members to take an active interest in foreign policy, let alone to challenge their leaders. It is not surprising that they prefer to leave foreign policy decisions to the top leadership and its foreign affairs specialists.

CONTRASTING LEADERS: VORSTER AND BOTHA

It is always tempting to treat foreign policy as though it were the private preserve of the national leader; to minimize the pressures and constraints, the manoeuvrings of bureaucracies, the shadowy influence of close advisers, and the sometimes astonishing intelligence gaps under which even a strong and well-informed leader must work. The temptation is all the greater in societies where political power is concentrated at the apex of the system, and where little is known about the workings of the ruling inner circle. How many 'insider' articles, press leaks, or memoirs by retired Politbureau members came out of Stalinist Russia? On the other hand, who could have doubted, even at the time, the towering influence of Stalin himself over the policies of that nightmare period?

South Africa has some obvious parallels: the dominant personalities of recent leaders, the concentration of state power in their hands, the secrecy of inner-circle deliberations, the public show of Cabinet unity. In both South Africa and the USSR it took a major political crisis to reveal the inner workings of a regime: Khrushchev's de-Stalinization campaign in the USSR, and the 'Muldergate' crisis at the end of the Vorster Administration in South Africa which will be discussed below. More is known about decision-making in the Botha government, largely because it is a more open administration with broader participation in the policy process. The conduct of South African foreign policy in the critical years since 1974 has to a large extent reflected the contrasting personalities and leadership styles of the two chiefs of state: B.J. Vorster (1966–78) and P.W. Botha since 1978.

Vorster was a classic example of what some sociologists have termed an 'inner-directed man'. He had always been led to believe that he was destined for greatness. Indeed, on her death-bed his mother called all her children around her and apologized for having always favoured John above the others because she had known early on that he was the one who would achieve great things. He was also superstitious: for example, he felt the number 13 had special significance in his fate, noting that he was the thirteenth child to be born to his mother, the thirteenth in order of precedence in the Cabinet and became prime minister on the thirteenth day of the month.

As Prime Minister, Vorster is generally regarded as having been a team leader: a 'chairman of the board' who consulted others, sought broad consensus within the Party and deliberated before making a decision, all in the interest of maintaining Party unity.[13] Ministers and department heads were given considerable autonomy. If 'board chairman' is an accurate description, however, Vorster was one who frequently took decisions on the counsel of one or another close adviser without consulting – and sometimes without informing – the full Cabinet. Nor did he draw broadly on the bureaucracy. Although he established a series of specialized Cabinet committees whose membership was kept secret from both the public and the bureaucracy, he usually reached major decisions after consulting only one or two ministers and close advisers.[14] He consulted selected bureaux and departments to the virtual exclusion of others. For intelligence assessments Vorster ignored the Military Intelligence Section (MIS) and security police and turned instead to the Bureau for State Security (BOSS) and the man he appointed to run it, Hendrik van den Bergh: an old and trusted friend with whom he had been interned for pro-Nazi activities during the Second World War.

Vorster's approach to policy decisions was thus marked by secrecy, *ad hoc* arrangements, and overdependence on close confidantes. All this had a major impact on his conduct of foreign policy. So, too, did his lack of direct experience in foreign affairs.[15]

Vorster came to the premiership in late 1966 with some definite ideas on foreign policy. In particular he set out to normalize the Republic's relations with other African states: his so-called outward policy. Within months of his inauguration he received Lesotho's Prime Minister in the first official visit to South Africa by a black African head of state. Shortly thereafter Malawi became the first (and so far the only) black African country to establish formal diplomatic ties with Pretoria.

More important than these symbolic achievements, however, was Vorster's secret *démarche* to Zambian President Kaunda. A world-class statesman of recognized stature and influence among both African and Commonwealth leaders, Kaunda was seen as a key factor in Pretoria's new African initiative: particularly the desire to see a peaceful resolution of the Rhodesian crisis.

The approach to Kaunda, who is a strong and outspoken opponent of white minority rule and a leading supporter of the national liberation movements in southern Africa, had to be conducted with subtlety and caution, however. And here Vorster's inclination towards clandestine, informal diplomacy was eventually rewarded. Following the collapse of earlier semi-official contacts in a bout of mutual recrimination, Vorster accepted the good offices of two leading businessmen with major Zambian interests: Roland ('Tiny') Rowland, chairman of the giant Lonrho enterprise, and Dr J.T. Marquard De Villiers, a member of Lonrho's board. In June 1974 they began to explore with the Zambians the possibility of a meeting between Vorster and Kaunda to discuss Rhodesia. The tactic was a good one. As De Villiers said later:

> So Mr. Rowland and I undertook to use our good offices to approach these two leaders and we had the advantage of not being connected to any particular political viewpoint or party. We could not exploit the thing to our own advantage and secondly *we could*

be repudiated by either party at any time. We were sufficiently small to be repudiated and that was always the strength of our negotiations.[16] [My emphasis.]

In this informal, *ad hoc* way, with no participation by South African officials, Vorster's important *détente* initiative was launched: an initiative that soon led to the first major break in the Rhodesian logjam discussed in Part III.

This loose and decentralized style of foreign policy conduct, in which there were no formal lines of responsibility, also had serious drawbacks. The most devastating foreign policy setback of the Vorster Administration was of course the invasion of Angola in 1975, which is analysed in Part III. There is no doubt that the Angolan débâcle occurred because of Vorster's inexperience in foreign affairs and his personalized and unsystematic approach to major policy decisions. The invasion was incremental, with no clear objective or end-point. Decisions with far-reaching political consequences were made by military field commanders on the spot. The Department of Foreign Affairs (DFA) might have provided an accurate assessment of the impact of the invasion in Africa and elsewhere, but it was not consulted. Instead Vorster acted on the advice of his Defence Minister, P.W. Botha, who believed that South Africa should move into the power vacuum left by the Portuguese and try to influence events to its advantage.

Vorster survived the Angolan affair, but his administration came to an ignominious end with the so-called Muldergate scandal: revelations of clandestine 'dirty tricks' directed at both foreign and South African opponents by the Department of Information, and of high living at the taxpayer's expense by officials of the Department. As in the Angolan venture, Vorster acted on the advice of one or two people, and no more than three senior officials knew the details of the Department's operations.

What the Angolan and Muldergate ventures suggest above all about Vorster's policy-making is his delusion of personal power and control. He apparently believed that he, together with one or two close subordinates, could themselves decide on such a major policy initiative and see to its execution without consulting the full Cabinet or drawing on the full range of relevant government departments. In neither the Angolan invasion nor the operations of the Information Department did Vorster appear to understand the enormity of the risks and likely political consequences.

Yet Vorster's confidence and subtlety as a leader had positive as well as negative results for South African foreign policy. He demonstrated a high degree of flexibility in conducting foreign relations, and carried out some far-seeing shifts in South African foreign policy. In the early 1970s Vorster broke ranks with his predecessors on the Namibia issue. Recognizing that growing world pressure would eventually force South Africa to release its vise-like hold and grant independence to the Territory, he agreed to discuss Namibia with the Special Representative of the UN Secretary-General in September 1972. This marked the first time a South African government had acknowledged the legitimacy of a UN role in deciding Namibia's future. A few weeks later Vorster took a symbolic step towards loosening the Republic's political bond to the Territory by formally abandoning the notion of its eventual annexation.

These were politically courageous steps, particularly in the light of the hard-line attitudes of Namibia's white minority. Although comprising only a small part of the Territory's population, whites have been extremely vocal politically. Many have worked through local branches of the National Party itself to oppose any loosening of South African responsibility for the Territory.

Vorster also came to see the inevitability of black majority rule in Rhodesia. In 1974, after propping up Smith's defiant white minority regime for almost a decade, Vorster signalled an abrupt change in policy. He perceived that South African interests lay in a speedy constitutional settlement in Rhodesia, and began cooperating with Western and African leaders to bring this about. This, too, was a bold move. It meant putting pressure on the Smith regime, which enjoyed wide sympathy among South African whites, and exposing himself to charges of 'selling out' Rhodesia's embattled white minority. Both the Namibian and Rhodesian policies are analysed at greater length in Part III.

Pieter W. Botha's accession to the premiership in September 1978 brought dramatic changes in personality, style and substance to the policy-making process. He is first of all a tough, pragmatic politician. To have risen through party ranks to become Defence Minister and head of the Cape branch of the NP, Botha had long since demonstrated that he was both loyal to the Party and trustworthy; that he was not too distant from the mainstream of Afrikaner opinion, despite some *verligte* (enlightened) notions. Yet members of his own staff privately label him a 'super-hawk', and fellow NP members gave him the nickname 'Piet Wapon' – Pete the Gun – both for his hardline views and for his alleged tendency to act impulsively and shoot from the hip.

Botha does not entirely demur from this label. 'We have a saying in Afrikaans that the highest trees catch the strongest winds', he told an interviewer. 'I cannot say I am a hardliner or trigger-happy or a hawk, but I do believe in principles. I detest weaklings in public life. I believe in straightforward and honest politics.'[17]

He also came to office with considerably more experience in foreign affairs than his predecessor. As Defence Minister he had travelled abroad, and during the waning months of the Vorster government he had exercised growing influence on foreign policy while the ailing Vorster focused his energies on trying to contain the Information scandal.

The most important difference, however, was Botha's belief in systems and organization. In contrast to Vorster's personalized, haphazard, secretive style of leadership, Botha immediately introduced system to the decision-making process and opened it up to broader policy input. He also set about enhancing the power of the prime minister (and later of the state president). He created for the first time an office of the Prime Minister, with a sizeable staff and a formal role in the policy process. He established a Cabinet secretariat to provide support and continuity to its work. And he set up five *permanent* Cabinet committees to replace the 20 *ad hoc* committees established (and frequently ignored) by his predecessor. The most important of these committees is the State Security Council (SSC), which is analysed below. For the first time a number of inter-departmental working groups were formed to work with the several Cabinet committees.

All these changes were introduced under the broad concept of a 'total national strategy': the notion that South Africa is the victim of a global 'total onslaught', and that all the society's resources must be mobilized to meet that threat. Botha, when he was Defence Minister, publicized the twin concept of total onslaught/total national strategy as a slogan in the late 1970s to win support for larger defence budgets and for a more aggressive military posture in the region. But the rationalization and streamlining of government operations to meet the alleged onslaught did not really begin until he became Prime Minister, as discussed in Chapter 6.

Botha also brought to his premiership a built-in antipathy to the West which has exerted a decisive influence on foreign policy. His anti-Western bias is to some degree a result of his personal experience of anger and humiliation when the US abruptly closed down its clandestine cooperation with South Africa during the 1975 invasion of Angola, but Botha's antipathy goes deeper. It seems to be based on a conviction that short-sighted Western leaders, yielding to political pressures at home and in the Third World, have turned their backs on South Africa: a state which he believes any right-thinking Western leader should see as a natural ally in the struggle against world communism. Furthermore, South Africa must take note of this defect in Western attitudes, he maintains, and stop trying to curry the approval of the West, since nothing short of black majority rule would satisfy Western demands. Botha's speeches have been laced with rhetoric inveighing against the untrustworthiness of the West and its alleged weakness in the face of the communist threat. Botha went so far as to criticize his own prime minister, John Vorster, in 1978 for the 'almost painful patience' the latter had shown toward the Western powers over Namibia.[18]

The accession of Botha to the premiership thus marked an end of significant foreign policy concessions by South Africa to the West. Botha has shown less sensitivity than his predecessor to the possibility of negative Western reactions to South African policies, and less interest in seeking joint endeavours with Western leaders. Whether this is due more to his personal mind-set, or to better intelligence assessments of Western attitudes and likely policy moves, the result has been that Pretoria has virtually written off the Western powers as being beyond its influence.

In relations with Africa, too, Botha has generally taken an adversarial approach. Neither in his speeches nor actions has Botha shown anything like Vorster's serious interest in reaching out to African leaders or collaborating with them in regional peace efforts. Botha's offers of mutual security pacts to South Africa's neighbours have usually been accompanied by threats of hostile action if cooperation should be declined. Even the abortive Botha proposal for a constellation of regional states was little more than a half-hearted launching of a trial balloon suggested by his foreign minister. Botha quickly dropped that (initially) broad idea and worked instead towards forging closer security links with a narrow group of Pretoria's client-territories (the nominally independent Bantustans, Namibia and, for a short time, Rhodesia). The mutual security accord with Mozambique, which has since all but collapsed, was less a peace initiative than a pact forced on a reluctant and suffering foe. Indeed,

South Africa's so-called 'destabilization policy' (analysed in Part III) is one congenial with Botha's personal inclinations, his long association with the military, and his general disdain for Western and African opinion as peripheral to South Africa's political imperatives.

A subtle but nevertheless important difference between Vorster's and Botha's foreign policies is the type and degree of risk each was willing to take. Although both men approved military ventures knowing they would provoke hostile reactions abroad, Vorster was the more cautious. Aside from the Angolan venture – which Vorster agreed to under the assumption it would have America's backing – an SADF raid on South West Africa People's Organization (SWAPO) camps inside Angola in May 1978 was the only blatant military action taken during Vorster's premiership. Under the Botha Administration, however, the war in Angola was immediately intensified, and countermeasures against the ANC began to include attacks on targets in neighbouring capitals.

Yet Vorster was more willing than Botha to take foreign policy decisions that would have political costs at home, such as withdrawing military support from the beleaguered Smith regime in Rhodesia and agreeing to a number of concessions on Namibia. Botha has so far avoided foreign policy moves which would cost him domestic political support. Zambia's President Kaunda, who has dealt with both men, sees this as a lack of courage on the part of Botha to take personal political risks with his foreign policy. In Kaunda's judgement: 'Vorster was a courageous man. Botha is an honest man, I believe; but he is not courageous.'[19]

COMPETING BUREAUCRACIES

The Department of Foreign Affairs has always held primary responsibility for conducting foreign relations, but this apparent advantage over other departments with a foreign policy interest is more formal than real. It has been more than offset by the Department's chronic inability to carry out its principal assignment: the defence of apartheid.

Working in an environment of foreign isolation, condemnation and often confrontation, South Africa's Foreign Affairs officials feel they are in the front line of a desperate and ultimately futile holding action. Thus one veteran ambassador remarked, 'I have always felt our foreign policy is essentially reactive and defensive.'[20] As South Africa has been ousted from a number of prestigious international bodies, from the Commonwealth to the International Red Cross, and as it has increasingly been subject to condemnation in the UN and to various sanctions over apartheid and Namibia, these setbacks have been seen in part at least as foreign policy failures.

As in other countries, domestic critics have charged the foreign policy professionals with being too cautious, too passive, and overly sensitive to foreign reactions and attitudes. In 1963 Prime Minister Verwoerd privately expressed his regret at having decided to grant nominal independence to the Transkei, attributing his decision – which caused serious divisions in his government – to his foreign minister's overly alarmist assessment of South Africa's international position.[21] Roelof ('Pik') Botha, who has been South Africa's foreign minister since 1977, acknowledged early on that not all of his NP colleagues shared his own perception of the threats from abroad or the need for internal political change to forestall hostile foreign actions.[22]

The perceived failure of South African diplomacy has led to frustration and impatience on the part of successive South African prime ministers, and to an inclination to seek the foreign policy counsel of individuals outside the Foreign Office. This, in turn, has encouraged ambitious men in other departments to try to move into the foreign policy arena, and to propose bold international initiatives that bypass the DFA.

The boldest of these was a 'provocative new propaganda campaign' proposed to Prime Minister Vorster in 1973 by Eschel Rhoodie, the brash Secretary of the Department of Information. Asserting that South African diplomacy as practised by the DFA was too low key and too passive in the face of foreign criticism, and therefore ineffective, Rhoodie proposed a massive 'unconventional' – that is, clandestine – initiative to influence foreign opinion-makers and leaders.[23] He presented his plan to a small closed group: his own Minister of Information, Connie Mulder; Vorster; and the Minister of Finance. The DFA was neither represented nor consulted.

Rhoodie, by his own account, made no attempt to hide his intentions:

> 'I said to [Vorster] that if it was necessary for me for example to influence a particular journalist to stop writing anti-South African articles, if it was necessary for me to send him to Hawaii with his girlfriend for a month's holiday at our expense, then I should be able to do so'.[24]

His scheme was approved by the three Cabinet ministers present, with a secret budget of some $70 million. In the next four years Rhoodie launched an astonishing variety of covert actions, including the purchase of a US newspaper; contributing to US Senate campaigns to defeat anti-apartheid legislators; bribing two British MPs to lobby for South African interests in the Commons and to report on anti-apartheid organizations; and establishing front organizations in Britain, Germany and France, to list but a few. In sum, it was an aggressive campaign in which South Africa tried to 'buy, bribe, or bluff its way into the hearts and minds of the world'.[25]

Much of the Department of Information's activity abroad was conducted independently of Foreign Affairs people, sometimes completely bypassing the local ambassador. This inevitably led to frictions between the two departments and, as Foreign Minister Botha later said, to 'the greatest distrust and ill-feeling' between the two.[26]

The downfall of Rhoodie and his Information initiative came about not as a result of foreign discovery of these activities and hostile reaction to them; indeed, many of these activities escaped notice at the time. The denouement, a scandal unprecedented in South African politics, followed the revelation of Information's clandestine activities *within South Africa*. The major initiative involved the use of laundered Swiss money to establish an ostensibly independent newspaper, *The Citizen*, to carry pro-administration propaganda to the unsuspecting South African public.

In 1977, as a national election campaign was getting under way, rumours that Department of Information officials had been guilty of wrong-doing and high living at the taxpayers' expense began to leak to the press. Audits of the Department's books revealed glaring misuse of public funds. Despite efforts by Vorster and Mulder to contain and dampen the crisis, it spread as rapidly and inevitably as the American Watergate scandal a few years earlier. Eventually the Muldergate affair engulfed both Vorster and Mulder, his favoured candidate to succeed him in the premiership, forcing the resignation of both men.

Bureaucratic politics played a discreet but important role in the unfolding of the Muldergate affair. A widespread, though unsubstantiated, belief among press and government people is that the early leaks about the affair came from South Africa's military in a surreptitious move to undermine Mulder's candidacy for the premiership and to boost the chances of their favourite, Defence Minister P.W. Botha. Some months later, on the eve of the NP caucus to choose the next prime minister, Foreign Minister Botha flew to Cape Town with a man who had come to him with inside information on the Information Department's secret funding of *The Citizen*. There the man repeated his story to P.W. Botha (who, in addition to his official role as Defence Minister, was head of the Cape Branch of the NP) and to the Party leader of the Orange Free State. They, in turn, confronted Vorster, who admitted the truth of the charges and his own knowledge of the whole affair. The full Cabinet was given the facts the next day.[27] The day after that the Party caucus elected P.W. Botha Prime Minister on the second ballot.

The Byzantine political infighting that was an integral part of the Muldergate crisis involved both bureaucratic and personal feuds of long standing. The military, and to a lesser extent the Foreign Office, had resented the close and privileged relationship of BOSS and its chief, General Hendrik van den Bergh, to Prime Minister Vorster. In addition to being Vorster's closest confidante on security and foreign policy matters, van den Bergh had won the right for BOSS to write the national intelligence estimates that were the basis for Cabinet discussions of security issues. During the decade of its existence (1969–78) BOSS grew from 500 to more than 1000 employees, and was assigned domestic as well as foreign intelligence functions.[28] Van den Bergh himself had been one of the few people closely involved with Rhoodie's covert operations overseas. The Military Intelligence Section avoided total eclipse only by bypassing BOSS and reporting directly to Defence Minister Botha, who is said to have clashed repeatedly with van den Bergh at meetings of the SSC.[29]

Alliances among the leading NP figures around Vorster were fluid rather than fixed, and sometimes coalesced over particular policy issues. Yet the last couple of years of his administration saw *de facto* hardening of two opposing groups: Vorster, Mulder and van den Bergh, who would sink together in the Information scandal, against the two Bothas, P.W. and Pik. These latter shared long-standing grievances over Vorster's *ad hoc* style of leadership and over their frequent exclusion from crucial decisions affecting foreign policy. They also came from the more liberal Cape wing of the Party, and represented its more *verligte*, pro-reform forces, impatient with Vorster's refusal to budge on domestic race policy.

The lines were not simple or clear-cut. Van den Bergh shared Pik Botha's dove-ish inclinations in foreign affairs, and vehemently opposed the hawkish tendencies of P.W. Botha. Indeed, among the more startling revelations to emerge in the aftermath of Muldergate were Rhoodie's detailed allegations that the defence minister had initiated dangerous military ventures behind Vorster's back.

While Vorster was attempting to establish friendly relations with the new Marxist government in Mozambique, said Rhoodie, P.W. Botha gave secret orders to MIS to supply extensive quantities of arms and ammunition to a pro-Portuguese group planning a coup against the new regime. Van den Bergh learned of the operation, however, and sent some of his own men from BOSS to immobilize the equipment before it could cross the border. Rhoodie further described an earlier occasion, when Vorster had withdrawn South African police from Rhodesia in accord with a pledge to Western and African leaders. In this instance a secret order given by P.W. Botha, without Vorster's knowledge, to airlift 500 troops to Rhodesia to help the beleaguered Smith regime was also aborted by van den Bergh.[30]

On policy towards Angola, too, there were serious differences. P.W. Botha and the military leaders, who favoured active military intervention in Angola's civil war in 1975, eventually won Vorster's support over the strong reservations of van den Bergh and the DFA. According to one observer, the Foreign Affairs Department was so far out of the decision-making on that issue that it first learned of South Africa's military thrust into Angola when its ambassador in Lisbon was handed a note of protest over the SADF action.[31]

The Angolan débâcle is viewed by South African leaders as primarily a *political* failure: a failure to consider various scenarios and their possible consequences in advance, a failure to consult all the domestic actors whose cooperation was eventually needed, and a failure to win prior commitments of firm Western and African support. The Defence Minister, Malan, who was SADF Chief at the time, later said that the Angolan war 'focussed the attention [of policy-makers] on the urgent necessity for the State Security Council to play a much fuller role in the national security of the Republic than hitherto'.[32]

THE STATE SECURITY COUNCIL (SSC)

The more systematized decision-making instituted by P.W. Botha under his national security management programme has, indeed, resulted in wider bureaucratic input to foreign policy, and less of the personal, *ad hoc* style favoured by his predecessor. But it has by no means put an end to bureaucratic infighting and manoeuvring for advantage over foreign policy issues and others. Indeed, by drawing more departments into the process at several levels, the new system has led to increased awareness among the bureaucracies about current foreign policy issues and the departmental interests that may be at stake.

By far the most important and influential institution under the system is the SSC.[33] Although this Cabinet committee was established in 1972 – that is, during the Vorster Administration – it met irregularly and confined its activity to narrowly-defined security matters under Vorster, but quickly became a pivotal organization when Botha assumed the premiership.

In formal terms alone the SSC clearly outranks the other Cabinet committees: it is the only one established by law, the only one chaired by the Prime Minister (now the State President), and the only one with a broad mandate to advise the government on policy and strategy relating to the 'security of the Republic'. Permanent members are the state president; the ministers of defence, law and order, foreign affairs and justice; and the senior Cabinet minister if not included in those listed. The senior civil servants representing security and foreign policy-related departments are also members: the directors-general of foreign affairs, justice and the office of the state president, plus the chief of the armed forces, commissioner of police and head of the civilian National Intelligence Service (NIS). Other Cabinet ministers and department heads may attend its twice-a-month meetings, but only on invitation of the state president.

The SSC is backed by a secretariat of some 50 permanent employees, compared to five for each of the other Cabinet committees.[34] The secretariat draws on a working committee of representatives from the several departments concerned with security matters.

Clearly, then, the SSC is a high-powered, well-staffed organ of the executive. But what role does it play in foreign policy? In particular, to what degree, if any, has it supplanted the Cabinet in foreign policy deliberation and decision-making? And what evidence is there regarding the contention of some critics that it has become a vehicle for military dominance in foreign policy?

Under the new (1983) constitution, the Cabinet has a number of non-white members, and thus no longer can function as a central, effective decision-making body on which only representatives of (white) NP supporters serve. Therefore, in the words of a South

African authority on public law, 'In much the same way that Charles II used a "cabal" or "inner cabinet" to make important decisions, the present government has used the State Security Council. This insures the retention of real policy-making power in the hands of an "inner" white cabinet.'[35] The perceived need to restrict policy deliberation and decision-making to a small number of trusted NP leaders would seem to be particularly imperative on sensitive issues of national security and foreign policy. There the danger of strong opposition to NP policy by members of other races and other parties, or of leaks to the public, would presumably be seen by the leadership as too great a risk to take. As a general practice, SSC decisions are conveyed orally to the Cabinet by the State President. If members have serious reservations, the SSC can be reconvened to give the issue further consideration.[36] But it is up to the State President to decide how much to divulge, to whom, and when. According to a former official in the office of the prime minister, SSC decisions are not required to be confirmed by the full Cabinet.[37] Furthermore the SSC continues to meet when Parliament is not in session and the Cabinet is not meeting regularly.

At best, then, most Cabinet members learn of SSC decisions *ex post facto*. Such decisions, reflecting both the State President's approval and a consensus among the top officials concerned with security and foreign policy matters, of course carry a great deal of weight. It would be a courageous Cabinet member indeed who would seriously question a decision of the SSC.

Moreover the SSC, like other Cabinet committees, is authorized to act on its own in a number of areas. In the SSC case, this independent mandate appears to be extremely broad. In December 1985 it was the SSC, not the State President or the Cabinet, which issued a formal threat to neighbouring states of the 'heavy price' they would pay if they continued to assist the ANC.[38] The SSC also has the authority to approve or deny Defence requests to launch major military offensives inside Angola.[39]

The question of military domination of the SSC is difficult to assess. On several occasions DFA officials are said to have publicly expressed thinly-veiled criticism of the military's influence. (One senior DFA official is reported to have remarked that 'the day of the generals is at hand'.)[40] The press has reported instances where the military's view prevailed over that of the DFA on policy in Angola.[41] Yet the Minister of Foreign Affairs, strongly backed by the Commissioner of Police, won SSC approval for the Nkomati peace initiative with

Mozambique over the objections of the Minister of Defence.[42] On another occasion, following an ANC car-bombing in Pretoria in May 1983, the SSC rejected an SADF plea that a reprisal attack be delayed so that intelligence could be collected about possible targets. In this case the SSC adopted the police view that an immediate attack was necessary to convey South Africa's outrage and retaliatory power.[43]

Such evidence is fragmentary and inconclusive, and may reflect little more than the usual bureaucratic grumbling when decisions go against the plaintiff's interests. Yet the South African military appears to enjoy an important advantage over other departments in the opportunities it has to get its views and assessments known and acted upon by the SSC.

For one thing, the General Staff writes the national threat assessment, which sets out the present threat to the Republic and recommends the steps needed to meet it. While stressing that the assessment reaches the full SSC only after its review by an inter-departmental working group, senior SADF officials none the less acknowledge that there is considerable advantage in being the authority responsible for drafting the only threat assessment to be tabled before the SSC.[44]

Of more tangible advantage are the key roles played by military men on the SSC Secretariat. Its head is a senior officer serving in the Defence Force: in November 1987 Army Major General Charles Lloyd became the latest SADF incumbent in this important position. The head of the Secretariat prepares the agenda for SSC deliberation, assigns papers and intelligence assessments to be written for the SSC, and decides which items proposed by various department heads should be placed before the full SSC. SADF officers hold a number of other key positions on the Secretariat, although they provided only 16 per cent of its total staff in 1984. Over half the personnel at that time came from the (civilian) NIS, and only 11 per cent from the DFA.[45]

The military also has been given a leading role in seeing that SSC decisions are implemented and coordinated locally. This is done through more than a dozen Joint Management Centres under the SSC's aegis. Most Centres coincide with SADF area commands, but several others deal with areas outside the Republic, including Namibia, Walvis Bay and certain African countries; that is, areas of foreign policy relevance. Each of these Centres is co-chaired by an SADF officer and a member of the South African Police.[46]

CRITIQUE OF THE PROCESS

In sum, foreign policy is no longer the exclusive preserve of a handful of insiders clustered around the head of state. The security management system of P.W. Botha is in place, functioning and able to draw a wide range of bureaucratic and other inputs into the foreign policy process. Formally, at least, no single group or department can monopolize foreign policy. At the same time, however, the system clearly enhances the power of the state president while diminishing that of the Cabinet in making policy. If he chooses to do so, the state president can approve and set in motion a major foreign policy initiative which has been reviewed only by the relatively small number of officials with statutory membership on the SSC; the rest of the Cabinet need not be brought in, or even fully informed, of a decision that conceivably could have profound political and economic consequences for the country.

Indeed the security management system of P.W. Botha has not insulated South Africa from foreign policy confusion and blunder. Neither has it prevented risky foreign ventures being launched without the participation or knowledge of all the departments affected.

Among the former is the policy towards Mozambique, analysed in Part III. After achieving a much-heralded mutual security accord with the Machel government in 1984 – a pact in which the prestige and credibility of President Botha himself were invested – the South African military continued to provide encouragement and logistical support to Mozambican insurgents, leading to the virtual collapse of that accord.

In 1983 a shadowy group of white South African mercenaries with direct ties to South African intelligence services launched an abortive coup attempt against the left-wing regime in the Seychelles. Their venture, as ill-conceived and ill-executed as the US Bay of Pigs débâcle two decades earlier, led to revelations of SADF collusion and bureaucratic infighting. More serious in terms of South Africa's deteriorating relations with the US was a clandestine SADF raid in Cabinda, Angola's oil-rich exclave, in the summer of 1985. After their capture, the raiders said they had been on a mission to blow up US-owned oil storage facilities. A more detailed account of these two misadventures appears in Chapter 8.

The abortive Cabinda operation was launched at a time when the Reagan Administration was engaged in a vigorous effort to block growing demands in Congress for sanctions against South Africa.

Indeed, the House had voted for sanctions only a month before. Because of the importance given by the Botha government to forestalling sanctions, and hence its intense interest in the sanctions debate in the US at the time, it is unlikely Botha would have approved an operation so certain to damage relations with the US if discovered. The Cabinda raid thus seems to have been another case where the Botha security management system failed to prevent actions damaging to important foreign policy interests.

The fact that these and similar episodes of clandestine and apparently uncoordinated foreign initiatives occurred under both the *ad hoc*, personalized style of decision-making of the Vorster government and the systematic policy-making procedures introduced by P.W. Botha suggests that this sort of event may be endemic to the apartheid system itself. The dual stress of maintaining white minority rule at home while facing isolation and hostility abroad would seem conducive to the development of the oft-cited 'laager mentality'. It can of course also lead to a paranoid view of the outside world. Foreign countries, whether they harbour South African guerrilla groups or merely engage in harsh rhetoric towards South Africa, are thus seen as enemies to be weakened or damaged by whatever weapons seem appropriate. It was no surprise, then, that the Muldergate revelations did not put an end to Rhoodie's secret Information projects abroad, 60 or more of which were taken over and continued by the Botha Administration.[47]

Such clandestine initiatives seem to be particularly congenial to authoritarian regimes, where they appear prominently among the repertoire of policy responses. In South Africa, especially under the 1983 constitution, awesome executive power is concentrated in a very few hands, and political opponents are virtually powerless to effect change from within the system. This condition seems inevitably to lead to an arrogance of power: a sense that the leadership can do whatever it wishes without consulting those outside the group, and with complete impunity. Indeed, this syndrome is not limited to authoritarian systems, as shown in the Reagan Administration's contempt for both Congress and US allies abroad in connection with the Iran/Contra scandal of 1986/7. But in authoritarian systems there are far fewer checks on executive action and fewer chances of bringing the government to account for policy débâcles.

A further explanation of the Botha Administration's frequent resort to clandestine and uncoordinated foreign policy actions is more personal than systemic. In part at least it reflects P.W. Botha's very close association with the South African military, dating back to his 12 years as Defence Minister. That experience, together with his personal preference for activist and aggressive responses to provocation, led him to view the SADF as the action arm of his foreign policy.

4 Foreign Policy in Defence of Apartheid

APARTHEID UNDER ATTACK

South Africa's domestic race policies under the National Party since 1948 have been by far the greatest single influence on its foreign relations; in few other cases has a country's foreign policy been so dominated and constrained by its internal policies.

The growing hostility to South Africa during the past 40 years is due not only to its apartheid policy – a policy that might have attracted little world attention in colonial times – but to the glaring discrepancy between that policy and post-colonial developments and attitudes throughout the world. South Africa's passage of a bewildering series of laws to enshrine the domination of a privileged white minority over a powerless black majority *on the basis of race alone* flew in the teeth of a post-1945 world in which colonialism was being rapidly dismantled and the ideals of majority rule, self-determination and human rights had been generally accepted.

In their almost single-minded dedication to implementing grand apartheid and maintaining white minority control, successive NP administrations aroused such serious international challenges to their leadership as to severely circumscribe South Africa's foreign policy options and to force its diplomatic activity to concentrate on defending the system against external pressures. Indeed, 'the foreign policy of South Africa has become almost totally a defense of its racial policy against the hostile pressure of nearly the whole world'.[1]

In 1946, two years before the NP came to power with its slogan of apartheid, South Africa's race policies had already come under attack at the first session of the UN General Assembly, when India sponsored a resolution condemning South African discrimination against its Indian population. In the same session South Africa refused to submit its League mandate over South West Africa (Namibia) to UN trusteeship, thereby precipitating its long (and still unresolved) dispute with the UN over that territory.

Apartheid itself came under increasing attack in the early 1950s, starting with a request by 14 Arab and Asian states that it be placed on the General Assembly's agenda as 'a threat to the peace' under the Charter. A surge of international condemnation followed the Sharpeville incident in March 1960, when police fired on a large crowd of unarmed blacks protesting against apartheid. Sixty-nine were killed and 180 wounded. Later that year the USA for the first time supported a UN Security Council resolution affirming that apartheid might endanger world peace and security. In April 1961 South Africa was forced to withdraw from the Commonwealth, and 24 African states introduced a General Assembly resolution urging the severance of diplomatic ties to the new Republic.

Third World countries, and particularly the newly-independent African states, led the campaign to isolate South Africa internationally. Gradually it was excluded from a number of important world bodies: the Food and Agriculture Organization (FAO), the International Labor Organization (ILO), the Economic Commission for Africa and the World Health Organization (WHO) among others. But revulsion against apartheid also affected South Africa's far more important relations with the Western democracies. In 1964 Britain, the US and other Western governments announced their acceptance of a voluntary arms embargo which the UN had adopted against South Africa a year earlier.

In the face of this growing hostility and isolation South African diplomats fought a futile holding action. On occasion the leadership was persuaded to take steps to make apartheid more palatable to the outside world, particularly the West. But such efforts only showed how little the leaders were aware of outside attitudes towards apartheid. Thus in 1962 the Prime Minister, Verwoerd, was convinced by his foreign minister that the gravity of South Africa's international situation required the government 'to do something dramatic and spectacular' to show the world that it was serious about political rights for blacks; otherwise damaging international action would be taken against the Republic.[2] Verwoerd responded by announcing plans to move the Transkei gradually towards independence. He explained to Parliament that allowing such ethnic entities 'to develop into separate Bantu states . . . is a form of fragmentation we would not have liked, were we able to avoid it'. But, he said, *'In the light of pressure being exerted on South Africa*, there is no doubt that eventually this will have to be done' (my emphasis).[3] Verwoerd saw this decision, which caused considerable dissension within the Cabinet and Party, as a major concession to external pressure. Later he expressed doubts that it had any impact abroad, and said he would move more slowly in responding to outside pressure in the future.

The growing international isolation was a setback to South Africa's ambitions to play a major role in African affairs. Until at least the mid-1950s South African leaders did not consider black Africa of intrinsic importance. When they spoke of an 'Africa policy' they were usually referring to their relations with nearby colonial regimes. But as the fateful 'winds of change' brought independence and black majority rule to a growing number of ex-colonial territories, these new states assumed growing importance in Pretoria on several counts.

First, successive NP administrations held it as an article of faith that an improvement in South Africa's relations with black African states, and particularly their acceptance of the political status quo in South Africa, would lead to an improvement in South Africa's more important ties with the Western powers. Second, South Africa has continued to seek international acceptance of its nominally independent Bantustans, which have remained the centrepiece of so-called 'grand apartheid' since the Verwoerd era, and has pressed the BLS states to recognize them as independent entities: pressure which these states so far have resisted. As expressed by South Africa's foreign minister in 1969, 'our Africa policy is in large measure determined by, and indeed flows logically from, our internal policy of separate development'.[4] And, finally, the defence of apartheid took on a security dimension in the mid-1960s as South Africa's leaders saw a need to establish friendly ties across the borders to help protect the country from armed attack by anti-apartheid forces.

APARTHEID AND NATIONAL SECURITY

During roughly the first decade of NP rule (1948–58) internal security concerns were paramount. Early apartheid measures had quickly led to organized resistance, including civil disobedience. The government saw this as communist-instigated, and responded with massive arrests and detentions. But sporadic protests continued throughout the decade, and in 1961 the ANC established a military wing, *Umkhonto we Sizwe* (Spear of the Nation), which conducted a limited campaign of sabotage and bombing during the next couple of years.

South Africa's leaders viewed these events against the backdrop of political upheaval and growing black nationalism elsewhere in Africa: a development they saw as part of a global communist strategy directed against the Western world. Thus the attack on apartheid was perceived as an integral part of a much larger offensive, in which South Africa and the West were linked as targets.

As long as the communist threat was seen to be vague and remote, as in the 1950s, South Africa concentrated on dealing with its internal security problem, while offering token forces to the global anti-communist struggle. In 1962, however, South Africa's Prime Minister Verwoerd reassessed the security threat. He discounted the likelihood of a global conflict in the short term, at least, and saw the main threat to be an Afro-Asian attack: an attack against which the Republic would have to stand alone. Although even that was an unlikely contingency, he said, South Africa must nevertheless prepare for it.

That a South African prime minister in 1962 would consider an 'Afro-Asian attack' anything other than a paranoid's fantasy is understandable only in the context of South Africa's isolation from the reality of developments in the Third World, and particularly in black-ruled Africa. This, too was a direct result of apartheid and the resulting exclusion of South Africa from the normal diplomatic, cultural, commercial and other exchanges available to most countries, at least in peacetime. The normally broad array of such contacts provides a country's leaders with a continuing flow of facts and informed opinion on the basis of which realistic foreign assessments can be made.

Nor were politicians alone subject to distorted notions of the security threat. South Africa's military leaders, equally isolated, urged a build-up in conventional weapons in part, at least, because they took seriously the extravagant rhetoric of African leaders in the late 1950s about creating a pan-African army to crush the apartheid state.

By the mid-1960s, however, fears of conventional attack had faded and the chief emergent threat was seen to be guerrilla incursions. The evidence was clear enough:

1961: Angolan nationalist guerrillas attack Portuguese settlers in northern Angola
1964: Frelimo guerrillas open war of national liberation in Mozambique
1966: SWAPO guerrillas launch first attacks in northern Namibia, and
ZANLA guerrillas and Rhodesian troops engage in firefight for the first time

1967: armed ANC operatives caught in Rhodesia *en route* to South Africa.

South Africa's leaders saw the need to initiate friendly overtures to Africa's independent black-ruled countries in the hope of creating a band of friendly and politically moderate states as a buffer against radical black influences from the north. Prime Minister Vorster's regional outward policy, inaugurated in 1967, led to diplomatic ties with one black-ruled state, Malawi, and to close economic ties with the BLS states. A development aid fund established under the Ministry of Foreign Affairs in 1968 made available some $50 million in loans to African countries during its first several years in operation. A customs union agreement between South Africa and the BLS states was renegotiated in 1969, giving the three smaller states free access to the South African market while at the same time making them more heavily dependent on the dominant member state.

The establishment of diplomatic ties with Malawi created much dissension within the NP. Some years earlier, before the UN General Assembly's resolution opposing diplomatic ties with the Republic, the Verwoerd government had rejected Ghana's offers of diplomatic ties, fearing that a Ghanaian embassy might become a centre for agitation against apartheid. Right-wing NP members raised the issue again with regard to Malawi. They were concerned that the presence of black diplomats, who would be immune from the strictures of apartheid, might have an unsettling effect on South Africa's black population. Divisions within the NP caucus over this issue were a contributing factor to the expulsion in 1969 of four National Party MPs who subsequently organized the right-wing HNP.[5]

The outward policy thus scored some initial successes: diplomatic links with Malawi and a customs agreement with the BLS states. But no other African states joined Malawi in extending diplomatic recognition; indeed, Malawi's action was heavily criticized by other African states. Neither did any government respond to Pretoria's offer in 1970 to conclude non-aggression pacts with Africa's black-ruled states. A Francophone proposal favouring dialogue with Pretoria was rejected by the OAU summit in 1971 by a vote of 28 to 6, with five abstentions. The six 'ayes' were Malawi, Lesotho and four conservative Francophone states.[6]

Black Africa's official response to the outward policy was the Lusaka Manifesto, drafted by Presidents Kaunda and Nyerere and adopted by the fifth summit conference of East and Central African states in April 1969 and endorsed by the OAU summit the same year. This joint manifesto, known officially as 'The Manifesto on Southern Africa', set forth black Africa's position towards the white minority-ruled territories (at that time South Africa, Angola, Rhodesia, Mozambique and Guinea-Bissau). While affirming that the independent African states would prefer to see majority rule come to these territories through peaceful means, they saw that way blocked by the actions of those in power in the white-ruled states. Hence there was nothing to talk about, and the African states were left with no choice but to give the peoples of these territories full support in their armed struggle. In regard to South Africa in particular, the Manifesto urged its diplomatic and economic isolation.

Astonishingly, neither Vorster nor his foreign minister was aware of the Manifesto – a document that is frequently cited by African states as their operative set of principles for dealing with South Africa – until it was brought to his attention by a South African businessman in 1975.[7] The Lusaka Manifesto showed once again the rock-hard resistance of black Africa against acknowledging the legitimacy or permanence of apartheid, and the readiness of these states to support wars of national liberation.

Promotion of the outward policy did not diminish South Africa's interest in its relations with the West, which were still viewed as important to national security. Once the major security threat had been redefined as guerrilla incursions, however, a military alliance with the West was no longer considered crucial although it was still desirable. The rapid build-up in South Africa's armed forces and indigenous arms production in the mid-1960s was concentrated on improving the SADF's mobility and striking-power to meet the new threat. In 1971 the defence minister described to Parliament the Republic's virtual self-sufficiency in producing infantry weapons, small-arms ammunition, explosives, armoured cars and simple communications equipment.[8]

South Africa still remained heavily dependent on foreign suppliers for tanks, aircraft and aircraft engines, helicopters, advanced naval vessels and particularly advanced electronics (such as avionics and radar). And, outside the communist states, most such items were manufactured either in the Western industrial countries or elsewhere under restrictive Western licensing arrangements. In order to have continued access to advanced military weapons and technology, it was therefore important that South Africa try to prevent or weaken moves by Western states to restrict the export of such goods. Indeed, until the imposition of a mandatory UN arms embargo in 1977, South Africa continued to purchase weapons and weapons technology openly from several European countries.

The causative linkage between apartheid, black protest and national security has continued to exert a dominant influence on South Africa's international position. The widespread racial turmoil following student protests in Soweto in 1976, and the Draconian security crackdown that followed in the autumn of 1977 were major factors leading to the UN Security Council's mandatory arms embargo against South Africa. The advent of the Reagan and Thatcher governments, both of which opposed punitive measures against apartheid, brought no more than a temporary respite in the early 1980s to South Africa's growing isolation. The resurgence of black protest in 1985–6 – the longest and most severe this century – led the Botha government to impose sweeping censorship and security measures, removing what few civil rights and restraints against police action had been available previously to protect political opponents. In 1986 the US, the West European nations, Japan, the Commonwealth states and virtually every industrial democracy imposed economic sanctions of varying severity against South Africa. South Africa's long-feared total isolation had come close to realization.

Part III
Shifting Foreign Policy Strategies

5 Deteriorating Security and Policy Reappraisal (1974–8)

DÉTENTE AND VORSTER'S RHODESIAN INITIATIVE

By the beginning of 1974 Portuguese power was crumbling in Angola and Mozambique, and in Rhodesia a growing guerrilla war was already sapping that country's manpower and budget. It was clear that South Africa could no longer count on the surrounding white-ruled territories as an effective and lasting shield against guerrilla assault on Namibia and the Republic.

To secure South Africa's borders in the future and to move regional developments in directions favourable to its interests, the Vorster government decided that it must intervene more directly in regional affairs. A first step had been the so-called *détente* initiative, begun a year earlier, to establish friendly links with moderate black African leaders. But after the Lisbon coup of April 1974 and the new Portuguese government's withdrawal from Angola and Mozambique, South Africa moved quickly on several fronts to project South African power and influence into the region.

In late 1974 Vorster became personally involved in trying to arrange Rhodesian peace negotiations between African nationalist leaders and Ian Smith, Prime Minister of the break-away British colony. In Mozambique Vorster declined to support a *putsch* by Portuguese whites against the new Marxist government, and instead offered economic assistance to President Machel. In Namibia Vorster organized a constitutional conference in September 1975 to set the Territory on the path towards an internal settlement. By August 1975 South African troops had invaded Angola in an ill-fated attempt to prevent the Marxist MPLA guerrillas from seizing power in Luanda.

Clearly not all these actions were consistent with the notion of *détente*. Indeed, *détente* became only one element, albeit an extremely important one, in a wide-ranging response to the shifting balance of power in the region. To the degree that Vorster could exert influence over regional conflicts and political developments, he could limit the damage that the collapse of Portuguese rule would otherwise inflict on South Africa.

The major focus of *détente* was Rhodesia. South Africa had been providing military support to the Smith regime since 1967, when some 2000 South African paramilitary police had been deployed inside Rhodesia to assist the government's counter-insurgency. The Vorster government had also permitted South Africans to meet their national service commitment by volunteering to serve in Rhodesia's armed forces. By 1974, however, Rhodesia's guerrilla war was heating up along both the Zambian border in the north-west and the north-eastern border with Mozambique. Vorster recognized that escalating warfare in Rhodesia would sooner or later bring chaos and disruption, and with it Soviet influence, southward to the border with South Africa, and that this would mean greater South African intervention in the fighting. Since none of this was in South Africa's interests, Vorster decided to seek a peaceful resolution of the Rhodesian conflict.

As early as 1968 Vorster had made secret overtures to President Kaunda of Zambia. He rightly viewed Kaunda as the only black African leader of stature who might be amenable to cooperating with South Africa in seeking a Rhodesian settlement. Indeed Kaunda had reasons of his own for seeking such a settlement. Zambia was host to Joshua Nkomo's ZIPRA guerrillas, a Soviet-supplied force of 10 000 or more whose size, armaments and training would have made it more than a match for Zambia's army in any confrontation. Moreover, as a major guerrilla sanctuary, Zambia risked (and soon would suffer) armed reprisals from Rhodesia. The Zambian economy, too, was affected since the closure of the Rhodesian border in 1973 severed Zambia's major rail link with the outside world.

Both Vorster and Kaunda were thus receptive to quiet efforts by senior executives of Lonrho Ltd, a British conglomerate with vast holdings throughout southern Africa, to bring the two leaders together for a joint peace initiative on Rhodesia.[1] These efforts led to a series of secret talks among South African and Zambian officials in late 1974 ranging over the gamut of regional *détente* issues. The result was a six months' '*détente* scenario' for the region. In regard to Rhodesia, South Africa agreed to withdraw its paramilitary police, and to pressure Smith into releasing black nationalist leaders from jail and lifting the ban on their political activities. In return the Zambians agreed that they, together with Botswana and Mozambique, would press the Rhodesian nationalists to cease their armed struggle and to engage in the process of seeking a political solution.

The Front Line states (at that time Botswana, Mozambique, Tanzania, and Zambia) were suspicious of Vorster's intentions, however. The true test of *détente*, they said, must be Smith's release of the nationalists and acceptance of independence under majority rule.

Vorster pressed Smith into releasing the nationalists in November. The political risks for Smith were such that he insisted the release be kept secret for a month: long after the nationalists had held their first meeting with the Front Line presidents in Lusaka. It was another three months, however, before Vorster could start withdrawing South African paramilitary forces from Rhodesia as he had agreed. Meanwhile the Front Line leaders discovered that the nationalists had fallen into deep and mutually hostile factions during their years of detention, and that it would be no easy task to get them to a conference table, let alone achieve unity among them.

An abortive cease-fire in December 1974 was followed by months of manoeuvring and futile efforts between Vorster and Smith and between the Front Line leaders and various nationalists to bring the warring parties together. Smith tried in various ways to derail the whole initiative. The several nationalist groups jockeyed among themselves for position and recognition. For them the crucial issue was who would lead the nationalist struggle. They viewed the talks with Smith as a side issue, particularly because they had no illusions that he was ready to relinquish power.

In August 1975 Vorster, Smith and Kaunda's special representative, Mark Chona, met in Pretoria and hammered out a loose agreement preparatory to a constitutional conference. Smith and the nationalist leaders would meet without preconditions. After an initial plenary session, which would only affirm the parties' desire for a peaceful settlement, they would form a number of joint committees to work inside Rhodesia. Later a formal conference would ratify the committees' proposals.

That Vorster and the Zambians would put their signatures to a scenario with almost no ingredients for success reflected their weakness and Smith's strength. Smith counted on nationalist disunity, and on the broad sympathy for his regime among South African whites, to forestall the need for real concessions on his part. The nationalists were confident that Smith's intransigence would prevail, leaving them free to pursue the war, which they saw as the only way to bring an end to white minority rule. Vorster was apparently prepared to apply more serious pressure to Smith, but only if there was a reasonable prospect that a moderate black majority government would succeed Smith. But divisions among the nationalists were so obvious and deep as to make it politically impossible for Vorster to convince Rhodesia's white community about the plausibility of a transfer of power to such a leadership.

The last act of regional *détente* took place in August 1975 in a dramatic setting: a white railway train poised midway between Rhodesia and Zambia on a bridge high above the Zambesi Gorge. There, while Smith met the nationalist leaders (Muzorewa, Nkomo and Sithole), Vorster and Kaunda held their first face-to-face meeting in a nearby car, where they talked amiably throughout most of the day. Zambian and South African officials trekked back and forth between the two opposing delegations with proposals for getting the talks moving. But Smith was unyielding. He declined even to discuss black majority rule, and flatly refused to grant amnesty for the nationalists to meet in joint committees in Rhodesia. After 13 hours the delegations departed without agreeing on anything. A South African participant later said the conference would have broken up in 20 minutes had Kaunda and Vorster not been present.[2]

Détente, in fact, probably had no chance of succeeding at that time. The Front Line presidents were in no position to deliver the nationalists to a serious negotiation, and neither had the presidents themselves reached a consensus about the feasibility of talks. Given the state of the nationalist side, the maximum concession Vorster was able to extract from Smith was the release of the nationalist leaders from jail. Smith played effectively on nationalist dissension, and also on the sympathy of South African whites, who saw Smith's defiance as a legitimate means of defending white rule from 'barbarism'.

In sum, the problem was too big to lend itself to a regional solution. South Africa and the Front Line states had too few carrots and only weak sticks at hand. They could not offer Smith legitimacy, or lift sanctions, or guarantee an end to the insurgency; and they lacked the clout to force Smith to concede majority rule. They were palpably unable to club the fractious nationalists into even a semblance of unity, let alone assure them that talks would lead to a transfer of power.

Despite the collapse of *détente*, the initiative led to important changes in the positions of the various actors, and to a shift in the balance of power between Smith and the black nationalists. Vorster had committed South Africa to support moves to bring Rhodesia under black majority rule. His successful pressure on Smith to release the jailed nationalist leaders led to a rise in national liberation consciousness and a boost in recruitment to the various nationalist groups. Smith's post-Victoria Falls initiation of talks with the nationalist Joshua Nkomo showed that Smith had come to accept the idea of admitting blacks to the government, albeit while retaining white control. These developments together brought greater symmetry to the conflict between the Smith government and the nationalists, thereby contributing to its eventual resolution.

For Vorster, his *détente* initiative was a major success because it propelled South Africa into deliberations with black African leaders over resolving regional conflicts. As Vorster had hoped, this led to a broader recognition that South Africa could play an important role in regional affairs; particularly with regard to Rhodesia.

Indeed, when the Rhodesian issue attracted US attention in early 1976, Secretary of State Henry Kissinger saw South Africa as the key to wringing concessions from Smith. Furthermore, the US and South Africa both had strong interests in avoiding the escalation and further radicalization of the Rhodesian conflict. South Africa was particularly concerned that the Cubans, following their successful intervention in Angola's civil war in late 1975, might be ready to intervene in Rhodesia as well.[3] Already faced with the spread of racial conflict and violence growing out of the Soweto uprising, the Vorster government was looking for cooperation, not greater contention, with the international community. By then Vorster had already reached the conclusion that black rule was coming to Rhodesia, and that South Africa's interests lay in facilitating the transition and seeing that moderate black nationalists prevailed over black radicals. In 1975 Vorster had authorized the distribution of a secret circular to members of the Broederbond, declaring that South Africa must abandon its traditional attitude of supporting white minority rule in Rhodesia, and instead accept the inevitability and imminence of black rule there.[4]

When Kissinger and Vorster met in Bavaria in June 1976, the South African was therefore ready to accept Kissinger's strategy of trying to coopt moderate black nationalists and isolate 'ideological radicals'. It was agreed between them that Kissinger would take the high-profile lead against Smith – a position which Vorster could not take because of the sensitivity of the issue in domestic South African politics – while Vorster would bring quiet but heavy pressure to bear.

It was also envisaged that the Front Line presidents would apply pressure to the nationalists; and, once Kissinger had brought Smith to heel, the UK would convene a peace conference.

Vorster began, without fanfare or publicity, to exert pressure on the Smith regime. Vital oil deliveries were cut back, and even the normal weekly trains carrying ammunition to the Rhodesians were disrupted.[5] Publicly South African officials blamed this on the closure of the Mozambican border with Rhodesia and the added strain this placed on South African rail facilities. In August South Africa delivered a diplomatic bombshell, when its UN delegation added a brief preamble to a speech the foreign minister had given in Durban a few days earlier: 'A solution to the Rhodesian issue on the basis of majority rule with adequate protection for minority rights is acceptable to the South African government.'[6]

Bowing to pressure, Smith agreed to meet Kissinger in September. But a few days before they met, Smith and Vorster held secret talks in which Vorster persuaded Smith to make a crucial concession: to accept the principle of majority rule within two years. In seeking his party's approval to meet Kissinger, Smith did not tell them of the concession.[7]

When Smith met Kissinger at the US ambassador's residence in Pretoria, Kissinger gave Smith a bleak assessment of Rhodesia's deteriorating security and economic prospects: an analysis that reinforced a confidential briefing given to Smith six months earlier by his closest advisers, who had warned him that conditions in the country would become intolerable if the war were not ended by June 1977.[8] Kissinger then presented a five-point package which amounted to an ultimatum. It called for Smith to agree to majority rule within two years; to meet the nationalists to organize an interim government; and to a mixed-race Council of State and Cabinet with a black majority. In return, sanctions would be lifted and the guerrilla war would end when the interim government took office.

Smith agreed to the proposals, subject to additional provisos that would guarantee white control over the interim government. With power remaining in white hands, Smith felt he could hold out for a constitution that would meet white requirements.

Kissinger then engaged in a game of calculated ambiguity with Smith and the Front Line presidents. He presented his five-point package to the latter without spelling out Smith's demands, then told Smith in extremely vague language that they had approved the package with Smith's provisos. Thus reassured, Smith made his stunning announcement to the nation that he had accepted Kissinger's proposals for moving towards majority rule within two years.

The Front Line leaders immediately repudiated the amended plan, the details of which they had learned only in Smith's speech. They demanded that the talks between Smith and the nationalists be organized by the UK, and that the shape and functions of an interim government be decided by the conferees, not by Smith in advance. The British, however, were reluctant to take responsibility for a conference based on Kissinger's package. They felt that their influence on the situation at that time was extremely limited, and that the conference had no chance of success.

In the end the UK agreed to chair the conference, which opened in Geneva in late October 1976. It was a fiasco that dragged on for seven weeks, due mostly to the unflagging optimism of its chairman, Ivor Richard, Britain's ambassador to the UN. Four separate nationalist delegations came to talk about a transfer of power. Smith insisted that his only mandate was to discuss the amended Kissinger plan. The conference ended without agreement on anything.

Meanwhile Vorster had concluded that Smith's major concession in agreeing to a short-run timetable for majority rule was as much as he could extract. Domestic political considerations prevented his exerting further pressure on the Rhodesians. Even before the Geneva Conference opened Vorster had ended the squeeze: oil deliveries were restored to their normal level, ammunition supplies were resumed and additional rail capacity was made available for Rhodesian freight.

In January 1977, a few weeks after the collapse of the Geneva talks, the Carter Administration took office in Washington, bringing with it a heightened interest in southern African affairs, a strong empathy for black nationalist aspirations, and a tougher attitude towards South Africa. At the same time Britain's Labour government appointed as Foreign Secretary David Owen, a brash young politician who was ready to push the UK towards a more activist role in Rhodesia. Owen believed, however, that a joint UK–US initiative was necessary, since only the US could bring pressure on South Africa to wring concessions from Smith.

After months of joint shuttle diplomacy to seek areas of consensus among African leaders, two senior diplomats – Ambassadors Low of the US and Graham of Britain – published their *Proposals for a Settlement* in September 1977. The Anglo-American proposals, which essentially called for a British resident commissioner to run a transitional government for six months prior to elections and independence, had little chance of success. For one thing, Smith had lost interest in an internationally-arranged settlement. He was already feeling his way towards an internal accommodation with moderate black leaders inside the country.

Moreover the UK–US plan contained a highly controversial clause, calling for the post-independence merger of the Rhodesian and guerrilla forces into a single Zimbabwe army 'based on the liberation forces'. This clause had been inserted at the suggestion of Tanzania's President Nyerere during a meeting with President Carter in Washington. For Smith, white control of the security forces was simply non-negotiable. The notion of guerrilla control of the future national army was something he could not have sold to his party or the Rhodesian white electorate even if he had wanted to do so.

Also working against the Anglo-US proposals was the deterioration in South Africa's relations with the US. Vorster and Defence Minister Botha were still smarting over the withdrawal of American support from their Angolan intervention of 1975–6. In a sombre New Year's address to the nation in 1977 Vorster said the West had 'lost the will to take a firm stance against the increasing communist menace', and the communist states knew from the Angolan experience that they could attack any country in Africa with impunity.[9] In May Vorster met the US Vice-President, Walter Mondale, in Vienna, where they had a particularly acrimonious discussion. Indeed, Mondale's iteration of the Carter Administration's strong anti-apartheid stance was seized upon by Vorster as evidence of Western hostility and interference, and was used as the NP's major appeal to voters in its landslide electoral victory in September. Relations were further strained in August 1977 when the US made a strong *démarche* to Pretoria over South Africa's apparent preparations to test a nuclear device. In November the US joined other UNSC members in imposing a mandatory arms embargo against South Africa.

According to US diplomats involved in the Rhodesia negotiations, however, Vorster was 'very forthright' about South African attitudes towards the Anglo-US plan.[10] When approached for his support, Vorster declined. 'We're not going to twist his [that is, Smith's] arm to accept the Anglo-U.S. plan or any other.' But, Vorster said, if Smith agrees to it, 'we will help you carry it out'. In short, South Africa would support Smith in whatever he decided. Vorster was none the less said to be scathing in his reaction to the contentious clause concerning guerrilla control of the security forces.

By early December Smith's discussions with several black nationalist leaders had led to an agreement on a constitution and an interim government. Three months later an interim government was installed with black members on its executive council and Cabinet. Smith remained as Prime Minister and kept *de facto* control of the security forces.

During 1978, while Smith and the interim government in Salisbury took various hesitant and ineffective steps to win black support and to end the war, Vorster did not try to pressure the US into supporting the internal settlement.[11] By then Pretoria's relations with the US had deteriorated to the point where Vorster probably felt pressure on the US would be futile and perhaps counter-productive. Moreover Vorster's fading energies were increasingly being spent on looming domestic issues: the burgeoning Information scandal, preparations for the September 1978 general election and his forthcoming retirement. The next moves on Rhodesia would be up to his successor, P.W. Botha.

SEEKING A SETTLEMENT IN NAMIBIA

When Vorster became Prime Minister in September 1966 Namibia had already been a source of growing friction between South Africa and the UN for more than 15 years. During the next ten years it ballooned into a major issue of contention between Pretoria and the West, and became the main focus of diplomatic initiatives in southern Africa.

The issues were complex. Essentially they involved, first, the South African government's refusal to place its League of Nations mandate over Namibia under the authority of the UN as successor to the League; second, South Africa's clear intention, until 1966, to annex the Territory eventually; and, finally, South Africa's moves in the 1960s to implement a system of so-called 'grand apartheid' in Namibia; that is, to carve it up into semi-autonomous ethnic 'homelands' like those in South Africa. The growing opposition to Pretoria's suzerainty over Namibia, both within and outside the Territory, was thus closely linked to the mounting antipathy to apartheid in South Africa, and to fears that apartheid would be extended to Namibia.

A month before Vorster took office SWAPO, a national liberation group formed in 1960, carried out its first armed attack inside Namibia. Shortly thereafter the UN General Assembly revoked South

Africa's mandate over Namibia and established a UN Commission to administer the Territory: moves which Vorster scornfully rejected.

Vorster could not ignore for long however, either the growing UN pressure or the rapid rise in SWAPO actions inside Namibia. Following the conviction of SWAPO leaders on terrorism charges in 1968, Namibia was placed under virtually total administrative control by the South African state president and Cabinet in early 1969: an action proposed by the Minister of Interior for security reasons. At the same time Vorster reaffirmed his government's readiness to talk to a representative of the UN Secretary-General 'on matters of mutual interest affecting [South Africa's] relations with the United Nations'.[12]

The pressure on South Africa was ratcheted up another notch in 1970, when the Western members of the UN Security Council declined to veto a Security Council resolution declaring South Africa's occupation of Namibia illegal. An even more stunning blow was delivered to South Africa the following year, when that UNSC resolution was found binding by the International Court of Justice. In 1972 Vorster received a special representative of the UN Secretary-General, thus for the first time giving *de facto* recognition to the UN's right to a voice in Namibia's future.

In sum, by the time of the Portuguese coup in April 1974, the Vorster Administration was already deeply involved in the Namibian issue. By then Vorster appeared to have accepted the idea of eventual independence for Namibia, although he still thought in terms of partition. He told Parliament in 1973 that the Territory's people would have 'to decide if they wanted confederation or a unitary state [as demanded by the UN], and *those who want to opt out can opt out*' (my emphasis).[13]

All this changed in 1974–5, however, as the Portuguese withdrew from Angola and the security situation there deteriorated. SWAPO took advantage of the new situation to move armed men from Tanzania through Zambia into the southern part of Angola, where they mixed easily with fellow Ovambo people who spilled over both sides of the Namibia border. Soon SWAPO guerrillas were moving into Namibia in large numbers; for example, a skirmish in late 1975 resulted in the deaths of 61 SWAPO and three South African soldiers.

Vorster was confronted by a burgeoning SWAPO insurgency, political disarray and assassinations of local political leaders inside Namibia, and a growing threat of sanctions if the Namibia issue remained unresolved. In fact, in June 1975 only a single Western veto prevented the UNSC from formally calling for the adoption of punitive measures against South Africa to force its withdrawal from Namibia.

Vorster therefore decided on a bold new Namibian initiative. In September 1975 – at the same time as South African troops were being secretly committed to a major military offensive inside Angola – Vorster convened a constitutional conference on Namibia at the Turnhalle building in Windhoek. Its mandate was to draft a constitution for the Territory as a whole, after which an interim administration would be established to lead Namibia to independence. The invited delegates were moderate leaders of Namibia's 11 official ethnic groups, including whites. Neither SWAPO nor any other political parties were invited to participate.

Although the Turnhalle conference was organized along strictly ethnic lines, it was nevertheless clear that Vorster had by then relinquished the idea of creating separate autonomous Bantustans in the Territory. Instead he sought agreement among the delegates on the future shape of a unified Namibia. In part this shift reflected Vorster's judgement that a territorial government would be better able to cope with the challenges of SWAPO and other political dissidents, whereas independent Bantustans – particularly an independent Ovamboland – would be vulnerable to political polarization and subversion. But the major impetus for Turnhalle was the need to head off UN sanctions by agreeing to Namibian independence, while making sure that the process was controlled from Pretoria, not from the UN. A third consideration was to pre-empt growing demands by Namibian blacks for a voice in the Territory's administration, while assuring that black political activity would be largely contained within each ethnic community.

While the Turnhalle delegates were hammering out a draft constitution during the next 18 months, South Africa conferred various degrees of self-government on half-a-dozen of Namibia's ethnic communities.[14] The draft constitution presented in March 1977 entrenched ethnicity by providing for a multi-ethnic, three-tier legislative system. Defence, foreign affairs and other national matters would be legislated by a 60-member national assembly, whose members would be appointed by the second tier; that is, by the legislative assemblies, tribal councils, and so on representing each of the 11 officially-recognized ethnic communities. Local and municipal councils would make up the third tier. Since the second and third tiers would have authority over such important local issues as housing, health and education, the new constitution guaranteed whites control over their own communities: a major concern of Namibia's whites, who make up roughly 7 per cent of the population. The proposed interim constitution was also designed to assure the various ethnic groups that the Ovambo people, who account for almost half the Territory's population, would not dominate the government of an independent Namibia.

The constitution called for South Africa to retain control over defence, internal security, foreign affairs, currency and other Territorial matters until independence. The Turnhalle drafting committee recommended that an interim government be established immediately under the constitution, and that formal independence be declared in December 1978.

The presentation of the Turnhalle constitution set in motion a rapid series of developments. Within Namibia whites approved the constitution in a referendum, but major black political and religious groups rejected it. The Western powers, fearing that South Africa might try to implement the Turnhalle constitution unilaterally, launched a major new diplomatic initiative towards South Africa. On 7 April 1977, a few weeks after the Turnhalle Conference ended, the five Western members of the UNSC – Canada, Britain, France, Germany and the US – delivered a strong note to South Africa, reiterating the demands of UNSC Resolution 385 approved a year earlier: free elections under UN supervision, withdrawal of South African forces, release of political detainees and scrapping of the Turnhalle plans for a pre-independence government. This was followed by a joint *démarche* in late April, when senior ambassadors from these five powers went to South Africa as an unofficial 'Contact Group' for private talks with South African leaders. They also met with Turnhalle delegates and various Opposition political groups in Namibia.

During two months of intensive discussions, the Contact Group achieved astonishing results. The group warned Vorster that the Western powers could not support the Turnhalle initiative, and that South Africa could no longer count on Western vetoes to stall sanctions. They persuaded him to agree to end apartheid in Namibia and also to agree to free elections in which SWAPO would participate. In return the West would not press for an early South African withdrawal from the Territory. They also persuaded him and the Turnhalle delegates that it would be futile to proceed with the interim constitution, which could not win international support. Instead it was agreed that Vorster would appoint a South African administrator-general, who would prepare Namibia for elections to a constituent assembly as called for in UNSC Resolution 385, and who would govern the Territory in the interim.

In June South Africa's Parliament passed a Bill authorizing the government to enact, repeal and amend South West African regulations and to appoint an administrator-general for the Territory. Vorster acknowledged to a stunned Parliament that this would open the path to election of a constituent assembly, and would eventually 'make the territory in its entirety independent'.[15] He explained this abrupt reversal in policy and the termination of Turnhalle as the result of external pressure. He praised the Turnhalle delegates for a remarkable achievement. But whilst 'one would have thought they would be applauded from all sides, especially by the Western powers . . . unfortunately they received, to put it at its highest, only a lukewarm reception'. The Turnhalle leaders, he said, realized that to have established an interim government would have prejudiced their chances for international acceptance.[16]

Vorster only hinted at the political costs of stopping Turnhalle in mid-flight. He noted that many existing laws would have to be repealed and new legislation enacted, particularly since local self-governing bodies were already functioning in a number of ethnic communities. Indeed the disappointment of local politicians who had been associated for two years with the Turnhalle negotiations, and who suddenly saw their political fortunes evaporate, contributed in no small way to the dissension and bitterness that have continued to dominate Namibia's internal politics.

In September South Africa installed Judge Marthinus Steyn as Administrator-General of the Territory, and the Contact Group held a third round of talks in Pretoria. By then, however, Vorster's attitude was hardening, and he balked at making further concessions. Major disagreements arose over the size of the proposed UN peacekeeping force; the size and deployment of South African forces during the transition; and the timing of elections to a constituent assembly.

Early in February 1978 the Contact Group presented SWAPO and the South African government with a new, comprehensive set of proposals, which became the basis for all subsequent discussions. Its main provisions were:

1. a cease-fire, in which South African forces would be reduced from

12 000 to 1500 and confined to one or two bases in the north, and SWAPO would be restricted to several camps in southern Angola;
2. appointment of a UN Special Representative and a UN military/civilian group (United Nations Transition Advisory Group, or UNTAG) to oversee the cease-fire and to work with the South African administrator-general during the run-up to elections;
3. elections to a constituent assembly to take place by 31 December under UN supervision.

'Proximity talks' about these issues began in early February in New York, where the Contact Group met separately with SWAPO and South African government representatives. Within a few days, however, the South African foreign minister, Roelof Botha, left the talks and flew home for consultations, after first declaring at a press conference that the proposals would lead to Namibia's being 'overrun and governed by Marxist terrorists'.[17] On 14 February, following a long and apparently acrimonious Cabinet meeting,[18] Vorster announced that South Africa would carry out its own plan for internal elections and (unilateral) independence for the Territory by the year's end.

South Africa's abrupt withdrawal from the talks seems to have been due in part to pique over a misunderstanding: one of many that were to plague the talks over the next few years. Weeks before the walk-out Austrian Major-General Hannes Philipp, the UN's choice to command UNTAG, was sent to Pretoria to work out with the South African military an agreed plan for the disposition of forces. Philipp met Malan, the SADF chief, whom he had known from earlier days when they had attended courses together at the US Army Staff College at Fort Leavenworth. The UN and Philipp had prepared for talks strictly between military men on logistical and other arrangements; but the South African side brought along foreign affairs people, who injected into the final document a number of stipulations that would have crippled SWAPO's political activity prior to the planned elections. South African forces would not be confined to one or two bases, but would be free to carry out operations during the electoral campaign, and the campaign period would be cut to four months.

In short, the South Africans effectively sandbagged Philipp into agreeing to an operational plan that would have been totally unacceptable to SWAPO and its African supporters at the UN. As a result the plan remained an internal UN document that was never circulated, and Philipp was fired (though some UN officials believe the blame should have fallen on his superiors for sending him on the mission unprepared). The South Africans, however, considered the plan officially agreed upon by the UN representative (Philipp), and therefore in final form to be submitted to SWAPO. When the document was shelved, they felt this was another instance of what they saw as UN double-dealing at their expense.[19]

Other, more fundamental, factors influenced Pretoria's decision to bolt the New York talks in February, however. One was the rapid deterioration in South Africa's relations with the West following the Soweto uprising. That event had led to global condemnation and to demands by Western governments for fundamental change in Pretoria's race policies. Indeed, on 4 November 1977 – three months before the start of the proximity talks – the UNSC had unanimously declared a mandatory arms embargo against South Africa. Confrontation over Vorster's nuclear intentions had further soured his relations with the West. The Vorster leadership thus felt that concessions on Namibia were of diminishing utility in bringing more favourable Western treatment of South Africa.

Another factor was sharp dissension within the Cabinet. Defence Minister P. W. Botha and the military insisted that South African security would be put at grave risk by a SWAPO electoral victory, which they asserted would lead to the introduction of Russians and Cubans along South Africa's border. Hence the military's position was simply articulated as 'No Red flag in Windhoek': a view they have continued to hold. The foreign minister and Vorster himself also saw national security as paramount, but they felt that an internationally acceptable settlement in Namibia might lessen the pressure on South Africa and perhaps reduce the risk of mandatory economic sanctions. Initially at least they appeared to believe that there was a chance of achieving such a settlement on terms that would prevent a SWAPO takeover.

During the first quarter of 1978 the South Africans saw the security situation in Namibia deteriorate. Several guerrilla raids into Ovamboland had led to South African 'hot pursuit' operations inside Angola. In February and March a series of kidnappings and assassinations of local political leaders was attributed to SWAPO. In mid-April the administrator-general was given sweeping powers of arrest and detention.

Thus by late March, when the Western Five offered 'clarified' proposals to South Africa and SWAPO, the South African military's reservations about a settlement had gained at the expense of Foreign Affairs' softer line. This was evident in the narrow mandate given the foreign minister to negotiate. On 25 April he announced South Africa's acceptance of the 'clarified' proposals, subject to several conditions: a (reduced) South African security force would be allowed to remain in Namibia following independence if invited to do so by the constituent assembly; the South African troop withdrawal would take place only after all hostilities had ceased; and responsibility for maintaining law and order during the transition period would rest with South Africa. Finally, Foreign Minister Botha insisted that the clarified proposals, including South Africa's new conditions, *must be agreed on as final*, and not subject to further negotiation or change. The Cabinet had apparently put the foreign minister on a short leash, with little room for manoeuvre in future negotiations.

The Vorster government's hardening line on Namibia was soon made evident in other ways as well. On 25 April, the day South Africa announced its qualified acceptance of the Western proposals, South African police arrested nine members of SWAPO's legally-functioning internal wing. Nine days later the SADF launched its first deep-penetration attack against SWAPO targets in Angola: an airborne blitz on a SWAPO base camp at Cassinga, 155 miles inside the country. Several hundred SWAPO people, including many civilians, were killed, and large quantities of weapons were destroyed in the raid. Settlement prospects were dealt a further blow in June, when Vorster announced plans to register Namibians for an internal election to be supervised by South Africa.

Intermittent talks resumed during the summer, but neither South Africa nor SWAPO appeared serious about negotiating a settlement at that time. Vorster's poor health, and his preoccupation with the urgent domestic issues already mentioned, were by then diverting his attention from Namibia. He was no longer in a position to engage his previously strong will and concern in the Namibia issue, nor to counter the hardline position of Botha and the military.

On 30 August the UN Secretary-General, Kurt Waldheim, officially presented the UN plan for Namibia. On 6 September the South African Cabinet deliberated the plan in a crucial meeting chaired by Defence Minister Botha in place of the ailing Vorster. The Cabinet formally rejected major elements of the Waldheim plan. The South Africans claimed that a UN force of 7500 troops and 1200 civilians was excessive, particularly since South Africa viewed these forces as hostile to its interests. The South Africans felt, probably correctly, that the longer SWAPO had to campaign inside Namibia, the greater its chances of winning; hence they were insistent that elections take place before 31 December, and not the following summer as stipulated in the Waldheim plan. This demand was of course unacceptable, since it would have allowed less than three months for establishing a cease-fire and making the necessary logistical arrangements for dispatching, deploying and maintaining a large UN force, organizing political campaigns, and so on.

On 20 September Vorster announced his immediate resignation as prime minister, and his Cabinet's decision to organize internal elections in Namibia before the end of the year. The following week P.W. Botha was elected leader of the NP, thus becoming South Africa's new prime minister.

Botha's election assured the ascendancy of the hardliners on Namibia. Indeed, during the final months of the Vorster Administration Botha had been assuming growing influence over the Namibia policy. Throughout the summer of 1978 he had repeatedly criticized Western and UN actions on Namibia, and had threatened further armed strikes into Angola.[20] To publicize his concern about the dangers of accepting the Waldheim plan, Botha – not Vorster – had removed General Geldenhuys, SADF commander in Namibia, from a South African delegation going to New York, and had instructed him to remain in place so as to 'keep the South African government *and everybody else concerned* informed about SWAPO's aggression from Zambia and Angola' (my emphasis).[21]

Following Botha's election to leadership of the NP and his succession to the premiership, a leading pro-government newspaper suggested that his hard line on Namibia had contributed to his political victory:

> Mr. Botha's aspirations to the Premiership probably received a boost with South Africa's rejection of the Waldheim plan for South West Africa [SWA]. He has repeatedly made it clear that he regards South Africa's role in SWA in warding off the Marxist orientated SWAPO onslaught as crucial . . . It is generally held that Mr. Botha was suspicious of the U.N. plan all along.[22]

Was the Vorster government at any time really serious about reaching an accommodation with the UN on Namibia? The evidence suggests that some senior officials, particularly in the foreign ministry, had originally urged Vorster to open negotiations with the UN to seek a settlement that would win international acceptance and ward off punitive sanctions. Vorster himself saw the desirability of reaching such an accord, if it could be had without sacrificing major South African political and security interests. He apparently hoped that mediation by the Western Five would dampen the influence of the more radical UN members and ensure that South Africa's concerns and interests were taken into account. Indeed Vorster was willing to make a couple of important and politically risky concessions – particularly terminating the Turnhalle exercise – in the interests of an agreement that would meet UN demands.

In a crucial ten-month period from November 1977 to September 1978, however, several events occurred which, together, reduced South Africa's interests and hopes in seeking such an accord. Deteriorating relations with the West; political turmoil inside Namibia as SWAPO guerrilla activities increased; a growing conviction in Pretoria that the negotiations were leading inevitably towards a SWAPO-dominated Namibia: all these factors diminished the prospects for an accord that would meet South Africa's growing security concerns, particularly those of the South African military. Even by the time of the Cassinga raid in May 1978 the Information affair was beginning to unravel, and it became apparent that the views of P.W. Botha and the SADF leadership were dominating the Namibia policy.

INTERVENTION IN ANGOLA, 1975–6

South Africa's military intervention in Angola in 1975–6 is generally credited with sounding the death-knell of Vorster's policy of *détente*, as well as being an aberration in that policy. The decision, or rather the series of decisions culminating in a major offensive by South African forces, was based on mistaken premises and shaky assumptions. In retrospect it seems incredible that Vorster could have thought it would succeed.

Yet given the Vorster leadership's assessments, both of developments in Angola and of the likely reactions of African and outside states to those developments, the Angolan intervention was no aberration. Indeed, it was initially perceived by Vorster as a move that would enhance his government's status with African and Western leaders and improve its relations with both regions. In short, it was seen as consistent and compatible with *détente*. Moreover, in the beginning there were at least some grounds for holding that view.

The *basis* for deciding to intervene, however, and the *process* by which that and subsequent decisions were made, were seriously flawed. The leadership was divided. It had no clear political or agreed military objective. The military was unprepared for the role it ultimately assumed. Involvement occurred through incremental stages, through decisions taken mostly by field commanders on the basis of immediate military developments. The end came on the heels of military reverses and the fading of hoped-for external support and collaboration.

Until the spring of 1975, however, the Vorster government showed little inclination to intervene in the troubled affairs of Angola. South Africa and the Portuguese authorities had exchanged intelligence on the activities of guerrillas since the early 1970s, and Vorster had secretly provided helicopters and other arms to the Portuguese during that period. In 1974, as the Portuguese were preparing to withdraw, South Africa expressed some interest in promoting a 'Groot Ovambo': that is, a greater Ovambo Bantustan straddling the Namibia–Angola border as a buffer against SWAPO.[23]

By June and July of 1975, however, a number of developments inside Angola had alarmed the South Africans as outlined below.

1. Under the terms of the Alvor Accord, which Angola's three national liberation groups signed on 15 January 1975, the Marxist MPLA established an office in Ngiva, only 30 miles north of the Namibian border. The South African military, in particular, feared this would lead to the spread of radical political ideas among the Ovambo people, and to growing support for SWAPO.
2. In July the commander of South African forces in Namibia warned that SWAPO was taking advantage of the growing chaos and collapse of Portuguese authority to consolidate its position in Cunene Province, which borders Namibia.[24] He spoke of SWAPO training camps housing several thousand Namibian exiles, and expressed concern about the the growing danger of SWAPO attacks on Namibian towns. Its guerrillas had already attacked SADF convoys inside Namibia during July.
3. Meanwhile, fighting among the rival Angolan movements spread south, sending 11 000 refugees ahead of it.[25] South African authorities, alarmed at the unsettling effect these refugees might

have in Namibia, established two refugee camps on the Angolan side of the border.
4. Vorster was also concerned about the two major dams nearing completion on the Cunene River just inside Angola: a joint project planned earlier with the Portuguese that would provide an important source of electricity and water for northern Namibia.

In June South Africa's defence minister, P.W. Botha, gave Vorster an options paper on Angola.[26] Although another three months passed before Vorster decided on a major SADF offensive, serious military operations inside Angola began in July. Following guerrilla harassment of engineers working on the Calueque dam, Vorster is said to have authorized P.W. Botha to instruct the Defence Force 'that the attackers should be decisively driven off'.[27] Accordingly SADF units drove to the nearby village where all three guerrilla groups had offices. While FNLA and UNITA operatives were disarmed, those of the MPLA were taken prisoner and their office sacked.[28] In early August SADF units established a permanent presence at the two dam sites.

Towards the end of August SADF activities moved beyond mere defence of the dams. The first offensive thrust came as an attack against the main MPLA headquarters at Ngiva, 100 miles east of the dams. This step, which represented a significant escalation in South African intervention in Angolan affairs, was taken without broad consultation in Pretoria. Indeed, the Department of Foreign Affairs first learned of it through a note of protest delivered by the Portuguese government.[29] Having targeted the MPLA as the enemy, the SADF launched a series of strikes against local MPLA forces, but left UNITA and the FNLA alone.[30]

In late September Vorster decided to provide weapons and vehicles, and a small number of advisers and instructors, to the forces of UNITA, FNLA and the ELP (the Portuguese Liberation Army, a small rag-tag group made up chiefly of former members of the Portuguese army and police).[31] This political decision to commit South African arms and personnel to the conflict was a victory for P.W. Botha and the military, whose conviction that South Africa should intervene militarily to influence the course of events in Angola finally prevailed over the counsel of caution urged by senior Foreign Affairs officials.[32] Once that decision had been made, the SADF drew up a four-stage operational plan for offensive operations, the final stage being the capture of Luanda.[33] To move from one stage to the next, however, would require a political decision by Vorster and P.W. Botha.

By then it was clear to the South Africans that they were not alone in supporting the FNLA and UNITA against the MPLA. As early as July, US arms were reaching both UNITA and the FNLA under a covert US assistance programme run by the CIA station chief in Kinshasa with the direct support and encouragement of Zaire's President Mobutu.[34] Indeed Mobutu was the major sponsor of the FNLA, which was headed by Holden Roberto, Mobutu's relative by marriage. UNITA, too, had a leading African patron: President Kaunda of Zambia, who had provided sanctuary and support to Savimbi for almost a decade. According to John Stockwell, chief of the CIA's Angolan task force in 1975–6, the CIA office in Lusaka ran intelligence-gathering operations in Angola that were coordinated with both Savimbi and Kaunda.[35] Similarly French cooperation in supplying arms for the two movements and in recruiting mercenaries to assist them was coordinated by the CIA stations in Paris and Kinshasa.[36]

Zaire and Zambia were not the only African states favouring UNITA and the FNLA. A number of conservative Francophone states, including Gabon, Senegal and the Ivory Coast, provided diplomatic support both to these groups and to their outside backers.[37] Other African governments, notably those in Tanzania, Nigeria, Egypt and the Sudan, appeared to support no particular group in Angola in early 1975, but were concerned about outside intervention. Since South African intervention was only beginning, and the US role had yet to surface, their chief concern at that time was the Soviet airlift of arms to the MPLA.[38]

In October the fighting in Angola rapidly escalated into conventional warfare as outside patrons stepped up their involvement. Early in the month 500–700 Cuban instructors and advisers arrived in Angola and immediately established four training camps for MPLA troops in the north and centre of the country.[39] In mid-October a South African-led combat group codenamed 'Zulu' crossed the border under instructions to 'recapture as many towns in southern Angola as possible'.[40] Originally consisting of an FNLA battalion, a Bushman battalion, and a dozen SADF officers and non-commissioned officers, the force was soon augmented by four squadrons of South African-manned armoured cars and an SADF heavy-mortar unit. Within three weeks the Zulu force had moved more than 300 miles, scattering the disorganized MPLA forces before it. It ran into its first opposition at the port of Benguela, where hastily dug-in MPLA and a handful of Cuban instructors offered but feeble resistance against the well-armed South Africans. The city was abandoned after a day's fighting, leaving some 700 defenders dead.[41] At that point four 88 mm guns were added to the Zulu force.

Meanwhile South Africa had organized a second combat group ('Foxbat'), made up of three companies of UNITA and FNLA, an armoured SADF squadron, 12 heavy artillery pieces, a platoon of mortars and an engineer regiment.[42] This force moved rapidly up the middle of Angola.

Not surprisingly the major supporters of UNITA and the FNLA made some attempt to coordinate their activities. The CIA stations in Pretoria and Kinshasa coordinated an airlift of US weapons and equipment, which arrived at Njili airport in Zaire at night to be met by two South African Air Force (SAAF) C-130s and flown to South African-led forces at Bie.[43] According to newspaper reports at the time, a small number of SADF personnel also took part in the separate FNLA offensive launched against Luanda from the north.[44] There is no evidence, however, that the two campaigns were coordinated, or that a master plan had been established for a grand pincer movement against Luanda.[45]

Lobito, a port less than 250 miles south of Luanda, fell to the Zulu column in early November. There the offensive halted for several days, apparently while Vorster decided whether to go forward with the fourth stage of the military operations plan; that is, to strike at the capital. Reports that Vorster sent a senior emissary to Washington at this time, and that Savimbi flew to Pretoria to urge the SADF to stay on, suggest growing South African ambivalence about further operations. An official SADF account published later referred ambiguously to the SADF awaiting orders to withdraw while 'mediation by go-betweens' went on during this period.[46]

On 11 November the Portuguese High Commissioner and all remaining Portuguese military personnel left, after an announcement that Portugal had transferred its sovereignty 'to the people of Angola'. The MPLA in Luanda declared the People's Republic of Angola, while the FNLA and UNITA declared a Democratic People's Republic of Angola from their headquarters in Huambo.

By then Vorster had decided to resume the SADF-led offensive. Within a couple of days the Zulu column advanced more than 75 miles to take the port of Novo Redondo, only 125 miles south of Luanda. Two new combat groups, 'Orange' and 'X-Ray', mounted attacks east along the Benguela railway and north along the main interior road to Luanda. By that time South Africa had committed 2000 or more of its troops to the Angolan offensive.[47]

Meanwhile an appeal by Agostino Neto, head of the MPLA, for urgent and large-scale Cuban intervention had led Castro's central committee to decide to send a combat brigade to Angola, a decision that was conveyed to the USSR on 5 November.[48] The arrival of three Cuban ships with hundreds of advisers, instructors and weapons supplies for the MPLA in early October indicates that the Cubans had already decided, at least by late September, on substantial military involvement in support of the MPLA.[49] But the first Cuban *combat* troops arrived in Luanda in two aircraft between 8 and 10 November, while three Cuban troopships carrying an artillery regiment docked in Luanda on 27 November.[50]

As the South African and UNITA/FNLA columns moved north in November and December they encountered stiffening resistance from MPLA forces and from the Cubans, whose forces probably numbered around 3000 by late November.[51] At first the Cubans slowed the South African advance by destroying bridges over Angola's steep-walled rivers. The SADF had stocks of bridging equipment in warehouses in South Africa, but had provided none to its forces in Angola: one of many signs of the lack of advance contingency planning by the leadership. SADF troops were therefore forced to cut trees and construct crude bridges for their vehicles.[52] The South Africans were also unprepared for the Cubans' 122 mm Soviet rocket-launchers. Outgunned South African artillerymen would move their pieces into range at night, open fire at dawn, then move beyond range of the Cuban weapons as quickly as possible.[53]

The SADF-led forces, although winning a couple of important engagements in early December, began to suffer heavy losses both of vehicles and personnel. In one engagement an ambushed column lost 14 vehicles and 200 FNLA/UNITA troops, who were killed inside their transports.[54] The offensive stalled at the Queve River, two hours' drive from Luanda.

By that time Vorster's Angolan venture had begun to suffer diplomatic setbacks as well as military reverses. On 25 November Nigeria added its name to the list of several African states which had already recognized the MPLA government in Luanda. The Nigerians said they did so because of the presence of South African troops in Angola.[55] At a press conference held in Luanda on 16 December, the MPLA presented two young SADF prisoners who blew the already-eroding cover on South African intervention. Three days later the US Senate passed the Clark Amendment which prohibited further American support to any of the Angolan combatants. NATO foreign ministers, who were meeting in Brussels in early December, were said by Britain's foreign minister, Callaghan, to want to 'avoid any suggestion that any NATO member become involved in support for UNITA/FNLA'.[56]

Both Vorster and P.W. Botha gave strong public hints that their continued involvement rested on Western support. Botha called a press conference on 27 November – that is, while the US Senate was debating American involvement in Angola – and told the assembled foreign journalists that he 'would like to see the Free World show more direct interest in getting the Russians out of southern Africa'.[57] In late December Vorster told the press that the USSR was sending sophisticated weapons into Angola: tanks, 122 mm rockets mounted in clusters of 50, and infantry-borne surface-to-air missiles. 'Only big powers can affect this arsenal', he said. 'It is certainly beyond our limits.'[58]

By then South Africa was publicly hinting that it was prepared for a conditional withdrawal. P.W. Botha was cited in the press on 30 December as suggesting that South Africa 'would almost certainly reconsider its involvement if its interests in southern Angola were guaranteed and if terrorists' attacks into South West Africa were halted'.[59] Whether this was a genuine peace feeler or only a bid to influence the US House of Representatives' vote on Angola policy, there were in any case no takers.

Savimbi, after being told by a local SADF commander on Christmas Day that the South Africans were planning to withdraw from their northern outpost of Cela, won Vorster's assurance that South African troops would remain in Angola until the outcome of the OAU summit (10–14 January) became known.[60] On 5 January, however, the SADF began withdrawing from Huambo, more than 125 miles south of their most advanced outpost.[61] A week later the OAU split down the middle on Angola: 22 states voted for a Nigerian resolution to recognize the MPLA as Angola's 'sole legitimate government', and 22 for Senegal's resolution calling for a government of national unity.

On 22 January South African forces began moving towards the Namibian border, and Vorster was telling the press that, without a more open Western commitment, SADF troops would be ordered to fall back to a defensive line along the frontier.[62] The US House of Representatives supported the ban on aid to Angolan combatants by a lop-sided 323–99 vote on 27 January, and in February the OAU recognized the MPLA as the sole, legitimate government of Angola. By then the Vorster Administration was expressing a guarded willingness to accept the new situation. Thus on 12 February P.W. Botha was quoted by the Associated Press as saying: 'If the region is stabilized and the Ovambo interests are not undermined by the MPLA – in other words, if they restrain themselves and stay where they belong – doubtless discussions could be held with them regarding our interests in that area.'[63] In early March the MPLA government gave assurances to Vorster that it would not interfere with work on the two Cunene River dams. Later that month the last of the SADF intervention force was withdrawn from Angola.[64]

In the aftermath of the Angolan débâcle angry questions were asked in Parliament and, rare in the closed NP leadership, public (albeit muted) recriminations surfaced among the bureaucracies. Official SADF casualties – 43 killed and around a hundred wounded – were surprisingly light given the campaign's six-month duration and the number of engagements fought. But these casualties came as a shock to South Africa's white community, which had been told nothing of the intervention until after the March withdrawal. Parents of young national servicemen complained that their sons had been sent to fight in a foreign country without parental consent. One result was a new Act, pushed through Parliament by P.W. Botha early in 1976, allowing the SADF to send personnel 'to perform service against an enemy at any place outside the Republic'.[65]

The military, smarting at what was widely perceived as a defeat for the SADF, criticized the 'political decision' to withdraw. Their frustration was reflected in the official SADF account of the campaign entitled 'We Could Have Gone All the Way'.[66] Two years later the new Defence Minister, Magnus Malan, asserted that the Angolan experience 'focused the attention of the leadership on the urgent necessity for the State Security Council to play a much fuller role in the national security of the Republic': an oblique criticism of Vorster's decision-making and the exclusion of the military from critical policy decisions on Angola.[67]

That was only one aspect of a seriously flawed policy, however. Even more fundamental was Vorster's lack of a solid mandate for the Angolan venture. The leadership itself was divided. From the outset P.W. Botha and the military pressed Vorster for a total commitment to the offensive. General van den Bergh, Vorster's closest confidant and adviser, had been in contact with UNITA and

FNLA leaders prior to South African intervention. Although initially he argued in favour of providing arms to both groups, he is said to have urged an end to South African participation after concluding that it could not succeed against the MPLA and Cubans without continued US logistical support.[68] The DFA, including both the respected Brand Fourie, Secretary of Foreign Affairs, and Roelof Botha, Ambassador to the US at that time, were opposed to South African involvement as a dangerous breach of Pretoria's traditional policy of non-interference.[69] Neither had Vorster built any sort of public consensus to support the intervention; hence his decision to intervene without informing Parliament or the South African public, and his accompanying instruction to the military that South African casualties must be avoided.[70]

The Vorster leadership also fell victim to flawed assessments of the will and capabilities of outside actors, including the two national groups it supported, UNITA and the FNLA. In its official post-mortem, the SADF noted that UNITA lost interest in the offensive once its own base area in the south–central plateau had been cleared of the MPLA.[71] South African military men also acknowledged later that they had counted on FNLA armoured units delivering heavy blows against Luanda from the north, not realizing that the only previous activity of those units had been to take part in parades in Kinshasa.[72] The hostility between UNITA and the FNLA, which on occasion flared into open conflict, was another unexpected factor weakening the joint offensive.

Both Vorster and P. W. Botha viewed the clandestine US initiative to aid the FNLA and (to a lesser extent) UNITA as a far more permanent and high-level policy commitment than in fact it was. Although Botha later complained bitterly about the US letting South Africa down, there were grounds early on for him to have had doubts about the nature of that commitment. John Stockwell, who headed the US intelligence task force on Angola, later wrote a detailed exposé of its activities in which he described how coordination with South Africa 'was effected *at all CIA levels*, and the South Africans escalated their involvement in step with our own'. He then went on, however, to note that the State Department effectively vetoed a CIA proposal to ship howitzer ammunition directly to South Africa. After that event 'CIA case officers continued to coordinate with the South Africans in Angola', but 'the CIA *stopped trying to expand that cooperation at the policy level.*'[73] Stockwell also 'saw no evidence that the United States *formally* encouraged [South Africa] to join the conflict' (my emphasis).⁷⁴ Although US involvement thus remained clandestine and low level, Vorster and Botha apparently were prone to believe that it represented a firm policy commitment by the Ford Administration.

Vorster similarly misread the degree and nature of African support for South African intervention. Private nods and winks from a handful of African leaders do not represent meaningful or useful support. When the initiative became bogged down amidst a rising tide of criticism of South African intervention, there was no African support to be found.

The evaporation of African and Western support showed once again the almost insuperable obstacle which any apartheid, white minority government in Pretoria faces in trying to win outside collaboration and support. At most outside states can provide only clandestine cooperation, which can quickly fade at the first sign of failure or public exposure.

The Vorster government also underestimated the chances of a rapid and large-scale Cuban military intervention to block the SADF/UNITA/FNLA offensive and assure an MPLA victory. The US, too, was caught by surprise. The SADF's claim that it 'could have gone all the way' to Luanda is thus only conditionally true. In early November the two major SADF-led combat groups probably had the momentum and capability to move on quickly to the capital. But the rapidly-growing opposition by MPLA and Cuban forces would probably have begun to inflict intolerably heavy casualties on the South Africans, leading to an early withdrawal. Furthermore, what would the South Africans have done upon reaching Luanda? Would Vorster really have been prepared to occupy and hold the capital while hoping for a turnaround in US policy and a favourable decision by the OAU? Presumably it was questions like these which prompted Vorster's growing caution in November.

In the end, the intervention was a costly one for South Africa. It put paid to *détente*, and to Vorster's efforts to project the image of South Africa as a benign, non-interfering power in the region. It led to widespread international condemnation, and weakened beyond redemption the chances for OAU recognition of UNITA and the FNLA as legitimate claimants to power in Angola. Rightly or wrongly, the campaign weakened the SADF's aura of regional invincibility. Most important, the intervention gave Cuba and the USSR a pretext for introducing a massive Cuban military presence in Angola, thereby bringing about the security situation most feared by successive NP governments: a large communist force north of the border.

The Angolan débâcle none the less had at least some positive results for South Africa's rulers. It led P.W. Botha to broaden the base of policy inputs and to bring much-needed structure to the decision-making process when he became prime minister in 1978. It also gave the SADF its first experience in conventional warfare since the Second World War, and showed its inadequacies in training and weapons, particularly long-range artillery and armoured firepower.

Finally, the experience in Angola left its mark on P.W. Botha. Clearly embittered by what he perceived as the US reneging on its commitment to support South African intervention, Botha carried his suspicion and distrust of the West, and the US in particular, into his own administration.

6 Growing Militancy and Isolation under P.W. Botha since 1978

THE ASCENDANCY OF A HAWK

The election of P.W. Botha to the premiership on 28 September 1978 brought no abrupt or dramatic shift in South African foreign policy. This is not surprising. For one thing, Botha's foreign policy options were limited by the same severe constraints that had restricted the actions of his predecessors. In his inaugural addresses in Pretoria and Cape Town the new Prime Minister spoke indirectly of Western demands on his government, and suggested that the price of improved relations with the West was too high: concessions in Namibia and in domestic race policy that were politically unacceptable. South Africa would remain in Namibia 'as long as the indigenous peoples required it to do so', he said. Nor would his government hand over South Africa itself 'to the forces of chaos'. After the obligatory assertion that change 'will not be forced on us from outside', Botha advised the rest of the world: 'sweep in front of your own door before you do so in front of ours'. In his only other references to foreign affairs Botha reiterated his conviction that South Africa's mineral wealth 'made her indispensable to many Free World countries', and he pledged to assist South Africa's neighbours.[1]

Foreign policy continuity under Botha was also to be expected because of his long apprenticeship in the National Party, where loyalty and adherence to the party line are essential attributes for advancement. Although Botha was outspoken and generally thought of as *verligte*, particularly with regard to South Africa's mixed-race group called 'Coloureds', he had never strayed far enough from the Party's mainstream to be considered dangerous or untrustworthy. Both as NP leader in the Cape and as Defence Minister for 12 years, Botha had shown that, aside from the unspoken assumption that NP rule must be maintained, party unity and national security were his highest priorities, and neither would be sacrificed in the interests of winning outside approval or favour.

Probably most germane to the continuity of foreign policy under Botha is the fact that he had exerted a major influence on policy in the last years of the Vorster Administration. The deteriorating security situation within and outside the country, exacerbated by worsening relations with the West, created an environment in which Vorster moved to a harder line towards the outside world and a militant posture in the region. He was thus increasingly receptive to the views of his hawkish and ambitious minister of defence, and less responsive to the more cautious views of the Department of Foreign Affairs.

Indeed 1978 witnessed an astonishing upsurge in South Africa's military preparedness under Botha's direction. Among other moves, the length of military service was doubled, an emergency military radio network established, construction of new army and air bases near the Mozambican border begun, and legislation introduced to clear a 10-mile zone along the frontier.[2]

Botha's influence increased dramatically as the Muldergate scandal unfolded in 1978. Among other things that crisis, discussed in Chapter 3, resulted in the political eclipse of General van den Bergh, Botha's arch political and bureaucratic foe. As head of BOSS, van den Bergh had long dominated the intelligence field, both domestic and foreign, and had exerted great personal influence on Vorster.[3] As van den Bergh's professional career shrivelled in the glare of the Muldergate revelations, however, he was no longer able to bring influence to bear against what he had long considered the dangerous adventurism of P.W. Botha.

Botha prevailed over the DFA's reservations in Vorster's decision to launch South Africa's first deep-penetration raid against a SWAPO camp in Angola in May 1978. The attack took place at a delicate stage in the Namibian settlement talks, effectively suspending them for several months.[4] Botha gave a number of public speeches during the summer of 1978 in which he criticized UN and Western actions in Namibia, warning that proposals for a UN force would mean a UN takeover of the Territory, and pledging that South Africa would never allow Namibia 'to be handed to SWAPO on a plate'.[5] In August Botha decided to pull his army commander in Namibia out of a high-level South African delegation *en route* to talks with UN officials.[6] Finally, at a crucial Cabinet meeting on 6 September, chaired by Botha in place of the ailing Vorster, South Africa formally rejected the UN peace proposals. Following that meeting there were reports of thinly-veiled complaints by Foreign Affairs officials about the military's growing political influence.

Indeed, by mid-1978 a *de facto* devolution of power to P.W. Botha and his military establishment had occurred. When the Western Five's foreign ministers went to Pretoria in October for urgent talks with the new prime minister, the Army chief of staff sat in on the discussions for the first time. Botha refused Western demands that he call off the internal elections scheduled for December. He did agree, however, to say those elections should be viewed as 'an internal process to elect leaders', and that his government would 'thereafter use its best efforts to persuade them to seriously consider ways of achieving international recognition' through the good offices of Mr Ahtisaari (the UN Commissioner for Namibia) and South Africa's Administrator-General, Steyn.

This was no more than a token concession: a vague undertaking to try to persuade post-election Namibian leaders that they should risk their newly-won offices in a second, UN-supervised election which they would almost certainly lose to SWAPO. The Botha statement did, however, leave the door open for future talks with the Contact Group. It also left executive authority in the Territory in the hands of the Botha government through its administrator-general, not in the hands of an internal administration.

Prospects for a negotiated settlement suffered a major setback in March 1979, when P.W. Botha issued a blistering condemnation of the UN and the Contact Group, charging them with 'scheming behind the scenes' to reach secret understandings with SWAPO and the Front Line states about the location and monitoring of SWAPO bases in the proposed transition period before independence.[7] Claiming that South Africa had been 'left in the lurch' by the West, Botha angrily rejected Waldheim's proposals, which would have allowed SWAPO to establish bases inside Namibia and only nominal monitoring of its bases in Angola. These proposals, he said, were 'drastic departures' from the proposals to which South Africa had already agreed.

This incident signalled an abrupt hardening in South African attitudes towards the West, and particularly towards the US, in the early months of 1979. A number of statements by the prime minister and his foreign minister depicted the West as unwilling to stand up to communist expansionism, and sly and dishonest in its dealings with Pretoria. From this it followed that South Africa could no longer look to the West for help in solving the problems of southern Africa, but must itself take the lead in seeking peaceful solutions and preventing further communist inroads in the region. Indeed since South Africa stood to gain so little from the West, they said, Pretoria should adopt a neutral stance between East and West.

THE 'CONSTELLATION' INITIATIVE AND THE FALL OF RHODESIA

These twin themes – the rejection of the West and the launching of a regional peace initiative by South Africa that would exclude the West – were elaborated by Foreign Minister Roelof Botha in a major policy speech on 7 March: the day after P.W. Botha's denunciation of the settlement talks in Namibia.[8] South Africa, he said, would consider a constellation of seven to ten southern African states embracing up to 40 million people south of the Cunene/Zambesi line. His government would set its own targets, including the attainment of peace and stability in the region and the establishment of a 'sub-continental solidarity' which could form the basis for close collaboration in all important spheres. From his subsequent statements it was clear he had in mind collaborative efforts in the political and security areas, as well as close economic links. He thus suggested to Parliament the possibility of organizing 'international secretariats' to regulate the affairs of the proposed constellation.[9]

Although the prospective membership was never spelled out, the constellation's maximal variant – ten states and 40 million people living below the Cunene/Zambesi line – would have had to include South Africa and its three nominally independent 'homelands' at the time (Bophuthatswana, Transkei and Venda); Zimbabwe–Rhodesia; Namibia; and the three BLS states. Only by including Malawi, a friendly state lying *above* the line, would the total come to 40 million, as shown in Table 6.1.

The notion of such a constellation simply was not credible, even at the time it was proposed. None of the prospective members appears to have been consulted, either about the forms such an association might take or their interest in joining. Botswana, Lesotho, Swaziland and even Malawi, the only African state to have diplomatic relations with Pretoria, reject apartheid and refuse to recognize the Bantustans as independent entities. The three BLS states, in particular, have resisted South African overtures for closer association over the years, and have made serious efforts to lessen their extreme

Table 6.1 Prospective constellation, 1979

Countries	Population (millions)
South Africa (including three Bantustans)	27.0
Zimbabwe–Rhodesia	6.3
Namibia	0.9
Botswana	0.7
Lesotho	1.2
Swaziland	0.5
Malawi	5.0
Total	41.6

economic dependence on the Republic. That they would willingly join a regional security alliance with South Africa at its centre, let alone take part in 'international secretariats' in which Pretoria would have the dominant voice, seems little more than self-delusion on the part of the Botha leadership.

Indeed, within a few months of Foreign Minister Botha's constellation offer, the Front Line states responded with their own plan for regional economic cooperation: the Southern African Development Coordination Conference (SADCC), from which South Africa was excluded as long as it practised apartheid. The BLS states and Malawi are among the nine member-states of SADCC.

Why, then, did the Botha government propose an arrangement with so little chance of acceptance? Was it, in fact, a serious proposal? If so, why was it put in such vague, general terms?

The constellation idea seems to have reflected several different, though overlapping levels of perception. At the rhetorical level it was virtually a knee-jerk reaction to the leaders' frustration in their dealings with the West and their growing unease over Western pressure on the Namibian issue. It is no coincidence that the speech in which Foreign Minister Botha first proposed the constellation began with a detailed denunciation of Western actions in the Namibia negotiations. This was not the first instance in which a deterioration in South Africa's relations with the West led its Afrikaner leaders to reassert their country's primary identity as an African country with paramount interests in Africa. As suggested earlier (see Chapter 2), this split image of South Africa as both European and African has allowed successive Afrikaner leaders to emphasize one or the other aspect at any given time, depending mainly on the state of Pretoria's relations with the industrial West. In spite of Roelof Botha's defiant rejection of the West in favour of 'neutrality' between East and West, and the declared intention to re-focus South Africa's foreign policy on its regional links, neither Africa nor any other region can replace the West as South Africa's crucial trading area and the source of the capital, technology and skilled manpower that are essential to its economic growth.

The constellation idea, however, has a geo-political aspect that far outweighs its rhetorical, anti-Western element. South African officials group African countries into 'inner and outer rings', defined in terms of security, geographical proximity and political affinity.[10] The innermost ring consists of the Republic (as the castle keep) and the nominally independent 'homelands' within its borders. The next ring, as of 1979, included the internal Democratic Turnhalle Alliance (DTA) administration in Namibia and the newly-installed Muzorewa government in Zimbabwe-Rhodesia, as it was then known. If South Africa were to let those two moderate administrations down, Foreign Minister Botha warned Parliament, 'the whole of Southern Africa would disintegrate'.[11] Just beyond this is a third ring, the three independent BLS states, which have close economic and historical links, as well as geographical proximity, to South Africa. South African sensitivity to the threat of radical or pro-Soviet influence emerging in these states was shown by the South African-engineered coup in Lesotho in 1986 (discussed in Chapter 8).

These three groupings or 'rings' were the entities which the Botha Administration sought to include within the expanded South African security perimeter envisaged in the constellation. The rest of Africa was loosely divided into states considered moderate and tractable (Malawi, Zaire, Ivory Coast and Zambia); radical and hostile or potentially hostile regimes (Angola, Mozambique and the Seychelles); and all others.

As the constellation appeal was quickly rejected, both by the BLS countries and other independent states in the region, the Botha government reconciled itself to a far smaller constellation: South Africa (including the Bantustans), Namibia and Zimbabwe-Rhodesia; and to looser links than those originally suggested. In November 1979 P.W. Botha outlined a modified constellation, saying that the concept 'does not primarily denote a formal organization, but rather a grouping of states with common interests in developing mutual relationships and between which a clear desire to extend areas of cooperation exists'.[12]

By that time South Africa was already involved in strengthening the position of the moderate, anti-Marxist coalitions in Zimbabwe-Rhodesia and Namibia. Indeed, in early 1978 – a year before Rhodesia's internal election – the Vorster government had already allocated 800 000 Rand (roughly a million US dollars at that time) in secret funds to the electoral campaign of Bishop Muzorewa's party, the United African National Council (UANC).[13] The Botha government increased this aid. In March 1979, as the date for an internal election approached and the civil war showed no signs of abating, South Africa dispatched a consignment of 11 Bell helicopters, purchased from Israel, to strengthen the Salisbury government's counter-insurgency campaign and to boost white morale before the election.[14]

To South African leaders Muzorewa's electoral victory and the installation of a nominally black-run administration was the optimal solution in Rhodesia, and one they had been urging on Smith for several years. They hoped that the West, too would support the new government, particularly by lifting sanctions.

It was soon clear, however, that the outside world was unwilling to recognize a government whose election was seen as seriously flawed and whose multi-racial composition failed to mask the reality of continued white control. As the Muzorewa regime failed either to win outside recognition or to wind down the war – the two critical measures of its effectiveness – Britain and the Front Line states gained growing world support for bringing Muzorewa and the guerrillas to the conference table to seek agreement on a cease-fire, a constitution and new, British-supervised elections.

The Botha government was apprehensive. The leaders feared the spill-over effects of growing black–white conflict in Rhodesia, and the domestic political repercussions of a victory by the Patriotic Front's guerrilla forces. They wanted to see a rapid and peaceful settlement, but one in which white interests were protected and radical black nationalists did not come to power. Their greatest concern, according to a senior South African diplomat, was to 'prevent chaos' along South Africa's border: that is, a situation leading to the flight south of Rhodesian whites and 'millions of Rhodesian blacks, as well'.[15]

South Africa therefore continued to support the Muzorewa government politically, financially and logistically during the Lancaster House peace conference in 1979. The Botha leadership had grave misgivings about Lancaster House which, according to one senior official, 'many of us felt was a reckless exercise'.[16] They warned Muzorewa of the risks he would run at the conference. They urged him to take a firm stand, as he had the most to lose in the negotiations. They persuaded him to take Ian Smith along as a member of his delegation, even though they knew the two were barely on speaking terms by then. A South African official later acknowledged that his government felt at the time that Muzorewa's political base would crumble once he stepped down as prime minister.

South African officials deny that they tried to influence the Muzorewa delegation once the conference was under way. To have done so, they say, would have led to charges of manipulating Muzorewa as their puppet. Yet Foreign Minister Botha made two brief trips to London, in October and November, and spoke privately with Muzorewa. On his second visit Botha urged the UK to close down the conference (because the intransigence of the guerrilla delegation had brought the talks to a standstill) and to accept the 'second-class solution': namely, recognize the Muzorewa government.

In late November an American who had served in the Rhodesian armed forces broke the news that South African troops were directly involved in the Rhodesian fighting on a scale far greater that anything previously suspected.[17] He alleged that SADF troops, wearing Rhodesian uniforms and using vehicles painted in Rhodesian colours, were effectively controlling the southern quarter of the country. Two SADF ground battalions and a squadron of Mirage fighter-bombers had been committed to the war, he said.

These allegations led Prime Minister Botha to acknowledge for the first time on 30 November 1979 that South African forces were operating inside Rhodesia: an admission that came as a surprise to the South African public. But he asserted that the involvement was limited to protecting transport routes – that is, the vital rail span connecting Rhodesia with South Africa at Beitbridge – and to intercepting ANC guerrillas moving towards the Republic.[18] Western intelligence sources at the time estimated that some 500–600 SADF forces were deployed in Rhodesia's south-east corner, plus 125 guarding the span at Beitbridge.[19]

Lord Carrington, chairman of the Lancaster House conference, had been aware for some time of South Africa's military involvement; but he had not known how extensive it was, nor had he wished to make an issue of it. Indeed the South African military presence, particularly its defence of the Beitbridge span, served the interests of both South Africa and Britain: destruction of the bridge would have disrupted the flow of oil, weapons and food to Rhodesia, thereby crippling the Muzorewa regime and encouraging the guerrillas to reject Lancaster House in favour of a military solution. Moreover it would have shattered the morale of Rhodesian whites, for whom the bridge was the major escape route should the cease-fire have collapsed.

Public exposure forced Carrington to address the issue, even though he had no means of forcing a South African withdrawal. He told the Rhodesian commander that the South Africans must be out by 12 December, when the British governor was due to arrive in Salisbury. The issue faded as Britain set in motion the train of events leading to a January cease-fire. And, in spite of continuing complaints by the Patriotic Front's delegates at Lancaster House, South African troops remained in place until February 1980.[20]

On balance, South Africa played an important role in making the Lancaster House settlement possible. Had the South Africans chosen to block the settlement they could have raised alarms, both genuine and fabricated, to persuade Muzorewa and Rhodesian whites to reject Britain's terms. That, together with offers of greater financial and military aid, would almost certainly have led to the collapse of the conference. Instead South Africa, whether intentionally or not, helped to bolster white morale and give the Muzorewa delegation the necessary confidence to go along with the settlement in the knowledge that the South Africans stood ready to intervene forcefully on their behalf if the cease-fire went wrong.[21]

In part the Botha government's low-key role reflected the leaders' consensus that the counter-insurgency could not succeed – a conclusion shared by the Rhodesian high command – and that the Lancaster House talks offered the best hope of ending the war and avoiding a total collapse of the society. Furthermore, South African leaders were lulled into complacency by their intelligence assessments which predicted a Muzorewa victory at the polls.[22] Some senior diplomats claim to have had 'serious doubts' about his electoral chances. But South African officials appear to have believed that, at worst, the votes would be so distributed among the several candidates that Muzorewa or Nkomo would be asked to form a government, thus denying Mugabe the premiership.

The Botha Administration secretly provided substantial support to the Muzorewa campaign. Four hundred motor vehicles, valued at $2.5 million, were dispatched for his use.[23] Muzorewa's campaign also received $5 million from the Anglo–American Corporation.[24]

Mugabe not only won the election: he emerged with a clear majority of 57 out of 80 contested seats in Parliament. This came as a surprise to almost everyone, not least the South Africans. For the Botha Administration the accession to power of a leader labelled simply a 'Marxist terrorist' was a worst-case scenario come true. Moreover, as a member of Botha's staff later acknowledged, 'The "constellation" is dead. It died with Mugabe's victory.'[25]

During 1980 the Botha Administration moved rapidly, however, to formalize its ties to the now shrunken constellation: the inner ring embracing South Africa, Transkei, Bophuthatswana, Venda and Namibia. The notion of 'confederation' gradually supplanted the term 'constellation' in official discussion of the policy. At a summit meeting of the group in July 1980 Prime Minister Botha spoke of coordinated action on 'interstate political relations, economics, social affairs, and security'.[26] The immediate focus, however, was to be regional economic development that would transcend political borders. Joint working-groups were established to deal with monetary and fiscal matters, economic development and small business development.[27] A Southern African Development Bank, capitalized at two billion Rand, came into being in 1983 to channel funds into long-term development projects. Although the bank concentrates its lending in South Africa's nominally independent black 'homelands', which have no access to outside sources of capital, its charter allows it to extend its activities to other states: a clear indication that the notion of a larger constellation had not died. (The bank's recent activity beyond South Africa's borders is discussed in Chapter 9.)

Namibia was of course included in the plans for a closer grouping of the remaining 'inner ring' of the constellation. Until its independence, however, it has been accorded only the status of an official observer in the various organizations created under constellation auspices. But the Botha Administration plans for full Namibian participation to follow independence.[28]

GENESIS OF THE NEW MILITANCY

The collapse of the constellation initiative left South Africa without a defined policy towards its independent neighbours. The constellation had been first proposed and subsequently elaborated by Foreign Minister 'Pik' Botha. It was an olive branch offered to the region, a bid to meet South Africa's perceived national security requirements through diplomacy and offers of economic and security assistance to its neighbours. It was thus a legitimate heir to the outward policy and *détente* of the Vorster era. Bureaucratically it was 'Pik Botha's best shot': that is, an attempt to establish the primacy of the diplomats over the growing influence of the military in shaping foreign policy. The initiative was neither carefully prepared nor vigorously followed up, however. And with the advent of the Mugabe government in Zimbabwe and the rejection of the constellation by the BLS states, the diplomats had no alternative, no fall-back plan to offer.

Indeed, the closest thing to a foreign policy platform had appeared somewhat earlier, in P.W. Botha's Twelve-Point Plan: a statement of his administration's policy plans and priorities which he presented to the Natal congress of the NP in August 1979, *before* the collapse of the regional constellation proposals.[29] While the main thrust of the Twelve-Point Plan set forth Botha's new course for domestic race relations, three of the points outlined his general ideas for combating the perceived threat to South Africa from within and without. The eighth point expressed the government's hopes of establishing 'a peaceful constellation of southern African states'. The ninth declared South Africa's determination to defend itself 'against interference from outside *in every way*' (my emphasis), to which the Prime Minister added that South Africa's defence capability was greater 'than ever before in [its] history'. The tenth point stated his administration's intention to pursue a policy of neutrality in the superpower conflict, and reiterated the priority to be given to South Africa's regional interests.[30]

South Africa's regional policy is not determined solely on the basis of its regional interests, however. Rather, it is the product of the leadership's shifting perception of its total security situation: in particular by the perceived security threat, internal and external; the state of Pretoria's relations with the Western powers; and domestic political imperatives.

By early 1980 events in all these areas were propelling the Botha Administration into a more militant, go-it-alone posture towards the region. The possibility of Western support, or of major Western concessions in the Namibia talks, had already been written off by Botha. Zimbabwe had become the sixth Front Line state. The loss of Rhodesia as a friendly buffer state, together with the neighbours' rejection of the constellation initiative, soured Botha's relations with the region and ruled out any chance of negotiating the sort of extended defence perimeter that South Africa sought to establish along its borders.

Of more immediate concern to the leadership was the worsening security situation in 1980, the early months of which witnessed a dramatic upsurge in guerrilla activity in Namibia. The rise in SWAPO infiltration was marked by sabotage of power lines, the destruction of several aircraft at an advance SAAF base by mortar fire, and attacks on civilian and military targets on a scale which forced vehicle traffic to move about the northern half of the territory in armed convoys.[31] South Africa, too, was the target of increased sabotage, including destruction of three oil installations in June by ANC operatives. In May and June South Africa also experienced a resurgence of black unrest, the most serious in several years.

These developments presented a challenge against which Botha had to be seen to act forcefully. For one thing, it was crucial to prevent South Africa's black population from coming to believe that sabotage and armed resistance could be effective against white minority rule, so the government had to strike hard at ANC and SWAPO.

The more important domestic political imperative, though, had to do with Botha's plans for domestic race reform-from-above. In the Twelve-Point Plan and elsewhere he had made clear that this was to be his highest priority. By 1980, however, right-wing opposition to his reform proposals had already surfaced within his own party. Reforms introduced in 1979 to give legal sanction to black labour unions and to increase black labour mobility were criticized by Treurnicht, head of the powerful Transvaal wing of the Party at that time, for undermining the position of whites. He accused Botha of 'creating confusion and uncertainty' in party ranks. In the June 1979 by-elections the NP lost votes to the far-right HNP.

As Botha prepared to introduce constitutional reforms, which would be even more controversial than the measures already put forward, it was essential that he win the broad support of his Party and of the white electorate. To do this he had to demonstrate that he was a tough, uncompromising leader; that he was in control of the reform process, and would not cave in to pressure, either from domestic or foreign critics; that he was acting from a position of military and political strength; and that South Africa would strike hard at its enemies, particularly against armed provocation. In a very real way, then, Botha's foreign policy became hostage to his programme of domestic race reform. His 'soft' domestic programme had to be balanced by a hardline stance towards the outside world.

Moreover, South Africa's military leaders had already sold P.W. Botha on the notion that the country was the target of a 'total onslaught' to which it must respond with a 'total national strategy'. The latter involved mobilizing the country's resources, both to meet the internal and external threat and, in Botha's words, 'wherever possible . . . to eliminate the fundamental causes which give rise to the threat': an indirect reference to the need to carry out domestic race reform.[32] In the early months of 1980 Botha began to promote and publicize the total onslaught to the country. He, as well as his foreign minister and minister of defence, analysed the perceived onslaught for Parliament. In March the prime minister asserted that, 'The main object . . . under the guidance of the planners in the Kremlin, is to overthrow this State and to create chaos in its stead, so that the Kremlin can establish its hegemony here.'[33] The present Soviet strategy, he continued, was to avoid a direct, conventional onslaught: 'the threshold is too high'. But, he added, 'an indirect strategy is being pursued by every possible means'. The military onslaught is being waged by proxy: by the Cubans, 'who are a crowd of slaves of the rulers in Moscow', and others. However, in a statement that anticipated his government's imminent shift to a far more aggressive response to the 'onslaught', he also warned of a conventional threat: 'there is the conventional military onslaught we have to bear in mind. There is a gradual buildup of more sophisticated arms in neighbouring states, especially in Mozambique, Angola, and Zambia. *Such equipment can be converted almost overnight into a credible instrument of Soviet aggression*' (my emphasis).[34] He said that Zimbabwe was also a threat, because it would be 'pressurized to play an active role in the onslaught on the Republic in the future'.[35]

Botha criticized the West for a 'paralysis of the mind' in failing to appreciate the importance of South Africa, and Malan, the Defence Minister, told Parliament that the West had 'accepted . . . that the white government of South Africa should be forced into a position where it has no other choice but to abdicate'.[36]

Thus P.W. Botha set the stage for a more militant policy towards his neighbours and a position of greater defiance and intransigence towards the West.

7 Namibia Policy and the War in Angola

THE SHIFTING WAR STRATEGY

By 1979–80 the Botha leadership faced a political situation in Namibia far more serious than that which had confronted the Vorster government a couple of years earlier. In Ovamboland, the northern border region where the Territory's population and major economic activity are concentrated, SWAPO had launched a campaign of sabotage, kidnappings, political assassinations and guerrilla attacks that were threatening to disrupt local administration and weaken the government's credibility with the dominant Ovambo people. Not only was SWAPO infiltrating in larger groups, Prime Minister Botha told Parliament, but it was using 'extremely sophisticated weapons, and its training was much improved'.[1]

Furthermore Botha saw that the DTA, the multi-ethnic coalition of moderate political parties put together by Vorster, had fallen into serious disarray. As its right-wing white parties lobbied effectively against desegregation and urged Botha to arrange an internal political settlement, the DTA looked ever less credible as a moderate political alternative to SWAPO. Indeed, in early 1980 South African officials began to see worrisome analogies with the recent Rhodesian elections, and expressed concern that the DTA coalition was showing signs of 'the Muzorewa syndrome': that is, being perceived as a puppet regime, powerless to bring about any real change inside the country.

The Botha leadership, however, had evolved no general strategy for dealing with these challenges. Even by the end of 1987, no coherent proposals for a settlement or for a post-independence political structure had yet emerged from the Botha Administration. Their absence reflected the lack of a consensus, in both the Territory and the Republic, on Namibia's future. The Botha leadership, like its predecessor, believes that South Africa's long-run security interests can be best served by an independent Namibia governed by a strong, moderate coalition committed to close military and security links to South Africa, but it has no clear or consistent idea of how to bring that about. Hence its policy moves have often been opportunistic and reactive, and occasionally improvisational.

In the absence of an articulated and consistent vision, the Botha Administration has followed an interim strategy composed of several elements: first, to destroy SWAPO as a credible guerrilla force so as to diminish its political appeal inside Namibia and weaken its claims to international support as an effective insurgent movement; second, to stretch out the UN-sponsored talks on Namibia, while simultaneously pressing for better terms and seeking a settlement that would bypass the UN settlement plan which calls for a cease-fire, a transition period and the election of a constituent assembly, all under UN supervision; third, to continue its efforts to strengthen and unify Namibia's numerous and fractious political parties into a credible anti-SWAPO coalition.

The war against SWAPO began in earnest in 1979. In March a joint land-and-air attack by the SADF destroyed more than a dozen SWAPO camps inside Angola and Zambia. In June 8000 South African reservists were called up to track down roving SWAPO units which had infiltrated Ovamboland.[2] By that time South Africa had also activated a covert SADF unit, the 32 Battalion, composed of black Angolans who had belonged to Holden Roberto's FNLA guerrilla movement until its defeat by MPLA and Cuban forces in 1975–6. Led by white officers (mostly European mercenaries in the early years), units of the 32 Battalion operated virtually full time inside Angola, where they carried out sweeps through villages, searching for SWAPO bands and destroying the local infrastructure: bridges, roads and houses. By late 1980 the 32 Battalion had created a buffer zone 20–30 miles deep in which abandoned villages and devastated countryside offered scant cover for SWAPO groups moving south towards Namibia.[3]

In June 1980, following a rash of SWAPO sabotage incidents (including the destruction of several military aircraft at the SAAF's main Namibian base), regular mobile units of the SADF launched a major attack against SWAPO camps in Angola. In four days of fighting and mopping up, the SADF claimed to have destroyed SWAPO's operational headquarters and to have killed 200 guerrillas and captured 100 tons of equipment, while suffering 16 SADF dead.[4]

An increasing share of the SADF's counter-insurgency fell on locally-recruited ethnic battalions. Recruitment of Namibian blacks to serve as border-guards was begun in the mid-1970s. By 1981, however, five ethnic combat units, totalling perhaps 4000 men and under the command of white SADF officers, were operational. Three – the Ovambo, Kavango and Bushmen battalions – had already engaged in combat.[5] In 1980 these battalions were placed under a new SADF command, the South West African Territorial Force (SWAT/F), and military conscription was instituted for all males aged between 16 and 25 to help assure a flow of new recruits. One unintended result of the new draft law was the flight of large numbers of young Namibian blacks, some of whom joined the ranks of SWAPO.[6] By 1985 these local ethnic battalions made up 61 per cent of the fighting forces in Namibia.[7]

By the end of 1982 South Africa's counter-insurgency measures against SWAPO were paying off. The SADF's aggressive operations prevented the establishment of permanent SWAPO bases in southern Angola, and the guerrillas were forced to operate from staging areas far north of the border. This complicated SWAPO's logistics, and reduced its opportunities to win recruits among the Ovambo people who straddle the border (and who make up a large majority of SWAPO's forces). Yet, while SWAPO attacks have decreased since 1983, it has not been eliminated as a guerrilla threat. Indeed, despite confident South African estimates each year on the numbers of guerrillas killed and on SWAPO's diminishing troop strength – from 16 000 in 1978 to 8000 in 1987, according to official statements[8] – SWAPO has continued to infiltrate between 1200 and 1500 operatives into Namibia at the start of each rainy season, including 1987–8.[9]

South African security concerns were by no means limited to SWAPO, however. In the summer of 1981, following the appearance of new Angolan defence installations in the southern part of the country, both the objectives and scale of SADF attacks in Angola shifted to a higher, more dangerous level. General Lloyd, then the SADF commander in Namibia, warned that the introduction of Soviet-made early-warning radar and ground-to-air missiles was making it more difficult to provide air support to South African ground operations inside Angola. He also reiterated Malan's warning to Parliament a few months earlier, namely that the build-up of heavy armaments in the southern part of Angola (Malan listed 300 Soviet-made tanks, 400 armoured cars and MiG-21 fighters) made a conventional war more likely.[10]

In late August, a few weeks after General Lloyd's warning, SAAF jets attacked Angolan radar and missile sites while South African armoured columns struck across the border in Operation Protea, the SADF's first deep penetration attack since the 1975 intervention.

Unlike previous engagements, the eight-day campaign led to heavy fighting between the South Africans and the Angolan army. The SADF's subsequent display of captured weapons left no doubt that the operation had been directed at the Angolan forces rather than SWAPO. Among the 3000 tons of captured arms were T-34 and PT-76 Soviet tanks, more than 200 scout cars, heavy trucks, 110 SAM-7 missile launchers and large quantities of 122 mm rockets. Of 38 prisoners brought back, 29 were Angolan regulars.[11] Angola's president reported that regular army units suffered 60 per cent of the casualties.[12]

Operation Protea was only the first of several deep assaults by the SADF during 1981–2. In November 1981 South Africa carried out a three-week attack, Operation Daisy, aimed at destroying a bunker complex near Cassinga, 160 miles inside Angola. In a January 1982 raid 190 miles north of the border the SADF clashed with Cuban troops for the first time since 1975. South African forces penetrated 175 miles during a month-long sweep against SWAPO bases in August 1982.

These attacks put heavy military and political pressure on Angola's dos Santos government. Already denied access to the southern third of the country, where operations by SADF units and UNITA guerrillas amounted to a virtual occupation of the territory, the government in Luanda by 1982 faced repeated conventional air-and-ground assaults by South African forces which it was powerless to stop.

The risk to Botha (that his aggressive strategy might provoke a direct intervention of Cuban forces in the conflict) faded during the SADF's deep penetration in August 1981, when an official statement in the Cuban press warned that Cuban troops would go into action 'with all forces available' *if* South African columns approached the Cubans' defensive positions.[13] In July 1982 Castro stated publicly that, if the South Africans 'strike deeply into Angola *and reach our lines*, we will fight with all our might against these parasitic, racist mercenaries' (my emphasis).[14] Clearly the Cubans were not seeking a more active combat role at that time.

Beyond the successful gamble against greater Soviet–Cuban involvement in the fighting, Botha's intensified military pressure against Angola also increased the urgency with which Angola, the Western powers, the UN and the Front Line states sought ways to dampen the conflict.

South Africa, too, had reason for concern over a continuing

escalation of the war. Its recent military operations had been running into serious resistance on the part of the Angolans. Casualties remained low by most standards: official data listed 107 killed in action between 1979 and mid-1983, although there is reason to suspect that actual casualties were substantially higher.[15] But by 1983 heavier and more sophisticated weapons were being used and the rate of casualties was accelerating; for example, in September the SADF reported the loss of 15 men in a single engagement when their helicopter was shot down over Angola. In December a Soviet UN representative privately warned his South African counterpart against further attacks on Angola, and in January the USSR announced that it had reached agreement with Angola to bolster Angolan defence capabilities.[16] Nor could South Africa be certain of continuing support and understanding from the Reagan Administration. In October, when the UNSC voted to condemn South Africa for its continuing presence in Namibia, the US chose to abstain rather than exercise its veto: a clear message to Botha that US patience was wearing thin in the face of South African intransigence.

Both South Africa and Angola were therefore ready to consider a cease-fire and mutual force disengagement when they were first proposed by the US late in 1983. American diplomats saw two advantages in pressing Botha to withdraw his forces from Angola. First, it would show the Angolans that the US has influence over Pretoria and was willing to use it to extract a major concession of advantage to Angola; and second, it would set the Botha leadership to 'moving more pieces around the board': that is, to considering ways of dealing with Angola other than military confrontation.[17]

On 15 December 1983 South Africa informed the UN Secretary-General that South Africa would start withdrawing its forces from Angola on 31 January, provided that the Angolans agreed to prevent SWAPO from taking advantage of the situation to infiltrate its forces into Namibia. Angolan, South African and US representatives met in Lusaka in early February to work out details. According to US diplomats, South African military leaders expressed strong reservations, particularly about the possibility that the Angolans might move radar and missile installations into areas vacated by the SADF.[18] Under the Lusaka Accord signed on 16 February, Angola agreed to notify South Africa of any moves in the demilitarized zone (DMZ) and to prohibit supplies for SWAPO from passing through the area. The Americans assured South Africa that, in the event of Angolan violation of the accord, the US would give diplomatic support to South Africa. A Joint Monitoring Commission (JMC) of Angolan and SADF representatives was established to patrol the border and prevent violations by any of the forces, including SWAPO, which had agreed conditionally to accept the terms of the cease-fire for its forces inside Angola.[19]

In anticipation of the cease-fire, and almost certainly in response to SADF leaders' reservations about withdrawing their troops from Angola, South Africa began a major, five-week campaign, Operation Askari, in December 1983. Officially undertaken to pre-empt SWAPO's annual rainy season offensive, the operation met unexpectedly heavy opposition from regular Angolan forces. Committing their T-54 tanks to battle for the first time, the Angolans counter-attacked an invading SADF armoured column and inflicted heavy casualties. SADF spokesmen acknowledged the loss of 21 men in the battle of Cuvelai: the largest number of South Africans killed in any single engagement up to that time. Western diplomatic sources say privately, however, that SADF casualties were higher.[20]

The February 1984 cease-fire was limited to a triangular area bounded by the Cunene River on the west, the Cubango River in the east, and a 300-mile strip of the Angola–Namibia border in the south. The South African withdrawal fell far behind schedule as SADF commanders charged SWAPO with continuing to infiltrate its operatives through the cease-fire zone. The SADF withdrawal was finally completed only in April 1985, a year later than agreed. During this period few, if any, clashes occurred between South African and Angolan forces. Indeed, representatives of the two armies cooperated in the JMC to intercept groups of SWAPO moving south.

In June 1985, two months after withdrawing, South African troops recrossed the border to attack SWAPO units 25 miles inside Angola.[21] In this, and in a similar operation in September, SADF officials asserted that the Angolans were told of the raid 'in its early stages' and did not interfere. SADF spokesmen also said that their forces were under strict instruction to avoid contact with FAPLA (Forças Armadas Populares de Libertação de Angola, the Angolan regular army) and to stay outside any town garrisoned by the Angolans.[22] The US-brokered cease-fire thus led to a period of some 18 months in which virtually no fighting between Angolan and South African forces occurred.

All this changed abruptly in late September 1985 when Angolan troops, equipped with newly-supplied Soviet helicopters and other weapons, launched a major ground-and-air offensive against the stronghold of Jonas Savimbi's UNITA guerrilla forces in the southeast corner of Angola, a few miles north of the Namibian border. That assault – the biggest in 10 years – raised the stakes of the Angolan conflict and posed an immediate and serious challenge to South Africa.

South Africa has been the major patron and supporter of UNITA in its war against Angola's Marxist government since 1975. Indeed, UNITA's activities, although undertaken in its own interests, have been an important element in South Africa's war strategy. With the help of sustained South African supplies of weapons including artillery and armoured cars, fuel and financial support, UNITA has maintained a punishing guerrilla offensive against the MPLA regime.[23] In 1983–4 UNITA moved out of its secure base in south-eastern Angola and conducted a series of hit-and-run attacks on towns and FAPLA outposts to within 125 miles of Luanda, Angola's capital. Its units also penetrated the northern diamond-mining area, and in late 1986 UNITA extended its guerrilla operations to Cabinda, Angola's northern exclave province, for the first time.[24]

UNITA has yet to hold any territory outside its southern stronghold, and neither has it threatened the capital; but its forays have created extensive economic and social disruption, effectively closing down production in Angola's rich central agricultural region. The government has been forced to maintain Cuban combat units in defensive positions around major towns and key installations to protect them from UNITA attacks, as well as against the threat of South African invasion.

UNITA has been useful to South Africa in other ways as well. According to South African military officials, the SADF counts on Savimbi's forces to defend a sizeable area of the border just inside Angola, extending east of the Cubango river.[25] Politically, too, UNITA's long claim to legitimacy as a national movement and to a share of power in the government puts additional pressure on the MPLA leaders. As long as UNITA survives militarily, it will almost certainly be a party to any Namibian settlement.

The Botha government's commitment to UNITA's survival has been reiterated by the leaders in both private and public statements. According to a confidential US State Department memorandum later leaked to the press, South Africa's foreign minister told US officials in April 1981 that his government 'sees Savimbi in Angola as buffer for Namibia, [and] believes Savimbi wants southern Angola. Having supported him this far, it would damage [South African government's] honor if Savimbi is harmed.'[26] Senior South African military men have suggested privately that they would like to see a federal solution in Angola leaving Savimbi in control of the southern region. With UNITA serving as a trip-wire, they say they would feel secure about the threat of a cross-border invasion of Namibia.[27]

South Africa's commitment to UNITA was first put to a critical test, however, in September 1985, when Angola's first major offensive against Savimbi's forces came close to overrunning the main UNITA base at Jamba. As Savimbi prepared to abandon Jamba and retreat to the bush, South Africa sent in a mechanized SADF battalion to reinforce his hard-pressed forces, while SAAF aircraft attacked the advancing Angolan columns for three days running.[28] President Botha indirectly acknowledged the SADF's intervention, telling a regional congress of his ruling National Party that his government could 'hardly sit still' while Soviet tanks, jets and helicopters were being deployed in a drive to destroy UNITA. If they succeeded in Angola, he said, the next target would be Namibia.[29]

The scale of the fighting was suggested by a reporter's description of the major battle area a few days after the Angolans had retreated:

Trees have been smashed by heavy vehicles and stripped by shells, and there were hundreds of foxholes, slit trenches, and underground bunkers, making the scene reminiscent of a World War I battlefield. The earth was scarred with shell craters and scorched areas where explosions started bush fires. *It obviously was a major conventional battle in what until now has been a guerrilla war.*[30] [My emphasis.]

The offensive, which resulted in heavy casualties among UNITA and FAPLA forces, held sobering lessons for both South Africa and Angola. SADF officials expressed concern a few months later over the USSR's willingness and capability to replace major Angolan equipment losses 'within a matter of weeks'.[31] Indeed, any doubt that Angola had maintained its goal of defeating Savimbi's forces militarily was removed by the chief of Angola's air force, who said in November 1985 that his country's recent acquisition of aircraft and radar installations was part of a plan to wrest control of the air over southern Angola from the South Africans. 'We have to go over to the offensive and liberate the territory occupied by UNITA and cut off its supply lines from South Africa', he said.[32]

By 1986 Angola had close to 100 Soviet fighter aircraft, including advanced MiG-23 fighter-interceptors, as well as 125 helicopters acquired from France and the USSR.[33] Angolan pilots were already flying MiG-21s in ground attacks against SADF raiders in southern Angola.[34] By then Angola's forward military bases in the south, from which future offensives against UNITA were to be launched, were ringed by surface-to-air missile sites and advanced radar, capable of monitoring SAAF flights in Namibia. Thus by 1987 Angola had the capability to provide air cover for assaults by its airborne and ground forces: a fatal omission from its 1985 offensive, when the SAAF attacked Angolan vehicles and helicopters virtually without opposition as they moved against Savimbi's main base.

In an article published in April 1986 the chief of South Africa's air force noted that the war in Angola had become 'a very high-intensity, sophisticated, high-technology conflict in which air power is paramount'. He warned that, 'as the air umbrella [over Angola] has become more effective, it is obvious that it is becoming increasingly difficult to neutralize it. And unless it is neutralized, *no long-range operations in the host country* [that is, Angola] *are possible without heavy casualties*' (my emphasis).[35] South Africa responded to the growing Angolan challenge to its air superiority by upgrading its aging Mirage III ground-attack aircraft with new weapons and Israeli-supplied avionics (electronic counter-measures) which allegedly make the renamed 'Cheetahs' superior to the MiG-23 and less vulnerable to Angolan radar and missiles.[36] The SAAF also acquired an improved air refuelling capability, giving its aircraft longer range, and unveiled two new, locally-assembled helicopters in 1986 and 1987.[37]

In 1986 and again in 1987 the Angolans consolidated their gains in several areas and reinforced their advance bases in the south from which any future assault on UNITA's main stronghold would be launched.[38] Meanwhile outside powers deepened their involvement and commitment to the opposing forces in Angola, thereby increasing the prospects for continued escalation of the fighting. In February the USSR, Cuba and Angola issued a joint communiqué on solidarity following a meeting in Moscow attended by Angola's defence minister. Later Fidel Castro pledged to match every increase in US involvement and to keep Cuban combat forces in Angola until the end of white minority rule in South Africa, or as long as the Angolans wanted them to remain.[39] In March and April 1986 the press reported that the US had begun 'covertly' to supply several hundred Stinger anti-aircraft missiles to UNITA.[40]

The war in Angola escalated further in the final months of 1987, when Angolan forces launched their second major assault on

UNITA's stronghold in the south-east. As in the Angolans' 1985 campaign, the SADF intervened directly to help UNITA inflict heavy losses on the attacking troops. But this time the SADF itself incurred substantial losses: a record 23 men killed in a two-week period, according to official SADF accounts.[41] No figures were given on numbers of wounded. Probably because of its unexpectedly high casualties, the SADF for the first time publicly acknowledged its combat role in support of UNITA. General Geldenhuys, Chief of the SADF, explained South Africa's interest in preventing UNITA's defeat by asserting that if the 'Russian- and Cuban-supported Angolan forces' were to gain control over the area now 'dominated by UNITA', SWAPO would be able to 'activate' Namibia's Caprivi and Kavango areas, and the ANC would have greater freedom of movement for infiltrating into South Africa.[42]

Angola responded to South Africa's increased military intervention by announcing that it had authorized Cuban combat forces for the first time to move south and start patrolling down to Angola's border with Namibia.[43] Previously no Cuban combat troops had been reported south of Lubango, some 160 miles or more above the border.

The fighting continued into the first four months of 1988, as UNITA and a South African force of several thousand men pressed a counter-attack against the town of Cuito Canavale, the Angolans' major bridgehead in the south. By late April the SADF appeared to be scaling back its intervention, suggesting that the counter-offensive had failed.

RESULTS OF THE WAR STRATEGY

The Botha leadership's war strategy had several consequences, not all of which were favourable to its declared objectives. The first objective, to weaken SWAPO militarily and politically, was largely achieved. SADF offensive operations disrupted SWAPO infiltration and logistics, caused heavy casualties and prevented SWAPO from occupying territory either in Namibia or in the southern part of Angola. In short, the counter-insurgency demolished any notion that SWAPO might open an effective guerrilla offensive, like that carried out by the Rhodesian guerrillas against the Smith regime in the 1970s. SWAPO's negotiating position in the intermittent peace talks was weakened, along with any basis for claiming to control territory in Namibia. Yet almost a decade of intensive counter-insurgency operations, in Namibia as well as Angola, failed to move SWAPO or its patrons to abandon their commitment to UNSC Resolution 435 as the basis for a settlement. Furthermore, the war strategy neither diminished SWAPO's popularity inside Namibia nor ended its capability to infiltrate small sabotage teams into the Territory each year.

The second major objective, to neutralize Angola's build-up of heavy weapons and remove the perceived threat of conventional attack, was not achieved. Indeed, South Africa's repeated assaults against targets inside Angola led to a sharp rise in Angola's air defence capabilities, including advanced ground-attack aircraft, thereby making SADF cross-border operations more costly both in terms of upgraded weapons requirements and likely casualties. Thus the 30 per cent rise in the South African defence budget for 1987/8 included a dramatic increase in air defence, which rose by $454 million: a whopping 55 per cent increase over 1986/7.[44] Although this was undoubtedly gratifying to the SADF leadership, it squeezed budgetary resources at a time when the economy was still struggling to emerge from four years of recession, and when the Botha Administration was committing far larger sums than before to social services, police and support to South Africa's four nominally independent Bantustans.

The continuing threat of South African attack, or of a major UNITA offensive with SADF participation and support, also ensured the continued presence of Cuban combat troops in Angola. This held certain advantages for South Africa's military leaders. It provided them with by far their best evidence that the long-touted 'total onslaught' was real, and that South Africa must prepare for a conventional attack. The Cuban troops – more than 40 000 in 1988 – thus helped to keep national security and the need for increased defence expenditure at the top of the Botha agenda, and further enhanced the influence of the military on regional policy.

By late 1987, however, the war strategy – particularly the continuing intervention on behalf of UNITA – was incurring far higher costs and risks than before. With Cuban combat forces deployed through southern Angola, the Botha Administration faced the prospect that future SADF incursions would result in SADF casualties on a scale likely to cause serious criticism of the policy by white South Africans.

Of more immediate concern to the SADF leadership was a protest by soldiers in two of its black Namibian battalions: the first such incident known. In late November 1987 SADF spokesmen acknowledged that 47 members of 101 Battalion, an ethnic Ovambo unit, had been discharged following a protest over their deployment. According to press reports from Namibia, the soldiers objected to being used as 'UNITA mercenaries' against their will.[45] The event, which SADF officials denied was a mutiny, had significant security implications: first, because South Africa counts on its Namibian ethnic units to bear the brunt of the counter-insurgency against SWAPO; and also because the 101 Battalion is composed of Ovambo, Namibia's dominant ethnic group from which SWAPO also draws its major support.

On the political and diplomatic fronts, South Africa's war strategy scored important points. At home it showed the government's determination to hit hard at guerrillas so as to prevent their developing into a credible military threat or a serious disruptive force in the Territory. The sustained campaign of armed raids and occupation of Angolan territory also placed the dos Santos government under tremendous strain. By 1981 it was spending half its total budget on defence.[46] Its efforts to cope with the fighting and devastation, particularly in the south, came to dominate the attention and resources of the government to the virtual exclusion of other issues. One measure of Angola's agony was its willingness to continue to seek US intervention to end the fighting: this in spite of frequent statements by Angolan leaders condemning the Reagan Administration's support of UNITA and officially rejecting US mediation. South Africa's repeated intervention on behalf of UNITA showed Angola, and Cuba and the USSR as well, that the campaign to defeat Savimbi would be long and costly, at best.

In 1987 a senior SADF official, speaking privately but apparently reflecting something like a mainstream military view, outlined alternative future 'scenarios' for Angola. A military defeat of UNITA, which he thought unlikely, would be a psychological blow but would not stop it from continuing the war. If the USSR and Cuba were to 'bow out', the government would collapse in two to four years, he said, and moderates within the MPLA would insist on negotiations with UNITA. He said that unofficial contacts between 'senior MPLA elements' and UNITA representatives occurred several times in 1986; 'in time' he believed the USSR would come to favour a settlement. He thought that the best hope for a stable Angola would be a federal solution based on the country's main ethnic groups, with a semi-autonomous Ovimbundu region in the south.[47]

South Africa's war in Angola was of course not conducted in isolation. Although Botha had no overarching strategic blueprint for

Namibia, the war strategy was closely linked with, and responsive to, political developments inside Namibia, the course of settlement talks with the UN and the Western powers, and US politics and policies.

BOTHA'S UN DIPLOMACY

The Botha Administration's Namibia diplomacy has had one overriding objective: to prevent the establishment of a SWAPO-dominated government. Both for security reasons and domestic political considerations, the South Africans have been unwilling to agree to any formula for independence which might lead to an outright SWAPO victory and the introduction of the Soviet and Cuban influence that they fear would inevitably follow.

The military in particular has consistently taken a hard line towards SWAPO, encapsulated in the oft-repeated slogan, 'No Red flag in Windhoek'. In confidential discussions held in April 1981 with Reagan officials, whose informal notes were subsequently leaked to the Press, Malan:

> flatly declared that the [South African Government] can't accept prospects of a SWAPO victory which brings Soviet/Cuban forces to Walvis Bay. This would result from any election which left SWAPO in a dominant position. *Therefore a SWAPO victory would be unacceptable in the context of a Westminster-type political system.* [South Africa] does not rule out an internationally acceptable settlement, *but could not live with a SWAPO victory that left SWAPO unchecked power.*[48] [My emphasis.]

But maintaining its military base at Walvis Bay is only one of several strategic interests South Africa has in Namibia. In a joint interview given to the influential Afrikaans newspaper, *Die Transvaler*, on 25 March 1981 Malan and Foreign Minister Botha argued that 'the security interests of South Africa and South West Africa are irrevocably and inseparably tied to each other'. A South African withdrawal from Namibia, they said, would:

1. 'substantially reduce the time-scale for large-scale hostile actions against South Africa';
2. encourage 'territorial expansion' by the USSR, with South Africa as the ultimate target;

3. place 'the enemy closer to the heartland of the Republic';
4. 'contribute in a high degree to the intensification of the revolutionary climate';
5. 'contribute substantially to the disintegration of South Africa's ability to withstand a full-scale attack'.[49]

There would be political costs, as well. A political analyst close to the South African military noted that the establishment of another Front Line state on its borders would be unwelcome, 'especially if this should come about because of apparent South African weakness and an election won by SWAPO through opportunities for intimidation. It would cause resentment among certain groups and parties in South West Africa and a further rightwing reaction in South Africa.'[50] A South African diplomat noted in particular that his government must avoid being seen by black leaders – particularly those in the nominally independent homelands, but also those in nearby African states – as having sold out the internal Namibian political parties.[51] Moreover, as one observer noted, by making the case against SWAPO and in favour of a continued South African military presence in such strident tones, the leadership has raised the potential domestic political costs of a SWAPO victory, and has made it more difficult for the government to accept such an outcome.[52]

There is no doubt, however, that the Botha government would like to see a resolution of the vexing Namibia issue, which remains a source of friction in South African relations with Africa and the West and a burden on South Africa's budget. Botha once referred to Namibia as 'an economic millstone' around the Republic's neck, and in 1984 he told Parliament that the costs of staying in Namibia were running at $1.5 billion a year, of which security costs alone were $300–$400 million.[53] Yet neither relations with the West nor the financial costs of remaining in Namibia have yet weighed heavily in Botha's Namibia calculations. For one thing, a Namibia settlement alone would not necessarily lead to any lasting improvement in South Africa's relations with the outside world as long as apartheid and white minority rule continue to exist in South Africa. Indeed, South African officials have often warned that the accession of a SWAPO government in Namibia would lead to increased global pressure on South Africa itself. The Vorster Administration's very real concern that failure to move towards a settlement in Namibia would bring on global sanctions never carried as much weight with Botha. In any event the imposition of limited Western sanctions in 1985 (over

Botha's domestic race policy, not over Namibia), and the obvious reluctance on the part of Pretoria's major trading partners to apply really tough sanctions, effectively removed the sanctions threat as a factor in the Namibia policy. Furthermore, Botha's statements on the financial burden South Africa bears in Namibia are only valid in part. As one expert has observed,

> foreign aid to an independent Namibia would probably be only a fraction of what the RSA currently contributes . . . Thus, if a drastic destabilization of Namibia's economy and a large exodus of whites is to be prevented (for internal political and psychological reasons) *even an independent Namibia would require substantial development aid from South Africa. Independence would thus not really 'save' all that much in defence and aid resources as is often suggested.*[54]

The notion of Namibia as a burden also is self-serving. It suggests to a sceptical world that South Africa really is serious about seeking a settlement and about carrying out the obligations of its self-proclaimed continuing trusteeship in the Territory.

In short, Botha's Namibia diplomacy has been dominated by the security and internal political factors already discussed. Neither financial concerns nor notions that a settlement might bring closer ties to the West have been enough to move Botha to commit his government to the UN settlement proposals.

Given its adamant opposition to risking an election that SWAPO might win, the Botha government has pursued a two-track diplomacy. In continuing to talk to the UN and Western Five about a settlement under UNSC Resolution 435, South African spokesmen have bargained hard for advantage, giving the impression that they are serious about seeking a negotiated settlement. At the same time South Africa has manoeuvred, both within the framework of the UN talks and in a series of unilateral actions, to weaken SWAPO's position and to strengthen that of the South African-supported internal coalition of Namibian parties. It has also attempted to reach a settlement that would bypass the UN process entirely.

Although the UN-sponsored settlement talks have gone on intermittently since 1977, South Africa has avoided making an unqualified commitment to implement UNSC Resolution 435, or setting final conditions for doing so. Its success in stretching out the talks for so long, and in winning substantially more advantageous terms for a settlement as time went on, reflects its strong bargaining position vis-à-vis its adversaries. While the pressures on Botha to avoid or postpone agreeing to the UN settlement plan have far outweighed the pressures to settle, the Western powers and the Front Line leaders have been eager to see an end to the Namibian conflict, which has spilled into at least two other countries and has threatened to make southern Africa the scene of a widening war-by-proxy between the superpowers. Both the Carter and Reagan Administrations, in particular, expended considerable energy and political capital in seeking an internationally-approved settlement.

In the talks South Africa employed a number of effective tactics to delay or avoid binding commitments. Time and again Western diplomats were left confused by South Africa's calculated ambiguity, and uncertain what it had agreed to. During 1979 and early 1980 the talks centred on the proposal to establish a DMZ 60 miles wide to straddle the Namibia–Angola border as a prelude to a cease-fire and UN-supervised elections. After both SWAPO and South Africa 'accepted the concept' of a DMZ, the South Africans made their formal acceptance conditional on satisfactory arrangements regarding SADF base rights, size of the proposed UN monitoring force and other specifics. By May 1980 discussion of these and other issues had substantially met South African reservations and narrowed the gap between the two opposing parties. When the UN Secretary-General then called on South Africa to discuss implementing the DMZ, Foreign Minister Botha neither accepted nor rejected the plan, but pledged that his government would 'cooperate with' it.[55]

Another of South Africa's tactics has been to raise a new issue or objection just when the two sides seemed close to agreement, and to withhold its final agreement pending a satisfactory resolution of the new issue. Thus Foreign Minister Botha made South Africa's 'cooperation' on the DMZ plan subject to a new demand: that 'those directly responsible for implementing' the UN plan must demonstrate their impartiality.[56] The impartiality issue, which was raised again in March 1988, was a useful one for South Africa, since South Africa, alone would set the criteria and determine whether they had been met.

In August 1980 South Africa responded to another appeal from the Secretary-General by reiterating the impartiality requirement and adding a new one: the internal Namibian parties must be included in all future talks. A UN team headed by Deputy Secretary-General Urquhart went to Pretoria in October to discuss the new South

African demands. On 20 October, the day Urquhart arrived, the SADF launched a heavy attack on SWAPO bases in Angola: the first such attack in four months. The timing, like that of several other attacks coinciding with moves on the diplomatic front, served to reassure Namibian whites and internal political groups in Namibia that South Africa was not about to make concessions under pressure from the UN.[57]

By then, in fact, the interests of the Botha leadership in the UN settlement talks had diminished, and the focus of its attention had shifted to the deteriorating political situation inside Namibia.

THE STALLED GAME-PLAN INSIDE NAMIBIA

The DTA, a coalition of white and moderate black parties organized and supported by the South African government, won a majority of seats to the new constituent assembly in Namibia's internal elections in December 1978. The constituent assembly lacked legitimacy, however, because Namibia's two major (and predominantly black) parties boycotted the elections, and a constitution drafted without their participation would attract little support within or outside the Territory. At the request of the DTA, which realized that it must prove itself as a political force, Botha in May 1979 converted the constituent assembly into a national assembly with broad budgetary and taxation powers. Executive authority, however, remained in the office of a South African administrator-general appointed by Botha.

Eager to win support within the Territory, particularly among the 90 per cent black majority, the DTA-dominated national assembly began legislating an end to various segregation statutes. It also publicly supported one-man, one-vote elections. On both counts it incurred growing and vocal hostility from Namibia's Afrikaans speakers and their right-wing political coalition, Aktur. Aktur withdrew its six elected members from the national assembly in protest, and petitioned the South African courts to nullify Botha's act creating the national assembly. Aktur also made direct appeals to Afrikaner 'friends' in the Republic, telling them of 'the total onslaught being waged' against their kith and kin in Namibia.[58]

Botha took administrative action to block Aktur's legal moves, but he could not ignore the revolt of Namibia's Afrikaner community and the threat of strikes by its aroused teachers and bureaucrats. Torn between conflicting demands of the politically-vocal Afrikaner community and the DTA, Botha temporized. He dismissed Judge Steyn, the Administrator-General who, by virtue of both his liberal family credentials and his support of desegregation measures in the Territory, had antagonized Namibian Afrikaners.[59] Steyn was replaced by Gerrit Viljoen. As chairman of the powerful Broederbond at the time, Viljoen brought the requisite credentials as a conservative and trustworthy leader of South Africa's Afrikaans-speaking community. To slow the desegregation process, Viljoen immediately revived the notion of a three-tiered government with strong regional and municipal elements: a move designed to assure whites of local control over the desegregation process, and to weaken the authority of the more liberal DTA-dominated national assembly.

At the same time the Botha government continued to support DTA activities, and to provide it with financial assistance estimated at $450 000 a month in 1980.[60] In May 1980 South Africa announced that the national assembly was to be given limited executive powers. In July Dirk Mudge, head of the DTA, was made chairman of a new Council of Ministers which was given administrative authority over some 20 government departments. In practice, defence and foreign affairs stayed under the control of the South African administrator-general.[61]

In November 1980 Namibia's whites took advantage of local elections – the so-called 'second tier' elections to ethnically-based legislative authorities – to register their strong opposition to the DTA's programme of desegregation and power-sharing with blacks. Neither South African support nor a vigorous DTA campaign were enough to prevent its ending up with only a third of the vote to the whites' legislative assembly. Two-thirds of the vote went to right-wing white parties.[62]

The DTA also failed to prevent an erosion of black support. Major black parties in the DTA lost out in the 1980 local elections, which were boycotted by most black groups outside the DTA. They criticized the DTA chairman, Mudge, for basing Cabinet appointments on ethnicity. Botha himself had urged Mudge to 'take a back seat' and let the DTA's black politicians play a more prominent role.[63]

The high-water mark of DTA prominence was the UN-sponsored 'pre-implementation meeting' held in Geneva in January 1981. The agreed purpose was to bring South Africa, the DTA and SWAPO together for the first time to work out final details for implementing a cease-fire and elections. It was quickly apparent, however, that the South Africans had agreed to the Geneva talks for one purpose: to push the DTA leaders into the limelight in the hope that they would gain international legitimacy and status as valid representatives of the Namibian people. South Africa failed in its bid to have the DTA accepted as a separate delegation at the talks. As a member of the South African delegation, however, Mudge was the major spokesman for his side. He used his appearance to make a number of specific demands for evidence of UN impartiality. But when delegates of the Western Five asked Mudge in private if he would support a General Assembly resolution to fund a UN peacekeeping force in return for major concessions on the 'partiality' issue, he demurred, asking for a delay of 18 months.[64] Two days later the conference was given the official *coup de grâce* by the head of South Africa's delegation, who said that it was 'premature' to start implementing the UN settlement plan.[65]

The DTA's Geneva performance did little to enhance its status inside Namibia. During 1981 and 1982 its popular support eroded further, as both the DTA and the national assembly it dominated were seen to have failed to bring an end to apartheid in the Territory. Mudge was unable to stop defections from the DTA, let alone achieve any cohesion or harmony among Namibia's 45 squabbling political groups. Leaders of black parties in the DTA failed to persuade Mudge to move away from ethnic politics in favour of a single national party that would have greater appeal to black Namibians. Peter Kalangula, president of the DTA and leader of the only Ovambo group belonging to the DTA, withdrew his party from the coalition in February 1982 and invited other groups to join him in creating a new national party for the Territory.[66] Within a few months Botha, impatient with Mudge's leadership, was manoeuvring to dump him and put the popular Kalangula in as head of a new, more effective, interim administration. In September Botha told the Transvaal Congress of the Party that 'it has become necessary for the National Assembly to become more representative and also that a more effective executive body be created'.[67] Botha went so far as to send General van der Westhuizen, head of Military Intelligence, to Windhoek to put together a new, broader coalition that would include parties to both the left and right of the DTA and would be headed by a black.[68]

The dispute between Pretoria and Windhoek sputtered along until January 1983, when Mudge and his Council of Ministers resigned in protest against Pretoria's interference and the national assembly was dissolved. A new administrator-general appointed the following month established 'councils of local citizens' to help him administer the Territory. In July he announced plans for a State Council, whose 50 members would be drawn from a broad spectrum of Namibian politics, to draft an interim constitution. Only a few parties agreed to take part, however, so that the Council turned out to be even less representative than the defunct national assembly. South African officials acknowledged privately that the main purpose was to give the internal parties something to do 'to stop the place falling apart'.[69]

Although the State Council accomplished nothing, a new political coalition, the Multi-Party Conference (MPC), emerged from it in November 1983. Initially the MPC incorporated all the significant parties except the internal (and legally-functioning) wing of SWAPO, which declined to join. SWAPO's refusal is understandable in light of the MPC's statement of objectives, which referred only indirectly to seeking 'internationally recognized independence' and made no mention at all of the UN or UNSC Resolution 435. Soon the MPC suffered serious defections. In March 1984 the Damara Council, whose inclusion was considered critical to any effective coalition, accused the MPC of being anti-SWAPO and opposed to Resolution 435. It withdrew from the MPC and allied itself with SWAPO. Another major party, SWANU (the South West Africa National Union) split over the issue of continued participation in the MPC, leading several SWANU officials to leave.[70]

Meanwhile Botha himself had called the MPC to Cape Town to propose the abolition of ethnic political institutions in Namibia and the establishment of a strong, centralized administration. He told them that the MPC must be involved in future talks with SWAPO on a level equal to that of the South African government.[71]

Botha's intense efforts in the early 1980s to stitch together an effective political coalition inside Namibia stemmed from renewed hopes that such a group might win international acceptance, and that a settlement might be worked out which would, in one way or another, ensure Namibia against future domination by SWAPO. These hopes were fuelled in large part by the advent of the Reagan Administration in January 1981.

THE REAGAN FACTOR

South Africa's leaders, whose antennae are finely-tuned to pick up even faint signals from Washington, had reason to be pleased by those emanating from the incoming Reagan team. Chester Crocker, the new Assistant Secretary of State for Africa, had already outlined a new, less confrontational US approach to Pretoria in a major article published in *Foreign Affairs*. His exegesis of the new policy of 'constructive engagement' emphasized the durability of the South African regime, the limits on US capability to influence it, and the need to work with its leadership to make that limited influence most effective. Crocker also ruled out economic sanctions, thus removing from consideration the one policy tool that had long been viewed as the greatest threat by successive South African administrations.[72]

The new Secretary of State-designate, Alexander Haig, gave strong hints that there would be less US pressure on the Botha government over Namibia. Questioned about Namibia during his confirmation hearings, Haig said that the US 'should not put in jeopardy the interests of *those who share our values* . . . above all, our interests in a strategic sense' (my emphasis).[73] This statement suggested that the Reagan Administration supported the Botha government's opposition to a SWAPO-run Namibia.

During the next few months a number of Reagan diplomatic initiatives showed a startling shift in US thinking on Namibia. The major premise was recognition that no settlement was possible without Pretoria's compliance, and that it was therefore necessary to ascertain its major concerns in Namibia and to seek ways of meeting them. In April Crocker proposed an all-parties conference to seek agreement on constitutional principles for an independent Namibia. This would have conferred on the internal DTA parties a legitimate role in the talks. It flew in the teeth of Resolution 435, which called for a cease-fire and elections to *precede* the drafting of a constitution. But Reagan officials argued that the UN plan had failed to win Pretoria's acceptance; that if constitutional principles, particularly protection of white minority rights, could be agreed upon, it should be possible to win South African agreement to free elections and independence.[74] When Crocker arrived in Pretoria for talks a few weeks later, he further distanced the US from rigorous adherence to the UN plan, saying that Resolution 435 'provided a basis, but perhaps not the complete basis' for a settlement, and adding that the UN 'undoubtedly still had a role to play'.[75]

Foreign Minister Botha's visit to the US in May – the first high-level contact between the two countries since 1978 – included a 30-minute meeting in the White House Oval Office at President Reagan's request. Botha later said that the administration's new proposals offered 'a real possibility of moving ahead' towards a Namibian settlement.[76]

The new US emphasis on trying to meet South African concerns gave the Botha government a significant psychological advantage, since it meant that the US was prepared to make concessions to Pretoria. This gave the South Africans hopes of an improvement in the settlement terms being offered, and the possibility of winning US support for bypassing the UN and Resolution 435. Indeed, South Africa's foreign minister responded to Crocker's proposal for an all-parties constitutional conference by declaring Resolution 435 dead, and calling for a new settlement plan to bypass the UN altogether.[77]

Meanwhile secret State Department documents, leaked to the Press, revealed the emergence of a strong East–West element in the Reagan approach to Namibia and southern Africa. In a confidential 'Scope Paper' prepared for Haig in May 1981, before his initial meeting with the South Africans, Crocker noted that Namibia is 'a primary obstacle to the development of a new relationship with South Africa', and suggested that US–South African cooperation in working towards an internationally acceptable solution 'represents an opportunity to counter the Soviet threat in Africa'. In another document Crocker proposed linking a Namibian settlement to a withdrawal of Cuban troops from Angola and an Angolan commitment to share power with Jonas Savimbi's UNITA.[78]

This so-called 'linkage issue' was raised with the South Africans for the first time in June 1981, when the then Deputy Secretary of State, William Clark, led a US mission to Pretoria to discuss the Namibian impasse. The talks went badly. When the Americans rejected South African arguments for shelving the UN plan, the talks deteriorated into mutual recriminations, and the US delegation prepared to leave. Recognizing that there could be no progress on Namibia without Pretoria's acquiescence, however, the Americans made a last-minute bid to win South African agreement to move forward with the UN plan. When Foreign Minister Botha was asked if he would be prepared to agree to the plan if a Cuban troop withdrawal were guaranteed, tensions fell away and serious talks began.[79]

The removal of the Cuban combat brigade from Angola had already become an objective of the Reagan Administration, having less to do with Namibia than with internal US politics: specifically, conservative Republicans' pressure on Reagan to push back Soviet expansionism in the Third World. In April 1981 Crocker told the

Angolans that US diplomatic recognition depended on the prior withdrawal of Cuban forces. A month later a US official made the linkage explicit, declaring that some commitment to a Cuban withdrawal must be part of the new negotiating framework for Namibia.[80]

Astonishingly, South Africa had not previously made a Cuban pull-out a precondition for agreeing to implement the UN settlement plan. In the months following the Clark mission's visit the South Africans did not press the issue, apparently preferring to let the US take the lead in introducing linkage into the negotiations.

The proposal ran into strong opposition from the Front Line states and members of the Contact Group. Indeed, the US soon refined the concept to one of 'parallel movement': simultaneous progress toward a Cuban pull-out and a Namibian settlement on the basis of Resolution 435. That concession failed to placate France, Canada and West Germany, all of whom rejected linkage as a condition for a settlement.[81] France stopped participating in the Contact Group's deliberations, and other members expressed frustration at their inability to influence the Reagan policy. Although the Western Five minus France continued to meet for the next six years (1982–7) some members admitted privately that meetings were *proforma*, and that they attended only 'to keep the structure in place' while awaiting a change in US policy.[82]

Only in mid-1982 did the South Africans themselves seize on linkage as a condition for agreeing to the UN peace plan. It was an ideal issue for Botha, who stood to benefit whichever way it was resolved. A Cuban departure would weaken right-wing opposition to a settlement, thus giving Botha greater freedom to commit his government to the US-led peace initiative. On the other hand, as long as the Cubans stayed on Botha had an excellent justification – and at least the tacit understanding of the Reagan Administration – for refusing to settle. Thus in mid-June 1982 Prime Minister Botha said his government was 'unwilling to complete all phases' of the UN settlement plan unless the Cubans departed.[83] In October Malan, the Defence Minister, went further, reiterating that South Africa could not accept an arrangement which led to a SWAPO victory. His added assertion that South Africa could not, in any event, withdraw from the Territory because of the 'tactical problems' that would create for the SADF, was amended a few days later to apply only to a *unilateral* South African pull-out.[84]

Discussion of other issues – voting procedures, logistical arrangements for a UN monitoring force and the composition of such a force – continued without resolution during 1982, while South Africa and Angola elaborated their respective positions on the conditions for a mutual troop withdrawal. By that time, however, critical developments within South Africa's ruling NP had become P.W. Botha's main concern, and had narrowed his freedom to manoeuvre on the Namibian issue. The long-feared NP split over domestic race reform finally occurred in March when Treurnicht, leader of the NP's *verkrampte* (ideologically hardline) wing and NP boss in the Transvaal, was forced to leave the Party together with 15 right-wing Party MPs who supported him. It was not a propitious time for Botha to alienate his right wing further by making concessions on Namibia, and the Angolans were not prepared to agree to a Cuban withdrawal without solid guarantees against South African attack, either direct or in the guise of a UNITA operation.

Early in 1983 it had become clear the linkage issue had brought the talks to an impasse, and the Contact Group's initiative had collapsed. By then a new initiative, involving direct negotiations between the US, Angola and South Africa, was already under way.

SEEKING ALTERNATIVE SOLUTIONS

Under this new triangular approach American and Angolan officials discussed terms for a Cuban troop withdrawal, while the South Africans and Angolans negotiated arrangements for a cease-fire. The new initiative was advantageous to South Africa: it kept the UN and the Contact Group out of the negotiations while engaging the relatively sympathetic Reagan Administration and South Africa in parallel talks with Angola. Throughout 1983 South African and Angolan leaders made offers and counter-offers regarding a mutual troop withdrawal, but failed to reach an accord. That impasse led to US pressure on South Africa and to Botha's dramatic announcement of a cease-fire in January 1984. But the really difficult issues – Cuban troop withdrawal, South African implementation of 435, and cessation of Pretoria's support for UNITA – remained unresolved.

During 1984 South Africa moved vigorously to take the Namibian initiative out of the hands of the US and UN, and to bring about a settlement on its own terms. Indeed a bewildering variety of hints, statements and moves, some of them mutually contradictory, emanated from Pretoria. First was Botha's surprise announcement on 1

March that Toivo ja Toivo, SWAPO's 59-year-old founder, had been released after 16-years' imprisonment. Official hopes that he could be induced to join the internal MPC coalition, or at least that he might bring about a split in the SWAPO leadership, were quickly dashed, however, when he denounced the internal parties and accepted a post as secretary-general of SWAPO.

At about the same time Foreign Minister Botha, in a blatant move to bypass the US/UN settlement process, proposed a regional peace conference to be held in Africa and attended only by African parties: South Africa, Angola, SWAPO, the MPC and UNITA. This proposal, which the US was not told of in advance, was rejected by Angola and SWAPO because of UNITA's inclusion.[85] It was also dismissed by the US.

In May, however, President Kaunda of Zambia followed up South Africa's March proposal by offering to host a meeting in Lusaka between SWAPO and Namibia's internal MPC coalition, which was included in the official South African delegation. UNITA was not included. The meeting was co-chaired by Kaunda and Botha's Administrator-General for the Territory, Dr Willie van Niekerk. Kaunda's hopes that the two opposing groups could agree on terms for Namibian independence were dashed when the two white parties in the MPC refused to endorse Resolution 435 and once again revived the issue of UN partiality. SWAPO, in turn, rejected MPC proposals that it publicly reject violence and agree to join the internal process to resolve the conflict. The Botha government said in advance that it would accept any agreement reached by the two opposing groups, but SWAPO delegates said they were convinced that the administrator-general in fact had no authority to commit South Africa to anything. The Lusaka meeting ended without even an agreed communiqué. Although the talks may have enhanced the legitimacy of the MPC as a party to a settlement, they also highlighted the deep divisions within the MPC, whose member parties had reached no consensus on an agenda for attaining independence. The Lusaka meeting also showed the pull of SWAPO on other political parties: SWAPO's 50-member delegation included representatives of several major internal parties which had left the MPC and associated themselves with the SWAPO position.[86]

In June 1984 press reports leaked yet another South African initiative, this one a secret offer to SWAPO, which would be given nominal leadership of an interim coalition government to administer Namibia until independence. Such key Cabinet posts as security, foreign affairs and finance would have been assigned to the MPC, however. This was part of a broader South African proposal aimed at winning the support of SWAPO and African leaders for a regional settlement in which Pretoria would drop its demand for a Cuban troop withdrawal in exchange for a weakening of Resolution 435 and a negligible UN role in the transition period.[87] SWAPO rejected the offer, however, saying they were being offered 'nice cars and nice apartments and asked to play the part of South African puppets'.[88]

Bilateral talks among the US, South Africa and Angola resumed in late 1984, but failed again to reach agreement on Cuban and SADF troop withdrawals. Prospects for progress received a further setback in December, when Foreign Minister Botha demanded that UNITA be included in any future settlement. Triangular talks lingered on in early 1985, but US warnings that rejection of its latest proposals by Angola and South Africa might lead Washington to end its mediation had little effect. By then both sides were losing interest. Angola was preparing for its big military push against UNITA in September, while South Africa was engaged in another attempt to shore up the sagging political structure inside Namibia.

Indeed, various moves by the Botha government from 1985 to 1987 indicated that it was preparing for an alternative settlement scenario. Foreign Minister Botha told Parliament in 1986 that the Namibian people 'cannot wait indefinitely for their independence'. If, in the end, he said, agreement cannot be reached on a Cuban troop withdrawal, then 'the parties most closely concerned with the present negotiations will have to consider how the area can obtain independence in a way which is acceptable internationally'.[89] Thus the government continued groping to create internal political institutions, including a constitution, which would be accepted by all Namibia's population groups and which would, through some means, eventually be accepted by the international community as well. A 'government of national unity', which was to serve as 'an interim mechanism for the internal administration' of the Territory 'pending internationally accepted independence' was established in June 1985. Its Cabinet and 62-seat national assembly were made up of the six ethnic-based parties of the MPC. Sixteen assembly members were appointed to serve as a Constitutional Council, assigned to draft a constitution 'acceptable to the majority of Namibia's people'.[90] The Council's chairman made clear his concern that the constitution be one which would gain external approval, noting that key elements favoured by the Western Five, such as a unitary state, a Bill of Rights and proportional representation, were acceptable to him.[91]

Tensions among the six MPC parties represented in the assembly continued to block the path to unity, however. President Botha himself backed the local NP's demand that the Namibian constitution must explicitly protect minority rights, meaning that it must guarantee Namibia's whites the right to maintain segregated schools and other facilities. In August 1987, after 17 months' work, the Constitutional Council published *two* draft constitutions: one, representing the majority of 14, was similar to Zimbabwe's, providing for a bicameral Parliament, a prime minister, a Bill of Rights and elections by a party list system. In a minority draft, submitted by the local NP's member, local ethnically-based councils would have considerable control, including the power to retain apartheid in their areas.[92] The issue remained unresolved, however, and in April 1988 P.W. Botha tightened Pretoria's control over the Territory by enlarging the authority of the administrator-general.

The Botha government thus continued to be plagued by its two conflicting objectives in Namibia. The first horn of its enduring dilemma was to promote an internal administration and a constitution which would represent a broad majority of the Namibian people. This was seen as indispensable to winning international acceptance for a settlement that would effectively exclude SWAPO from power. The second was to retain the essential elements of separate development so as to avoid a political confrontation within the MPC coalition between the majority favouring rapid desegregation and right-wing whites represented by the local NP.[93]

The prospects for resolving this dilemma, at least by the end of the decade, remained dim. Botha's Namibia diplomacy, together with his hard-hitting counter-insurgency, postponed the holding of free elections which SWAPO would almost certainly have won.[94] But his failure to develop a consensus in Namibian politics, and to articulate a coherent plan for its future political development, reflected his inability to find a formula that would meet his government's conflicting interests in Namibia.

8 Regional Destabilization

SADF RAIDS IN NEIGHBOURING STATES

By 1980 the ANC had won permission to establish local administrative headquarters and to maintain sizeable numbers of personnel in six countries bordering South African territory: Angola, Botswana, Lesotho, Mozambique, Swaziland and Zimbabwe. Angola and Mozambique offered virtually full sanctuary to ANC operatives. The other four restricted the ANC presence to non-military personnel, and prohibited the use of their territories as bases for attacks against South Africa. But except for Zimbabwe, which closely monitored ANC activities and controlled the size of its local staff, these states lacked the capability and in some cases the will to do either. Botswana and Lesotho have only small security forces (Botswana's *total* police and paramilitary number 4000) with which to patrol borders with South Africa that are over 1000 miles long.[1]

Operating from neighbouring sanctuary states, the ANC in 1980 opened a campaign of highly visible, and in some cases seriously damaging, sabotage and bombing attacks inside South Africa. Major targets included symbols of apartheid authority, especially police stations and government departments responsible for implementing security and apartheid legislation. Others were targets of economic significance, such as power stations and fuel depots. Some attacks were more symbolic than destructive: in August 1981 ANC operatives lobbed a brief barrage of rockets into South Africa's central army base near Pretoria. But a sophisticated attack on the Koeberg nuclear power complex in 1982 used limpet mines, timed to detonate at intervals, and caused damage to one reactor and two transformers amounting to more than $20 million.[2]

As ANC incidents rapidly increased (from 19 in 1980 to 55 in 1981, according to official count), the Botha government responded with blatant attacks against suspected ANC offices and residences in neighbouring capital cities. The first, a January 1981 raid on ANC quarters in Maputo, was carried out by a motorized SADF column disguised as Mozambican troops. A dozen ANC members were killed and several captured.[3] In December 1982, following the ANC attack on Koeberg, SADF special forces assaulted suspected ANC residences in Lesotho's capital, Maseru. A devastating ANC car-bomb attack on SAAF headquarters in Pretoria in May 1983 led immediately to an SAAF reprisal bombing of a Mozambican missile site and alleged ANC camps near Maputo. In October the SADF struck a third time at Maputo, as airborne commandos attacked an alleged ANC planning office.[4]

Both the timing of the SADF attacks and the official publicity given to them, however, suggest that aggressive strikes at the ANC had a strong domestic political imperative, and sometimes only a dubious military rationale. The first raid on Maputo occurred two days before Botha announced a general election for whites. Indeed, the Afrikaans newspaper of South Africa's far-right HNP accused Botha of postponing that attack until the election announcement in order to win votes.[5] The attack on Maputo in October 1983, which was not in reprisal, was launched two weeks before South African whites were to vote on Botha's controversial new constitution and multi-ethnic Parliament. A further indication of the domestic political element in the SADF raids was the absence of any prior low-key diplomatic moves; instead, they were often preceded by highly publicized threats from South African officials, including those delivered in Parliament by Botha himself.[6] The popularity of the cross-border attacks was shown in a 1982 opinion poll of South African whites, 80 per cent of whom approved assaults on the sanctuary states. Among Afrikaners, 86 per cent approved.[7]

The initial foreign reaction to the SADF attacks was mostly rhetorical, and presented Botha with no real deterrent to his policy. The late President Machel invoked Mozambique's treaty of friendship with the USSR, Article IX of which stipulates that, 'if situations arise that threaten the peace', the two states 'will immediately get in touch in order to coordinate their positions in the interests of eliminating the threat that has arisen'.[8] The USSR responded by dispatching two warships to Maputo three weeks later. That largely symbolic action removed any fear that the Soviet Union might view the attack as an opportunity to confront the South Africans or to raise its military stake in Mozambique. Indeed, in a speech heralding the warship visit, the Soviet ambassador said: 'We are not threatening anyone . . . [but] If anyone attacks us or our friends, we will give a suitable response.'[9] Protests were voiced in the UN and OAU, which sent representatives to the funeral of ANC officials killed in the attack, and at a meeting of Front Line leaders. In the US the newly-installed Reagan Administration, which was still groping for internal consensus on an Africa policy, failed to condemn the attack. In fact, three days after the Maputo raid Botha gave a press interview in which he hinted that the Reagan Administration's tough stand against terrorism was a factor in the decision to launch the attack.[10]

The first dividends from the sanctuary attacks came in 1983, when several of the neighbouring states began to exercise closer control over ANC personnel. Following the May 1983 raid on Maputo, Mozambique announced that ANC refugees would be prohibited from carrying arms. In Swaziland the police began to raid the homes of ANC members to search for weapons. In a secret deal the previous year Swaziland had signed a mutual security pact with Pretoria in exchange for a promised slice of territory on which South Africa later had to renege. In August 1983 Lesotho announced that South African military and economic pressures had forced it to expel 3000 South African refugees.[11] In March 1984 Mozambique was forced to agree to a mutual security accord with South Africa; but, as discussed below, this was due more to pressure from Mozambican National Resistance (MNR, or Renamo) activities than to SADF attacks. Mozambique announced the expulsion of 200 ANC personnel following the signing of that accord.

By 1984 the raids had resulted in a drastic shrinkage of the ANC's sanctuaries. Its military planners were forced to move to Zambia which was too distant from South Africa's borders to enable them to plan and oversee the execution of sophisticated sabotage attacks. ANC leaders acknowledged that a new strategy was required. The change occurred in 1985, in the wake of the uprising in South Africa's black townships. Moving to associate itself with those activities and to bid for a leadership role, and acknowledging that the short-term prospects for a Rhodesia-type insurgency were nil, the ANC decided at a conference in Kabwe, Zambia, in June 1985 to call for a 'people's war'. As described by the leading academic authority on the ANC, this would involve a:

> broadening out of the base of guerrilla operations with the recruitment of 'part-time guerrillas' who would operate within their normal home areas, who would be provided with basic training through short courses in the use of simple weaponry and explosive devices, and who would concentrate their activity at this stage on attacking the representatives of apartheid political institutions and the forces of law and order within their communities.[12]

The ANC managed to adapt to the loss of protected sanctuaries, and in 1985 doubled the number of attacks inside South Africa. But in place of sophisticated sabotage, the new part-time recruits in the 'people's war' carried out simple operations, particularly mining remote farm roads. This was a dangerous new development. Previously the ANC had attempted with some success to avoid causing large-scale civilian casualties. Before 1985 the only incident leading to substantial civilian loss of life was the car-bombing of SAAF headquarters in Pretoria in May 1983, killing 16 people and injuring 200. It seemed inevitable that the new 'people's war' strategy would mean less centralized ANC control over operations carried out in its name, and hence a greater likelihood of civilian casualties.

As ANC attacks increased, South African cross-border raids continued. In June 1985 SADF troops staged a raid on residences in Botswana's capital, Gaborone, in which 11 ANC supporters and five people with no ANC links were killed. In December South Africa threatened to invade Zimbabwe in pursuit of ANC guerrillas. Later that month commandos in black-face attacked a residence in Lesotho's capital, Maseru, shooting nine people. Following the attack South Africa's State Security Council accused *all* the neighbours of harbouring ANC operatives and threatened them with retribution, thus implicitly acknowledging that South Africa could not be certain where ANC attacks originated.[13]

The SADF attacks on Botswana and Lesotho were widely condemned; indeed, the Reagan Administration recalled its ambassador from Pretoria in protest over the Botswana raid. Yet South Africa continued to apply strong military and other pressures against its neighbours. In early 1986, while blockading Lesotho (analysed below), South Africa threatened to take 'appropriate measures' against Botswana unless its leaders agreed to provide detailed biographies of all South African residents in Botswana and to allow a South African official to attend the screening of refugees.[14] Botswana responded by asking the few remaining ANC representatives to leave, and by closing down a news service run by South African exiles. Zimbabwe sent military officers to meet their SADF counterparts to discuss alleged ANC border incidents.

Perhaps the high-water mark of South Africa's campaign of raids on alleged ANC sanctuaries was the May 1986 simultaneous assault by the SADF on Gaborone, Harare and Lusaka. The choice of multiple targets and the timing of that assault had more to do with South Africa's worsening external relations, and particularly with external pressure for political change inside South Africa, than with the ANC threat. The raiders struck several alleged 'operational and information centres', according to the SADF, but no key installations or command centres, and caused only a few casualties. The attacks, for which Botha took 'full responsibility', were in no sense random, however. They were directed against three Commonwealth states, and were launched on the same day that a delegation of senior Commonwealth officials, known as the Eminent Persons Group (EPG) had returned to South Africa from talks with the ANC. The EPG's mission, on behalf of the Commonwealth, was to establish a basis for talks between the ANC and the Botha government.[15]

The multiple raid, which was seen as Botha's defiant rejection of the EPG peace initiative, led to condemnation by virtually all Western, Commonwealth and African states, and gave increased momentum to the international pressure for sanctions. Argentina severed diplomatic ties. Canada recalled its ambassador and tightened sanctions. A bipartisan coalition of US Senators and Congressmen called for stiffer US sanctions, and the EPG declared that tougher sanctions might be the only way to avert the worst bloodbath since the Second World War. A number of Western countries withdrew military attachés from South Africa.

EPG officials and senior US diplomats believe that the Botha government was surprised by the strong international reaction to the May 1986 raids.[16] Undoubtedly it was in part responsible for the diminution of cross-border attacks since that time, and for the pains taken by South African officials to categorize and justify subsequent armed actions. Thus, according to an SADF officer close to policy-makers, a distinction is now drawn between *pre-emptive* attacks, directed at *ANC* targets, and *retaliatory* attacks, directed at *governments*. He noted that the latter 'are kept to a minimum, because they are more risky internationally'.[17] Accordingly, when SADF commandos attacked two residential buildings in Zambia's border town of Livingstone in April 1987, South African Army spokesmen were careful to describe the assault as 'armed reconnaissance on terrorist infiltration routes through Zambia and Botswana', thus suggesting its limited scale and objective.[18]

Cross-border attacks by no means ended, however. Four people in Botswana's capital were killed in a raid by SADF commandos in late March 1988. While officially-acknowledged cross-border attacks by the SADF diminished in both frequency and scale during 1986–7, South Africa appeared to have turned instead to a deliberate campaign of assassinations of ANC officials in foreign countries by anonymous 'hit squads'. Assassinations, by letter-bomb and other means, have long been part of the secret war against the ANC. But the number of killings rose dramatically in 1986–8, suggesting an official shift in South African tactics. Indeed, Foreign Minister Botha acknowledged in late 1986 that his government had kidnapped ANC agents in Swaziland and that it would attack the ANC in London if South African security were at stake. Thirteen people, most of them known or suspected ANC members, were gunned down in neighbouring Swaziland in roughly the first nine months of 1987, and more than a dozen ANC-linked exiles were assassinated in Lesotho between late 1985 and 1987. In July 1987 five white men were detained in England on charges of conspiring to blow up ANC headquarters in London and to kidnap ANC leaders.[19] Following the assassination of a long-time ANC representative on a Paris street in March 1988, the ANC's Washington spokesman said the Federal Bureau of Investigation had warned him to be alert to the possibility of South African hit squads operating in the US.[20] Whether these more blatant acts of counter-terrorism would lead the ANC to undertake deliberate terrorist acts against South African whites or South African officials abroad remained to be seen, but the war against the ANC in its sanctuaries was only one element in the comprehensive destabilization strategy.

RENAMO AND OTHER PROXY FORCES

By the early 1980s South Africa was involved in supporting groups of armed dissidents operating against Angola, Lesotho, Mozambique, Zimbabwe and perhaps Zambia as well. Of the various groups trained, armed, financed and in some cases directed by South Africa, its greatest political commitment was to UNITA, the Angolan nationalist movement, as discussed in Chapter 7. But other South African proxy forces have been important agents of destabilization, particularly in Zimbabwe and Mozambique.

Mugabe's sweeping electoral victory in Zimbabwe's 1980 independence election over the South African-backed candidate, the docile and conservative Bishop Muzorewa, was a worst case scenario come true for white South Africans. Indeed, following Mugabe's election, South African officials began using the term 'Muzorewa syndrome' to express concern over the prospects for South African-supported black leaders in Namibia and South Africa. Thus a coolly correct exchange of communications at the time of Mugabe's accession, including his assurances that he would not allow guerrilla bases in Zimbabwe, did not remove Botha's mistrust. Mugabe, a recently-emerged national leader who was virtually unknown in South Africa, was perceived as a political radical: a self-declared Marxist, the austere and uncompromising leader of a large and effective guerrilla army, and an outspoken foe of apartheid.

Within six months of Zimbabwe's independence and Mugabe's accession to power in April 1980, he accused South Africa of carrying out airdrops of supplies to dissident ex-guerrillas who had been trained in South Africa and sent back into Zimbabwe to foment unrest. Western diplomats believed the charges to be true.[21] By 1983 small groups of armed dissidents were engaged in a rampage of banditry and murder in Zimbabwe's Matabeleland province. Mugabe sent a Korean-trained army brigade to pacify the region, but its campaign was marked by indiscriminate destruction and violence, which exacerbated long-standing ethnic tensions between Matabeleland, home of the minority Ndebele people, and the Shona-dominated government. Dissident activity had virtually ended by 1985, only to re-emerge in 1987 as more than a dozen people, including farmers, government workers, tourists and missionaries were killed in separate incidents. The dissidents were believed to number fewer than 200; but their sporadic attacks were enough to cause alarm among the local people and to increase political and ethnic tensions.[22]

According to a senior Zimbabwe security official speaking in 1986, security relations between Pretoria and Zimbabwe remained uneasy, but regular meetings between military officers from each side provided an important channel for refuting SADF charges of Zimbabwean complicity and oversight in ANC attacks. Despite frequent public threats against Zimbabwe by South African officials, the SADF seemed sufficiently relaxed about its Zimbabwe border to allow most patrolling to be done by Zimbabwe forces on their own side.[23]

Lesotho, the tiny enclave state in South Africa, has been a major refuge for blacks fleeing South Africa. During the 1980s the Botha government grew increasingly uneasy with Leabua Jonathan, an unpredictable autocrat who had come to power with South African help two decades earlier. His growing defiance of South Africa – especially the opening of Soviet, Chinese and North Korean embassies in Maseru in 1983, and his rejection of South African requests for a mutual security pact – led to increasing South African intervention in Lesotho's affairs. There had already been reports that sabotage against the Jonathan regime by a group called the Lesotho Liberation

Front (LLF) had been launched from South Africa with official knowledge, if not sponsorship. Some 500 troops from the LLF engaged Lesotho forces in an eight-hour battle in September 1983.[24] In early 1984 South Africa's foreign minister and other officials met dissident Lesotho political leaders to help organize a new alliance and to offer financial support for a campaign to oust the Jonathan government. The group promised that, once in power, it would sever relations with communist countries.[25] Nothing came of this initiative, however, and ultimately South Africa opted for applying extreme economic pressure – its so-called 'railway diplomacy' – to bring about the downfall of the Jonathan government.

The activities of South African-supported dissidents in Zimbabwe and Lesotho, however, were far less damaging to the target countries than the operations of the MNR in Mozambique. The MNR was formally organized by Ian Smith's Rhodesian intelligence service after Portuguese rule ended and Frelimo nationalists came to power in Mozambique in 1976. At that time a group of Mozambican mercenaries, originally hired by the Portuguese to fight against Frelimo, fled to neighbouring Rhodesia along with other opponents of Frelimo. Organized, trained and armed by Rhodesia, MNR operatives were sent back into Mozambique to harass the new government and to disrupt guerrilla attacks being carried out against Rhodesia from Mozambican sanctuary.[26]

With the end of white minority rule in Zimbabwe in 1980 the MNR was airlifted to South Africa, where its forces were reorganized and trained in a Transvaal camp under the direction of the SADF's Directorate of Military Intelligence (DMI). Although lacking the credentials of a legitimate national movement, Renamo was nevertheless useful to South African security objectives. According to captured MNR documents, which Western diplomats believe to be genuine, DMI officials directed the MNR 'to interdict rail traffic [in southern Mozambique], establish bases inside Mozambique adjacent to the South African border, open a new military front in Maputo province, and provoke incidents in Maputo and Beira'.[27] Thus in addition to harassing the Frelimo government, which South African leaders considered to be actively supporting ANC operations against South Africa, the MNR was specifically directed to disrupt ports and rail links that were vital to Zimbabwe and important to the other regional countries as well.

By late 1983 Renamo had penetrated almost all of Mozambique's ten provinces, and had removed large areas of Mozambique's far-flung territory from any vestige of government control beyond the main cities. The MNR's estimated 5000–8000 heavily-armed forces operated in groups of 100 or more to carry out traditional guerrilla attacks: sabotage of rail and pipe lines and assaults on isolated villages and army posts, killing and kidnapping villagers. The economy, already reeling from the impact of several years of drought and economic mismanagement, was quickly brought close to collapse by Renamo's depredations.[28]

Recognizing that there would be no outside help to defeat Renamo or to prevent direct SADF attacks, three of which had occurred since 1981, President Machel asked the US to approach Pretoria about a rapprochement. The result was a mutual non-aggression pact, the Accord of Nkomati, signed by Presidents Botha and Machel on 16 March 1984. The accord pledged each party to prevent the use of its territory as a base for aggression against the other, and to end support, sanctuary and recruitment for groups or individuals planning acts of violence against the other. A Joint Security Commission was established to monitor the terms of the agreement.[29] For Machel the embarrassment of signing a pact with the detested apartheid regime was softened to some extent by a parallel series of agreements on joint economic ventures in Mozambique.

The Botha Administration saw the Nkomati Accord as a major step toward its long-cherished goal of creating a belt of regional states linked to South Africa by mutual non-aggression pacts and bilateral economic cooperation agreements. For Botha and the SADF the pact vindicated the destabilization policy: particularly because Mozambique was a Marxist state with an active mutual cooperation treaty with the USSR, as well as being the main staging area for ANC attacks. The pact was signed with much pomp and publicity, and with statements by Botha and his foreign minister that it marked a turning-point in regional relations. A career diplomat appointed to serve as South Africa's trade commissioner in Maputo called the accord 'crucial to our whole foreign policy': 'Imagine the effect an economically prosperous Mozambique would have on the attitudes toward South Africa of other neighboring states.'[30]

The accord brought immediate benefits to South Africa as Mozambican authorities expelled more than 800 ANC activists, including commanders of its military wing, and reduced the ANC presence to a 10-man office in Maputo.[31] But the accord failed to bring the relief from MNR attacks that Mozambique had expected. Indeed, when the SADF was ordered to clear out the MNR's Transvaal camps, it sent at least 1500 heavily-armed and trained MNR troops across the border, where they opened a campaign to isolate Mozambique's capital. Moreover the SADF, presumably with Botha's approval, organized a massive resupply operation, dropping tons of supplies by sea and air as a 'golden handshake' to Renamo.[32]

In an abortive effort to end the fighting, Foreign Minister Botha hosted proximity talks between the Machel government and the MNR in October 1984. But the resulting Pretoria Declaration was little more than a unilateral expression of South African hopes for a cease-fire in which neither side was interested. Machel rejected negotiations with Renamo, and offered the MNR only a general amnesty. Mozambique did agree, however, to take part in a joint technical commission to organize a cease-fire. The MNR, apparently with the support of highly-placed backers in Portugal, walked out of the talks and rejected the terms for a truce.[33]

By late 1984, amid growing reports of clandestine South African support for Renamo, Machel accused Pretoria of deliberate violations of the Nkomati Accord.[34] Foreign Minister Botha denied the charges. Fearing Mozambique was about to renounce the accord, however, he prevailed on P.W. Botha to authorize a security investigation of South Africa's Portuguese community and of the SADF, too. In February 1985 the foreign minister acknowledged for the first time that 'elements' in South Africa were involved in helping Renamo. The police had uncovered a 'Mafia-type' syndicate which had aided Renamo through smuggling and other illicit activities. The syndicate had also enlisted the help of a dozen MNR sympathizers in the SADF, all of whom had since been transferred or dismissed.[35]

The first official hint that senior SADF leaders might be implicated was Malan's thinly-veiled reaction to the security probe. He objected strongly, he said, to aspersions being cast on (unnamed) heads of the SADF for allegedly obstructing the government's Mozambican peace initiative.[36] The issue blew wide open in September 1985, after Mozambique released diaries and other documents captured in a surprise assault on Renamo's main headquarters at Gorongoza. The Vaz Diaries, which Western diplomatic and intelligence authorities generally believed to be genuine, disclosed that senior SADF intelligence officials met MNR leaders secretly and made arrangements for clandestine arms shipments as late as August 1984: five months after the signing of the Nkomati Accord. Among its entries the diary (which was translated from the Portuguese) describes a meeting at MNR headquarters on 16 August, where a brigadier and a colonel in DMI responded as follows to a request for ammunition:

> As regards war materiel, AK-47 ammunition, we have this for you . . . but at the moment there are transport difficulties. We can no longer use the C-130 aircraft, as these aircraft are under Air Force control, nor can we use the Navy as there might be an information leak . . .
> To overcome this difficulty we are going to use civilian aircraft. So Col. Vanikerke [sic] will go to Gorongosa on 22/8/84 to meet the President of Renamo so as to organize landing strips to make it easier to use civil aircraft that can land and not drop parachutes . . .
> As for material for urban guerrilla warfare we shall send this, but not all the kinds asked for, since some bombs were assembled in SA, and it would compromise us with the Inkomati [sic] Accord.[37]

Following the revelations in the Gorongoza documents, Foreign Minister Botha acknowledged publicly in September 1985 that his government had been guilty of 'technical violations' of the accord, including airdrops of 'mostly humanitarian aid'.[38] He defended the post-Nkomati contacts with Renamo as part of an effort to arrange a settlement between the MNR and the Machel government. That explanation appeared at odds with entries in the Vaz Diary, however, including a message allegedly from General Viljoen, the SADF Chief, to the MNR the previous September, in which he counselled Renamo to maintain its military strength and to reject Machel's offer of amnesty, assuring its leader that 'we want Renamo to win the war'.[39]

General Viljoen held his own press conference at which he admitted, as had the foreign minister, that many of the facts in the Gorongoza documents were correct; but Viljoen charged that some of the information had been doctored. He confirmed the diary's evidence that Louis Nel, a deputy foreign minister, had made three secret trips to Gorongoza under Military Intelligence auspices without the knowledge of either the foreign minister or the defence minister. He disagreed, however, with the foreign minister's assertion that technical violations had occurred, and criticized his handling of the abortive peace talks the previous year.[40]

These developments, which bear some of the elements of the US Iran–Contra scandal a year later, revealed, at the very least, unresolved bureaucratic conflicts between the military and the DFA over policy towards Mozambique. Some months earlier Foreign

Minister Botha had attributed South Africa's difficulties in implementing the Nkomati Accord to 'conflicting elements' which were initially opposed to the pact. This had continued to be the case, he said.[41] But whether the military was a loose cannon, pursuing an agenda of its own to undermine the Nkomati Accord, or was only carrying out a duplicitous policy approved by the top leadership, is uncertain. President Botha tried to bury the issue when he addressed a Party congress in October 1985. Asserting that his government had 'kept faithfully' to the accord, he went on to affirm his faith in General Viljoen's honesty, thus indirectly denying any personal knowledge of the events in question:

> Whatever you say of [General Viljoen], you can surely say that he is an honourable and brave officer. I asked him in front of witnesses whether he was guilty of transgressing the accord. He denied it and assured me that he kept to the government's decisions. I believe General Viljoen, and no communist attempt to discredit him . . . will succeed.[42]

While formally observing the Nkomati Accord, SADF leaders clearly had strong reservations about supporting the Marxist regime and closing off the military option. Thus a strong case can be made that the military, which had trained and directed Renamo's forces for four years prior to Nkomati, were reluctant to abandon a 'contra' force with which they had worked closely: particularly a force that had been so effective in harassing and weakening the Marxist government in Mozambique. If Renamo could be kept alive, there would remain at least the possibility that its operations might force the regime to greater concessions than those it had agreed to at Nkomati.

Moreover, independent initiatives by the military, if such they were, would have been easier to conduct at a time when President Botha was occupied with domestic political reform and growing black rebellion, as was the case in 1984 and 1985. With growing demands on the SADF to patrol South Africa's turbulent black townships as well as to increase its efforts to intercept ANC infiltrators along the border, Botha would have had good reason to avoid inquiring too deeply or publicly into activities which might have led to unfavourable publicity for the SADF and embarrassment for his administration. Yet a repudiation of the Nkomati Accord by Mozambique would also have been embarrassing.

The DFA viewed Nkomati as a diplomatic coup, and had a strong bureaucratic interest in seeing it implemented. If it was seen to bring peace and economic cooperation between South Africa and Mozambique, the accord might attract other nearby states into entering similar arrangements with Pretoria. This would mean a shift from military to diplomatic initiatives and a lowering of tensions between South Africa and its neighbours, thereby enhancing the status and influence of Foreign Affairs relative to the military.

Official South African ambivalence toward Mozambique continued to be evident in 1986. In April US Secretary of State Shultz told a congressional committee that the South Africans were not 'keeping their side of the bargain' with regard to Nkomati.[43] A senior South African diplomat led a delegation to Maputo in September to try to 'improve communications' with the Machel government, but the following month South Africa announced plans to repatriate thousands of Mozambican workers in retaliation for ANC cross-border attacks allegedly originating in Mozambique.[44]

In September 1986 Mozambique's security situation took on a regional dimension as several Front Line states, particularly Zimbabwe and Tanzania, made a strong commitment to assist the government against Renamo. A joint *démarche* to Malawi, threatening to close its borders and cut off trade unless it expelled MNR forces encamped inside the country, led to the expulsion of several thousand Renamo guerrillas. But these heavily-armed forces crossed into Mozambique's thinly-populated Zambesia province, where they quickly occupied several towns and key bridges over the Zambesi. After Zimbabwe raised its troop strength in Mozambique to between 6000 and 12 000, its forces kept open the vital road, rail and pipe lines running from Zimbabwe to the sea, and helped the Mozambicans to clear Zambesia of the MNR early in 1987. Tanzania provided 500 troops to retrain Mozambican units and to hold villages cleared of MNR forces by the Mozambicans. Even neighbouring Malawi, the only African state to maintain diplomatic relations with South Africa, signed a mutual cooperation agreement with Mozambique and dispatched a small contingent of Malawian soldiers to guard the Nacala rail line connecting Malawi with Mozambican ports.[45]

This joint military cooperation put considerable pressure on Renamo, which suffered serious reverses in 1987. In January Mozambique claimed to have foiled a South African plan to resupply Renamo by sea, and by February the MNR had been driven out of Zambesia Province, the only area where its forces actually controlled any territory.[46] Thus South Africa appeared to face the choice of seeing the military fortunes of its former proxy group continue to fade, or intervening militarily on its behalf.

Relations between South Africa and Mozambique, already strained over the MNR issue, deteriorated further in late 1986 when President Machel died in a plane crash in which Mozambican authorities accused South Africa of complicity. Officially, the Botha government declared its support for the new Chissano administration and for Nkomati, but a May 1987 commando attack in Maputo which caused the deaths of three innocent Mozambicans was blamed on South Africa: a charge which the US State Department supported.

In August 1987, however, Mozambique and South Africa revived the Nkomati Accord and reactivated the Joint Security Commission to confer on issues in contention, including the question of aid to the MNR.[47] Renamo's fortunes suffered a further setback in the summer of 1987 when the Reagan Administration resisted right-wing pressure to extend support and recognition to the MNR, and instead reiterated its support for the Chissano government. But the MNR was far from finished as a guerrilla force. It continued to cause serious economic disruption by cutting supply lines to major cities and launching hit-and-run attacks on rail lines and motor convoys. It also carried out mass murders of civilians in remote rural areas.

RAILWAY DIPLOMACY

As South Africa's economic power has grown during the past 25 years, its leaders have increasingly projected an image of South Africa as a regional superpower, the natural hub of a regional economy dependent on South Africa for employment opportunities, trade, transport, technology and expertise. This image is usually portrayed as benign: a prosperous and friendly South Africa ready to share the benefits of its considerable economic and technical accomplishments with nearby states. But it has another aspect, far from benign: the potential economic leverage over the neighbours, and the leaders' willingness to use it.

Vorster used the economic weapon sparingly, probably because he saw no great need for it. He also used it without fanfare. In his efforts in 1975 to persuade Ian Smith to release black nationalists from jail, Vorster simply slowed deliveries of diesel fuel critical to Rhodesia's war against the guerrillas. Two years later Vorster's annoyance with Lesotho's leader led him to withdraw South Africa's grain export subsidy and to delay paying Lesotho its quarterly share of joint customs revenues.[48] In both cases the absence of threats or public announcements gave Vorster a basis for plausible denial, thus reducing the potential political fallout from his moves.

Economic pressure came into far greater use under P.W. Botha, where it joined military action as a major weapon of destabilization. The first target was Zimbabwe. Relations between the Botha government and the Mugabe Administration had deteriorated after independence (April 1980), in spite of mutual assurances that each government desired correct relations and had no hostile intentions towards the other. In July 1980, after Mugabe accused South Africa of recruiting thousands of white Rhodesians to destabilize southern Africa, Botha withdrew South Africa's diplomatic mission from Zimbabwe and said he could not guarantee a normal economic relationship once the mission was closed.[49] In September Zimbabwe severed diplomatic relations, although maintaining its highly advantageous trade arrangements with South Africa.

By 1981 the levels of rhetoric on each side had grown shrill, as South African leaders threatened Zimbabwe if Mugabe 'persists in his support of ANC terrorists', a charge which Zimbabwe denied. Zimbabwe warned that it would defend its territory 'with the utmost vigour' if Pretoria carried out 'its long-conceived plan to invade'.[50] This war of words reflected both the Mugabe government's real fears of South African intentions and the Botha Administration's growing annoyance with Mugabe. That annoyance went beyond a suspicion that Mugabe was not doing enough to curb ANC activity. His decision to restrict the repatriation of profits by foreign firms in Zimbabwe was seen as a move directed at South Africa, since the bulk of direct private investment in Zimbabwe was South African. The sources of greatest resentment, however, were Mugabe's extravagant anti-apartheid utterances, his UN votes for sanctions against Pretoria, and his refusal to deal officially with the South African government or to acknowledge Zimbabwe's heavy economic dependence on South Africa.

In early 1981 South Africa recalled 150 of its railway technicians working in Zimbabwe and announced that it would not renew the leases on 25 locomotives on loan to Zimbabwe. Since at that time more than a quarter of Zimbabwe's own locomotives were out of service for want of maintenance, the South African action posed a grave threat, particularly to Zimbabwe's ability to market a bumper grain crop. At about the same time, South Africa announced that it would not renew its preferential trade pact with Zimbabwe when it expired in March 1982. The clear political intent of these moves was confirmed by Botha's minister of transport, who said in an SABC interview that the rail problems could be solved and an additional 60 locomotives provided if Zimbabwe's transport minister would contact him or Foreign Minister Botha directly.[51]

In late 1981 the crisis eased, following a quiet *démarche* to Pretoria by Chester Crocker, the US Assistant Secretary of State. According to senior US diplomats, Crocker made clear that the Reagan Administration was displeased, and that it could not associate itself with any moves to destabilize Zimbabwe. In response to South African officials' insistence that Mugabe must cease his rhetoric and agree to formal contacts, Crocker suggested they pay more attention to substance and less to rhetoric.[52] A few weeks later two Zimbabwe officials of sub-Cabinet rank made an unpublicized visit to South Africa, where they concluded an agreement to renew leases on the locomotives. In January South African officials announced their willingness to negotiate a renewal of the preferential trade agreement, which was concluded two months later.[53]

Economic relations between the two states continued without serious disruption until August 1986, when six Commonwealth nations – Zambia, Zimbabwe, Australia, Canada, India and the Bahamas – voted to impose limited economic sanctions against South Africa, including the termination of air links and imports of South African agricultural products. Although it was extremely unlikely that the two African states would, in fact, implement sanctions, South Africa immediately imposed a steep levy on all goods passing through South Africa *en route* to Zambia and Zimbabwe, and announced a slowdown of lorry traffic at the border so as 'to obtain a statistical picture of the nature and extent of trade traffic from certain neighbouring states'.[54] Foreign Minister Botha said that the import levy would oblige Zambia and Zimbabwe 'to put their money where their mouth is'.[55]

A summit meeting of Front Line leaders in late August commended the actions of Zambia and Zimbabwe, but failed to agree on joint sanctions. The hard line of Mugabe and Kaunda softened further in late 1986. Food riots in Zambia in November forced the government to give greater priority to the country's economic needs. In December Zimbabwe was forced to call on South Africa to deliver an extra 34 000 tons of relief fuel to help overcome internal transport difficulties. As economic ministers in Zambia and Zimbabwe urged a more pragmatic and cautious approach to sanctions, the 1 January 1987 deadline for the two states to impose sanctions passed without action or comment. Meanwhile traffic restrictions had been eased.[56]

By far the most blatant act of railway diplomacy was the Botha government's total blockade of Lesotho in January 1986. The blockade followed several years' growing friction between the two governments. Its immediate trigger was a landmine incident near the Lesotho border two weeks earlier which had claimed the lives of six South African civilians. In response to the local Afrikaner community's demand for revenge, an SADF assault team stormed residences in Lesotho's capital on 20 December and killed nine people, six of whom were ANC members. A fortnight later South Africa shut down Lesotho's border to all commercial traffic, demanding that Lesotho hand over ANC personnel to its security forces. In spite of British and US demands that Pretoria lift the blockade, South Africa persisted. The tiny enclave state was brought to a standstill in a couple of weeks. On 20 January Lesotho's military deposed Prime Minister Jonathan in a near-bloodless coup.[57]

The new military council of Lesotho immediately met South Africa's foreign minister and agreed to expel all ANC members. On 25 January 60 ANC 'activists' left Maseru by plane for Lusaka, and South Africa lifted the blockade. General Lekhanya, leader of the coup, told a press conference that his government would continue to offer sanctuary to South African refugees, but would eject active ANC cadre. There would be consultation about this with South Africa, which would have to substantiate any charges that guerrillas were among the refugees. The General 'saw no need' to sign an Nkomati-type pact, however, nor would his government close down Eastern bloc embassies in Maseru. He also announced that Lesotho would no longer support sanctions against South Africa.[58]

SADF MISADVENTURES

The extent of SADF clandestine military operations in support of destabilization may never be known, nor can there be any certainty about how many of these ventures, and which ones, were authorized by P.W. Botha and the State Security Council. It is known, for example, that any military offensive inside Angola important enough to be given a codename – such as Operation Protea – required advance approval by the SSC. Yet in some cases an assault initially designated by SADF officials as only a limited search-and-destroy mission against SWAPO, and therefore not requiring SSC approval, expanded into a major campaign lasting several weeks and involving combat with Angolan regular army units. One can only speculate whether the SADF launched some of these ostensibly 'limited' missions with more ambitious objectives in mind but sought to avoid asking approval from the SSC, where an assault might be vetoed because of the risks of diplomatic fallout.

Although much of the SADF's clandestine activity remains the subject of speculation and of allegations impossible to verify, several clandestine operations aborted in a way that led to public disclosure. These known misadventures involving SADF personnel offer some insights into SADF attitudes towards the military's role in the region; that is, the sort of operations military men were willing to undertake, even where the risk of discovery was considerable and its likely political consequences serious. Where the official policy is one that sanctions clandestine armed assaults, the line between officially-approved acts and those carried out at the initiative of subordinates is often so blurred as to make the distinction meaningless.

The Angolan operations of the 32 Battalion, composed of Angolan ex-guerrillas and originally staffed by white mercenary officers, have already been discussed. The disclosure of their existence by defecting officers revealed for the first time South African use of proxy forces, as well as the extent of direct military intervention in support of UNITA. Similarly, after publication of the Gorongoza documents the Botha government no longer could deny that it had been providing military support to Renamo, whether or not the continuation of such assistance after Nkomati had been authorized by Botha and the SSC.

By far the most bizarre misadventure involving the SADF was the abortive Seychelles coup in November 1981. Colonel 'Mad' Mike Hoare, an ageing professional mercenary notorious for his role in the Congo troubles of the 1960s, organized a motley group of 45 men to oust the Marxist government of the Seychelles. Disguised as rugby players on holiday, the group landed at the Seychelles airport where security officers discovered large quantities of weapons in their baggage. An immediate shoot-out followed in which several people were killed and three of the attackers captured. The rest hijacked an Air India plane to fly them back to South Africa.

Under pressure from the West, the Botha government reluctantly put the plotters on trial for hijacking. Testimony by Hoare and by one of his group captured in the bungled coup attempt revealed a tangled web of involvement by officers in the SADF and NIS. The force included 23 South Africans, most of them reservists in elite 'recce' units of the SADF, plus foreign mercenaries.[59] AK-47s and other weapons were acquired from Defence Force armouries, delivered in an SADF truck, and signed for on SADF stationery.[60] According to Hoare's testimony, he had been led to believe that the coup had the active backing of the government. In a detailed account that had an eerie echo in the US Iran–Contra hearings five years later, Hoare told of meeting senior officials of the NIS who assured him that the Prime Minister supported the venture. Later he was told that an order from the Prime Minister's office had turned the project over to Military Intelligence, and he was introduced to two brigadiers from DMI, who arranged to procure weapons and a training site for the group.[61]

Although the government offered no denial of these allegations, Botha declared that he, the Cabinet, the SSC and the NIS had known nothing about the coup plot. Botha rejected demands for a parliamentary inquiry. The Defence Minister, Malan, conducted a secret inquiry within the SADF which concluded that 'no responsible officer gave authority for assistance in the coup'. Both he and the head of the NIS invoked national security laws to cut off further investigation and reporting on the affair.[62]

Yet the conclusion of the trial judge, the Judge President of Natal, that 'it would be naive to suggest that the National Intelligence Service was not aware', was widely shared, even among the ruling party. Thus *Die Vaderland*, a newspaper closely identified with the NP, complained that the Prime Minister's assurance 'does not clear up the obvious suspicion that people in responsible positions acted irregularly or at the least neglected their duty'.[63]

Less than a year after the Seychelles fiasco a Zimbabwe army patrol surprised an SADF column of 15–20 men about 20 miles inside Zimbabwe, killing three white South African soldiers. The others escaped, abandoning a variety of Soviet weapons and unmarked tins of food. The three dead turned out to be army sergeants and former members of the Rhodesian army. After an SADF inquiry, the Chief of the Defence Force said that the group had entered Zimbabwe on an unauthorized mission apparently aimed at trying to free friends being held in a detention camp.[64]

The official explanation failed, however, to still Mugabe's fears that Zimbabwe was the target of a deliberate South African campaign to undermine his government. Indeed, the incident came less than a month after unknown saboteurs had set off a series of explosions which destroyed ten jet fighter aircraft at Zimbabwe's main air base.[65]

In May 1985 Angolan forces ambushed an SADF commando unit in the far northern exclave province of Cabinda, a thousand miles north of the Namibian border. In a brief skirmish two South African soldiers were killed and a third captured. They were carrying high explosives, communications equipment and weapons with silencers, and were intercepted in the vicinity of a US-owned oil installation. It was apparent that the unit had been assigned to blow up the installation. The official South African explanation, that the group had been on a mission to gather intelligence on SWAPO and the ANC, found little acceptance. Indeed, US diplomats dismissed it as totally disingenuous.[66]

ASSESSING DESTABILIZATION

The destabilization policy was neither accidental nor *ad hoc*. The Botha government declared in 1979 that it would set about arranging its own solutions to the perceived external security threat to South Africa. During the years 1979–1988 it attempted to do just that, using its military and economic power to try to impose regional *détente* on its own terms and to formalize it through bilateral security accords: in short, a *Pax Pretoriana*.

In terms of the most obvious goal – clubbing the neighbours into submission – destabilization must be deemed a success. Botswana, Lesotho, Mozambique, Swaziland and Zimbabwe together expelled hundreds of ANC personnel, in some cases including guerrillas and military leaders. All these states were compelled to exercise more rigorous surveillance over ANC activities along their borders. Swaziland and Mozambique were forced to sign mutual non-aggression accords. Mozambican and SADF officers began serving together on a joint security commission, and Zimbabwean and South African military men consulted on border violations. In a sense the US tacitly acknowledged the success of destabilization by brokering the talks leading to Nkomati.

In terms of domestic political objectives, the Botha government's well-publicized military and economic warfare measures against the neighbouring states' alleged offences demonstrated to the electorate the administration's ruthlessness in the face of outside provocation, thereby vitiating right-wing charges that Botha was ready to sell out white interests in Namibia and along the border. The hardline policy was also meant to show South African blacks that armed resistance would not be allowed to succeed.

Yet SWAPO, despite heavy losses over the decade, continued to infiltrate saboteurs into Namibia and to inflict casualties on the SADF. Similarly, continuing ANC incidents, together with occasional discoveries of arms caches in South Africa's black townships, showed that the ANC was very much alive in spite of its loss of sanctuaries in nearby countries. Newspaper editorials and letters to the editor indicate white disappointment over the government's failure to put an end to ANC and SWAPO incidents, and also over growing SADF casualties in Angola. The public appears to have viewed Botha's policies as largely successful in that they prevented SWAPO and the ANC from posing serious military threats and from developing into Rhodesia-type insurgencies. But whites appeared less sanguine about the future. In a 1984 survey of South African elites, a majority of businessmen, academicians, journalists and diplomats thought that a bush war would in time develop inside South Africa. While most of the elite groups surveyed felt the war against SWAPO could be won, journalists and academicians were evenly divided on that question.[67]

The destabilization policy isolated the government further from the outside world, particularly from the West, and contributed to public support in the West for sanctions against South Africa. Thus, in reaction to SADF raids into nearby states, in May 1986 the Reagan Administration expelled a South African military attaché; a bipartisan coalition of US Senate and House members called for stiffer sanctions against the Botha government; and Argentina severed diplomatic relations with Pretoria. In spite of the Botha Administration's efforts to influence Western opinion against the ANC, in 1986 both the Thatcher and Reagan Administrations held high-level talks with the ANC, which a senior US official characterized as 'a legitimate voice in the black community . . . one of the important players'.[68] In 1986–7 Britain, the US and other Western governments made clear their support for the Chissano government in Mozambique and condemned South Africa's clandestine aid to Renamo. The UK doubled its programme to train Mozambican field-grade officers in 1987. Indeed, the only issue on which US and South African regional policies were aligned was that of support for UNITA, South Africa's long-time client, which became the recipient of substantial deliveries of American weapons starting in 1986.

A number of sympathetic statements and moves by senior Reagan Administration officials, particularly in the early 1980s, helped to nurture the Botha government's illusion that it was perceived to be playing in southern Africa the same role as the US in Central America; that is, the local superpower-as-policeman, defending the region from communist penetration. Thus a commentary on SABC, South Africa's state-owned radio, the day before an SADF raid on Lesotho spoke of a 'joint commitment' with the Reagan Administration to 'a Monroe doctrine for the region' which recognized South Africa's 'special responsibility' to maintain stability in southern Africa, like that of the US in Central America.[69] Unlike the US invasion of Grenada, however, which at least a few Caribbean states approved in advance, no state in southern Africa sought or approved South African attacks against Angola, Botswana, Lesotho, Mozambique or Zimbabwe.

By 1987 the Botha Administration appeared to have recognized that the more blatant aspects of destabilization were incurring high costs, particularly in the adverse effects on relations with the West. But the likely long-term consequences of the chaos and disruption let loose by destabilization were probably not foreseen. The seemingly endless and futile conflicts launched with South African sponsorship in Mozambique and Angola; the deaths of an estimated hundred thousand Mozambican civilians whom the US State Department says were 'systematically' killed by Renamo in 1986–8;[70] the flood of refugees uprooted by the fighting in neighbouring countries; the ethnic tensions and suspicions fuelled by South African support of dissidents in Zimbabwe and elsewhere: such forces, once set in train, cannot easily be slowed or stopped, as shown by the Botha government's ambivalent relations with Renamo after Nkomati. By 1988 these had become chronic problems that all the regional states, including South Africa, would have to deal with for a long time to come.

Part IV
Deteriorating Relations with the West

9 Foreign Policy Responses to the West

FADING HOPES FOR CLOSER TIES

In his annual New Year's Day address to the nation, Prime Minister Vorster told the South African people in January 1977 that they no longer could count on the support of the West in their struggle against communism. Citing the collapse of Western cooperation in the Angolan affair, which he attributed to a 'loss of will', Vorster concluded with a bleak warning: 'If therefore a Communist onslaught should be made against South Africa, directly or under camouflage, South Africa will have to face it alone, and certain countries which profess to be anti-Communist will even refuse to sell [us] arms . . . This is the reality of our situation.'[1] This theme of the alleged unreliability of the West, and of how the West – particularly the US – had 'left South Africa in the lurch' in Angola, was reiterated by P.W. Botha.

Further strains in relations with the West came quickly. In April the UNSC's five Western members (Britain, Canada, France, West Germany and the US) delivered a strong note to Vorster on Namibia, and threatened sanctions if he persisted in his plans for an interim government. A few months later Vorster and US Vice-President Mondale met in Vienna, where their confrontation over South Africa's race policy led Vorster to adopt the theme of foreign meddling as the major issue in his successful re-election campaign of 1977. A more serious contretemps occurred between August and October 1977, when the US, France and the UK issued strong warnings to Vorster over a suspected South African nuclear test site. In November the UNSC adopted a mandatory arms embargo against the RSA.

Relations continued to worsen after P.W. Botha assumed the premiership in 1978. Western pressures and diplomatic manoeuvring over Namibia led Botha to denounce the Western-led peace effort. In Rhodesia, where the Western powers had earlier found Vorster useful in bringing pressure to bear on the Smith regime, a British initiative brought independence and a Mugabe electoral victory in

1980. With its intervention no longer needed, South Africa temporarily lost its former status as a regional actor whom Western leaders took into their confidence in seeking to resolve that conflict. Moreover, Western powers accepted the Mugabe victory with relative equanimity, though without enthusiasm; but for South Africa the victory of a self-declared Marxist guerrilla was seen as the fall of yet another domino, this time with active Western help, and as a further widening of the gulf between Pretoria and the West.

The advent of the Reagan Administration led to a temporary remission of US pressure and to some revival of South African hopes for improved relations with the West, particularly during Reagan's first term, 1981–4. A cardinal and explicit principle in the new US policy of constructive engagement was the need to take account of South Africa's security concerns. To the Botha leadership this suggested that the US was coming to accept South Africa's identification of a communist onslaught as the real threat to regional security.

Early statements and actions by Reagan officials seemed to support this assumption, as well as to indicate a more sympathetic US stance towards Botha's internal reforms and towards his destabilization moves. Alexander Haig, Reagan's first secretary of state, spoke of 'shared values' and 'shared strategic concerns' with South Africa. Following a major SADF assault inside Angola in August 1981 – an assault which may have been designed to test the new US administration – Haig declined to blame South Africa and the US, alone among the Western powers, vetoed a UNSC resolution condemning the attack.[2] In 1982 it was disclosed that the Reagan Administration had granted visas to officials of South Africa's defence force, police and intelligence services, thus reversing a previous ban on such visits in accord with the spirit of the UN arms embargo.[3] The press also revealed that the Reagan Administration had approved the sale of highly sophisticated computers with possible military end-use to South African parastatal organizations, and aircraft to the SADF.[4] The US was reported to have resumed swapping intelligence information with South Africa in the early 1980s.[5]

This prolonged honeymoon with the Reagan Administration finally ended, however as misunderstanding and unrealistic expectations on each side led to mutual recriminations and a cooling of relations by 1985. The catalyst was the explosion of protest and violence in South Africa's black townships in late 1984 and the government's Draconian response, including shooting of unarmed protesters and mass detentions without trial.

Reagan, faced with growing domestic criticism of constructive engagement (even among conservative Senators) and with calls for sanctions against Pretoria, spoke out strongly against South Africa for the first time in December 1984. He warned that forced removals, detentions without trial and other abuses of apartheid threatened to extinguish 'any hope for peaceful, democratic government' in the future.[6] Within a few months, as South Africa's state of emergency led to ever-tougher security measures, Reagan signed a Bill banning the sale of computers to South African security forces, and White House spokesmen were publicly charging that apartheid itself was 'largely responsible for the violence' in South Africa.[7] Following an SADF foray into Botswana in July 1985, Reagan recalled the US ambassador from Pretoria. Two months later Reagan imposed limited economic sanctions against South Africa: a move that the administration, despite its deep opposition to sanctions, felt forced to take in the hope of forestalling considerably tougher sanctions by Congress.

By June 1986, as Congress moved inexorably towards a comprehensive sanctions package of its own, the US was 'reassessing' its policy towards South Africa. As part of a move to forge closer ties with South African black leaders, senior Reagan officials by then had already held discussions with the ANC.[8] Thus US–South African relations had reached such a nadir that even the Reagan Administration, the most sympathetic to Pretoria's problems yet to come along, was helpless to prevent sanctions and was, moreover, discussing South Africa's future with the most militant South African nationalist group, the ANC.

Pretoria's relations with other Western states also were deteriorating. In 1985 the Commonwealth heads of state, having failed to agree on sanctions, appointed an Eminent Persons Group (EPG) of Commonwealth political figures to visit South Africa to try to 'promote a political dialogue aimed at replacing apartheid by popular government'.[9] After detailed discussions with various government and opposition leaders in South Africa, the EPG concluded that effective economic measures against South Africa 'may offer the last opportunity to avert what could be the worst blood bath since the Second World War'.[10] After a Commonwealth meeting in August 1986 seven member states – the UK, Canada, Australia, India, Zambia, Zimbabwe and the Bahamas – announced various national sanctions measures against South Africa. Japan and the 12 EEC nations also imposed modest sanctions in 1986, and Sweden and Norway adopted a total trade ban against South Africa the following year. Meanwhile Britain had, like the US, opened a dialogue with the ANC.

How, then, has South Africa responded to pressure from the West, and particularly to the long-feared imposition of sanctions? In what ways has its foreign policy been influenced by external pressure?

DIPLOMACY UNDER PRESSURE

Foreign policy communities in the West, particularly in the US, remain seriously divided over the issue of whether pressure against South Africa works. On one side of this continuing debate are those who assert that threats, diplomatic pressure and sanctions only increase South Africa's isolation, drive its rulers into the *laager*, and create a confrontational environment which is hostile to dialogue and concessions. On the other are those who say pressure is the only way to wring concessions from an unresponsive and near-totalitarian regime, whose leaders tend to interpret Western goodwill gestures as signals of approval.

Although the argument usually focuses on internal policy – that is, can pressure move the leadership away from apartheid? – it is equally germane to Pretoria's foreign policy. The question is particularly important because, as one observer has noted, 'while South Africa's foreign policy formulators are relatively unfettered by domestic interest group pressure so common in Western states, they are probably subjected to more intense external pressure than their counterparts in any other country in peacetime'.[11] Since virtually every government seeks to portray itself as being in full control of the nation's destiny, none likes to acknowledge bending the knee to foreign pressure. And so it is with South Africa. Moreover, the National Party's long sense of ruling under siege has imbued the leadership with an urgent need to appear strong, unified and monolithic against perceived enemies. Yet ruling groups are seldom monolithic, nor do they necessarily close ranks under pressure. A leading academic analyst of South African politics has described how the process of consolidating white power created contradictions which have led to serious cleavages within the ruling group: 'Changing perceptions [of interests among the ruling group] lead to new alliances and splits, far removed from the static image of South African politics so frequently portrayed . . . It is to these issues of a divided ruling class that any outside intervention must be sensitive.'[12]

Diplomats in the Reagan Administration believed that the Botha leadership group was itself divided over domestic and foreign policy issues. They therefore sought to identify the more 'reasonable', or softline senior officials, and to provide them with data and arguments to use against the hardliners.[13]

Indeed some of South Africa's recent foreign policy moves appear to have reflected such divisions. Responses to Western pressure, in particular, have often seemed hasty and impulsive: the result, perhaps, of a temporary bureaucratic victory extracted by one group or another. These responses have been of three general sorts: concessions; counter-pressure; and repudiation of the West and of South Africa's traditional Western orientation.

Concessions

The most striking concessions to Western pressure were those agreed to by Vorster in negotiations on Namibia (see Chapter 5). Under threat of sanctions, Vorster acknowledged a UN role in Namibia, abruptly terminated a process that was leading towards an internal settlement there, and agreed in principle to free elections and independence under a unitary government for the Territory. These moves amounted to a dramatic reversal in the direction of South African policy towards Namibia. Senior officials who were close to Vorster admit that this involved considerable political costs for him, particularly in terms of relations with internal political groups in Namibia; but Vorster, fearing sanctions, 'felt he had to look after South Africa's interests first'.[14]

Vorster's concessions to the West on Rhodesia, where he put pressure on Smith to negotiate a settlement with black nationalists, were of a different order. By agreeing to joint diplomatic action with Kissinger in Rhodesia, Vorster gained status as a regional leader whose cooperation and intervention were sought by the leading world power. Moreover Vorster, like Kissinger, wanted to see the Rhodesian conflict resolved before it brought Cuban and Soviet involvement, as in Angola. South African diplomats also noted that 'Smith wanted to carry on the war, but expected South Africa to foot the bill'.[15] Thus in Rhodesia South Africa's own interests were served by cooperating with the US, particularly since Kissinger personally took the lead in forcing a showdown with Smith and bore the brunt of white Rhodesian criticism for doing so.

Under P.W. Botha the most significant concessions to Western pressure were his agreement in December 1983 to withdraw South African troops from their *de facto* occupation of southern Angola, and his quiet termination of economic warfare measures against Zimbabwe. (These events are analysed in detail in Chapters 7 and 8.) The SADF withdrawal was agreed to under considerable pressure from the US, and in the face of strong reservations on the part of South African military leaders. American diplomats say they made four *démarches* a week to Pretoria, pointing out to the Botha leadership that South Africa could 'only get what it wants from the US', and warning that the US would only go so far in blocking UN actions against South Africa. In the end Botha seems to have been sold on the usefulness of a dramatic peace gesture in Angola. But he first demanded an American guarantee that, if Angola violated the agreement, either by allowing Cuban troops to enter the DMZ or missiles to be placed there, the US would raise no objections to SADF counter-measures.[16]

In the case of South African economic pressures against Zimbabwe in 1981 the US said bluntly, but privately, that it could not associate itself with moves to destabilize Zimbabwe. Even without US pressure, however, it is doubtful that South Africa would have maintained its economic squeeze on Mugabe much longer. The withdrawal of South African locomotives from Zimbabwe railways at the critical grain harvesting time and the refusal to renew a preferential trade agreement were meant as signals of annoyance at Mugabe's anti-apartheid rhetoric and as reminders of Zimbabwe's heavy economic dependence on South Africa. To have sustained these measures would have precipitated a severe economic and political crisis in Zimbabwe, with attendant risks of social upheaval and foreign intervention. There is no reason to think this is what the Botha government had in mind. In short, terminating these measures was an easy concession for Botha: a way to show his government's willingness to cooperate with the Reagan Administration, particularly since the US *démarche* had been made without publicity. And it was what South Africa had planned to do from the start.

Counter-pressure

By far the most ambitious counter-pressures were those carried out under the Information Department's clandestine propaganda offensive of the 1970s discussed in Chapter 4. That multi-million-dollar campaign of secret and in many cases illegal projects at home and abroad had as its goal nothing less than turning world opinion around to support the positions of the ruling NP. Although the campaign undoubtedly had some impact on opinion in Europe and the US, which were the major targets, its influence was probably greatest among ultra-conservatives, who were already disposed to support the South African regime. It was bound to fail in its larger objective, however, simply because apartheid was not saleable.

More recently South Africa employed a variety of counter-pressures to forestall the imposition of economic sanctions. Until mid-May 1986, P.W. Botha and his foreign minister attempted to persuade Western governments that South Africa was in the process of dismantling apartheid and that sanctions were therefore not only unnecessary but counter-productive. In late April, just before the Commonwealth's Eminent Persons Group returned to South Africa for further talks, Botha sent a message to Free World leaders attending the economic summit in Tokyo, urging them to support his programme of racial reforms and his conditions for the release of Nelson Mandela.[17] His action apparently was taken to win broad Western backing so as to weaken the demand for sanctions which the EPG was expected to issue.

In mid-May, however, following Cabinet-level discussions with the EPG, Botha apparently decided that the EPG's demands for freedom of assembly, release of Mandela, unbanning the ANC and PAC and allowing free political activity were far too risky for his government to undertake, and that there was no possibility of meeting those demands half-way. An eminent Afrikaner political philosopher described the leaders as '[feeling] they were being pressured into negotiating themselves out of power, so they decided to call a halt and face the threat of sanctions now'.[18] When the EPG next met Foreign Minister Botha on 13 May they found him 'distressed', and noticed 'a hardening of the government's position'.[19] That position was confirmed two days later in a speech by the State President, who pointedly referred to 'meddling groups visiting our country'. Any lingering doubts about Botha's attitude were banished by the SADF raids on three Commonwealth countries on 19 May while the EPG were still in South Africa.

The government followed this up with a series of counter-pressures against the threat of sanctions. In July 1986 the government appointed Fred Bell, former head of Armscor, to run a quasi-clandestine organization to help South Africa evade sanctions. In June Foreign Minister Botha warned that South Africa would strike back at neighbouring states if sanctions were imposed on the Republic. He threatened to expel foreign workers and to deny nearby countries access to South African rail and port facilities.

In August, after the Commonwealth announced that agreement had been reached on a package of limited sanctions against South Africa, the Botha government introduced a transit tax on goods passing through South Africa *en route* to Zambia and Zimbabwe, whose leaders were outspoken advocates of sanctions. South Africa also adopted a system of import permits for all goods purchased from Zimbabwe, and began conducting exhaustive 'security checks' at border points, causing several days' back-up of commercial traffic between Zimbabwe and South Africa. These restrictions were removed following a summit meeting of the Front Line states, which had pointedly avoided committing themselves to sanctions as a group.[20] Indeed, in the early months of 1988 Presidents Mugabe of Zimbabwe and Kaunda of Zambia – both *formally* committed to the idea of comprehensive sanctions – were expressing doubts in private about the potential effectiveness of the sanctions campaign.

In early October 1986, a day or two before the US Senate overrode President Reagan's veto of sanctions by the lop-sided margin of 78–21, South Africa's foreign minister made a blatant, last-ditch attempt to influence the voting. He personally telephoned a number of key Senators from the grain states, threatening to cancel South African grain purchases if the sanctions bill was approved. A week later South Africa announced plans to repatriate thousands of Mozambican migrant workers. Although that move was officially said to be in retaliation for a landmine incident near the Mozambican border, it seems also to have been part of South Africa's campaign to demonstrate to both Africa and the West that sanctions are a two-edged sword: further sanctions against South Africa might lead it to take damaging action against its neighbours.

Repudiation of the West

South Africa's Afrikaner leaders have held a split image of themselves and their society as being both European and African to a degree not present among ruling groups in the former white settler societies of Africa. In foreign policy, as in other aspects of their corporate lives, they have identified South Africa as being among the modern, advanced European states, but with long roots in Africa that give them claim to a special understanding of Africa and a special role there.

Occasionally the twin images have been integrated. In the mid-1970s Vorster played an active role as mediator between black and white Rhodesian leaders, and as a partner of the US in trying to arrange a peace settlement in Rhodesia. But in the decade of the 1980s the images became increasingly split. As a senior South African diplomat explained it, 'a reciprocal is at work'. Like the carved fair- and foul-weather figures on a Swiss barometer, when relations with the West are down, those with the region are up. He characterized relations with the West as being at an all-time low in 1987, with little chance of improvement in the short term. Like others in the Botha Administration, he condemned the Reagan policy of constructive engagement for failing to prevent the imposition of sanctions. South Africa 'won't nibble at that bait again', he said, but 'will put as much distance as possible between itself and the Western powers.'[21]

Hence, as relations with the West soured, the Botha leadership increasingly reacted by renouncing the West and its policies, and emphasizing South Africa's links to Africa. In part this purposeful distancing was rhetorical: a defiant response to Western actions which it was powerless to prevent. The constellation initiative of 1979–80, accompanied by Botha's assertions that the RSA should pursue a policy of neutrality between East and West, was such a response: a policy statement hastily cobbled together which was almost certain to be rejected by the African states to whom it was ostensibly directed. In August 1986 Botha blamed unnamed foreign powers for trying to isolate South Africa from its neighbours through the creation of SADCC.[22] The following month, in a speech directed at the non-aligned states, Botha called for pan-African cooperation and issued an unusually sweeping condemnation of the Western powers, which are 'far removed from the misery they had helped cause [in Africa and the Third World]', and which now 'hide their guilt behind the campaign against South Africa'. Third World leaders, he said, should: 'stop being blindfolded and exploited by the major powers. They care for nothing but their own wealth and interests . . . Let us, as the leaders of this continent, come here together, here in Africa, and not on other continents, to reflect on our problems and seek solutions.'[23] Botha criticized both East and West, and called on the outside world to 'stop pretending that the problems of the sub-continent can be solved by the destruction of the existing order in South Africa'.

This rejection of the West, in response to the West's rejection of Botha's domestic and foreign policies, had far more than rhetoric behind it. In Namibia, after it became clear that the Western powers would not abandon the main outlines of UNSC Resolution 435 as the basis for a settlement, Botha tried without success to launch a number of unilateral peace initiatives in which South Africa would have dealt only with the African parties to the conflict, bypassing the UN and West entirely. Similarly the *de facto* dismissal of the EPG mission in 1986 signalled a rejection of the principle of negotiating with outsiders over South Africa's future political dispensation.

Botha's most surprising diplomatic move was a 1988 peace overture to the USSR. In March Defence Minister Malan, citing recent developments in Afghanistan, announced that South Africa could live with a non-aligned government in Angola. If the USSR agreed to that, he said, and if UNITA and the MPLA government could reach an accord, South African forces would withdraw from Angola.[24] A few days later President Botha gave an exclusive interview to an American editor in which he speculated on the shift in Soviet perceptions of southern Africa under Gorbachev. Asserting that the Soviets 'now admit we are a regional power of importance', Botha said:

> Gorbachev seems anxious to cut down the high cost of propping up and arming poor nations. Regional conflicts like Afghanistan and Angola are draining the USSR and Cuba. But change is slow and I don't think Moscow is about to ditch Angola, but they seem to be shopping for a compromise.[25]

When asked why the signal to Moscow was sent by Malan rather than the Foreign Minister, Botha noted the SADF presence in Angola and the need to make clear that South Africa has 'no claims whatever against Angola'.

The peace offer thus appears to have been prompted mainly by the expanding war in Angola and the prospect of growing SADF casualties. It may also have reflected Botha's concern that the Reagan administration, eager to achieve a peace settlement during its final months in office, might agree to terms which would force South Africa to make a politically risky choice on Namibian independence. The overture quickly faded, dismissed by the US as unrealistic and by the USSR as irrelevant: the only thing Afghanistan and Angola have in common, said a Soviet official, is that they both begin with the letter 'A'. Indeed, the USSR appeared willing to continue giving diplomatic support to the US peace initiative and military aid to Angola. The notion that Gorbachev would negotiate an Afghan-type deal with Pretoria, or be seen to accept Botha's formula for a settlement, seemed unlikely.

During 1986–8 South Africa took steps to expand its economic links with nearby African states. In spite of strained relations with Mozambique over South African support for the MNR and Mozambican failure to root out ANC operatives, by late 1986 South Africa had established a permanent trade representative in Maputo, and in May 1987 foreign affairs officials announced that South Africa would make available $1.5 million for upgrading and expanding Maputo harbour.[26] The Botha government, under pressure from South African mining companies and farmers, had meanwhile backed off from its earlier threats to repatriate thousands of Mozambican migrant workers. In October 1987 their work permits were being renewed, and the expulsion drive was limited to illegal migrants.[27]

Pretoria's ties with Lesotho were strengthened by the exchange of permanent trade representatives in June 1987, and by the conclusion of a treaty on the Lesotho Highlands Water Project: a $2 billion development plan to harness Lesotho's rivers and provide water to drought-prone South Africa. South Africa will eventually contribute around $100 million to the project, the bulk of which will be financed by the World Bank.[28]

The Southern African Development Bank was established by South Africa in 1983 primarily to provide economic development financing to the four nominally independent black 'homelands' of South Africa and to local black authorities. Although these remain the bank's priority customers, it has recently expanded its financial and technical support to projects in the neighbouring independent states. In the spring of 1987 the bank had loans under appraisal for the Lesotho water project, a river basin development in Swaziland, and a forestry development plan in Mozambique. Its officials have also extended their professional contacts with the BLS states, where they have arranged seminars and reviewed development projects amongst other activities.[29]

The Botha government also took action in 1987 to improve its ties with Zimbabwe. In October it quietly dropped its demand for Cabinet-level talks before agreeing to renew the leases on South African locomotives requested by Zimbabwe. Coinciding with that gesture, a senior foreign affairs official in Pretoria was sent to

Zimbabwe where he asserted his government's wish for improved relations between the two countries.[30]

These moves to seek *détente* with several neighbours were chiefly triggered by deteriorating relations with the West, but other factors also seem to have played a part. For one thing, Botha's destabilization measures had forced all the neighbours but Angola to adopt tougher measures towards ANC activities, and to confer jointly with South African officials about border violations. Botha and his military leaders therefore had less reason by late 1987 to insist on maintaining a hardline policy towards these states: particularly in the face of sanctions, which enhanced the neighbours' economic importance to South Africa as countries where points of origin and destination of South African commerce could be disguised so as to evade sanctions.

SEEKING ALLIES ELSEWHERE

Of greater importance to South Africa economically and militarily, however, has been the expansion of its trade and technical links to Israel and several Pacific nations, particularly Taiwan. South Africa had been developing these ties for a long time; but they became more important after the UN arms embargo in 1977, and particularly after the imposition of Western sanctions which started in 1985–6. South Africa's success in establishing close and advantageous relations with Israel derives from several mutual affinities. Each leadership sees in the other an analogy with its own security situation, since each faces weak but hostile neighbours who reject its legitimacy and who have access to Soviet weapons. Diplomatically, too, each state has found itself largely isolated and a target of Third World condemnation at the UN: South Africa almost since the UN's founding, Israel since black African and other Third World states abandoned it in favour of the Arab countries following the 1973 Yom Kippur war.[31] Beyond these current issues, the Afrikaners and Israelis see themselves as sharing a similar historical experience as a minority people struggling for national survival in a hostile environment. Furthermore, South Africa's Jewish community of around 120 000 has close ties to Israel, and to the thousands of South African Jews who have settled there.

A bilateral economic cooperation pact in 1976 led to a rapid upsurge in trade and investment between the two countries. South Africa is Israel's main source of coal and a major buyer of Israeli machinery and electronic equipment. Joint ventures by South African firms in Israel have helped gain them entry to European markets. As one analyst noted:

> Local processing of semi-finished goods enables South African businessmen to re-label their products and bypass the severe controls on imports from South Africa imposed by the European Economic Community. Israel has come to provide, whether consciously or not, a vital bridgehead for South African exports in Europe and the United States.[32]

Such ventures would of course be of even greater importance to South Africa since 1985–6.

Israel has also been an extremely important supplier of advanced military technology and equipment. South African purchases are 'unofficially' estimated to have reached several hundred million dollars in 1986.[33] But even that total, which makes South Africa Israel's leading arms customer, understates the importance of Israeli arms to South Africa's defence.[34] Israel sold South Africa advanced navigational and electronic equipment, which enabled the South Africans to upgrade their Mirage jet fighters so as to evade Angola's advanced Soviet radar and surface-to-air missiles. In 1986 Israel supplied the SAAF with two converted Boeing-707 in-flight refuelling tankers, effectively extending the range of air strikes to 1200–1600 miles, well beyond the Front Line states.[35] Israel also helped South Africa develop a surveillance aircraft. South Africa's navy has nine missile attack craft, the first vessels (Reshevs) acquired directly from Israel and the rest (Saar-class) assembled in South Africa with Israeli components and technology.

The prospects for continued South African access to Israeli weapons and technology dimmed somewhat in 1987, when the State Department presented to Congress a mandated report on arms sales to South Africa in which Israel was charged with being a major violator of the arms embargo.[36] Congress called for the report with a view to cutting off US military aid to violators. Although no one expected the findings to result in a Congressional cut-off of aid to Israel, the findings were a blow to Israeli relations with the US, particularly with the Congress. Coming hard on the heels of the Pollard spy case, the report was taken extremely seriously in Tel Aviv. The Israeli government had anticipated the report, and had already announced that no new military contracts would be signed with Pretoria.[37]

Whether Israel would, in fact, implement that decision remained to be seen. A former senior adviser to the Israeli government said in private that Israel would be unlikely to subvert its announced ban: for example, by supplying upgraded models of previously-contracted weapons. He cited the Cabinet's conviction that the US relationship is too vital to put at risk. Moreover, South Africa is no longer as important to Israel as it was a decade ago. Arms sales to South Africa, once a major factor offsetting Israeli financial losses in the production of weapons (particularly tanks), are no longer that crucial, and the reliability of South African coal supplies is no longer considered critical. Finally, Israel's ties with black Africa had improved significantly by 1987.[38] In sum, by 1987 Israel had less incentive to continue violating the arms embargo, and more to lose in doing so. In September 1987 the Israeli government announced moderate, but significant, sanctions against South Africa which included bans on investment and borrowing as well as on official visits, and the termination of South Africa's use of Israel as a conduit for exports to other countries.

The imposition of Western sanctions led to a dramatic rise in South Africa's trade with the newly-industrialized states of Asia, particularly Taiwan and Korea. Like its relations with Israel, South Africa's links with the 'pariah' state of Taiwan had been growing for some time. On a five-day official visit to Taiwan in 1980 P.W. Botha praised its leaders for their stand against communism and drew parallels with South Africa's experience. By then bilateral agreements had been concluded on trade, air transport, agriculture and fishing, and technical cooperation. Trade – uranium, ferrous metals and food in exchange for Taiwan's machinery, manufactures and technology – was approaching $300 million annually in 1980.

In 1979 the two governments agreed to collaborate on a number of joint projects in defence technology and atomic energy.[39] A report by the US Defense Intelligence Agency in 1981 described nuclear cooperation among a 'pariah state network', and stated that South Africa's nuclear development had received 'critically important technology' from Taiwan.[40] Other defence experts suggested that an implosion process developed by Taiwan for fusing metals might be adapted to trigger a nuclear weapon.[41]

By 1987 sanctions had helped boost South Africa's trade with Taiwan to a billion dollars, more than double the previous year's total.[42] Taiwan, Singapore and Hong Kong were reported to be serving South Africa's increasing need for trans-shipment points that would conceal the origin of its exports. These states none the less accounted for only 4 per cent of South Africa's trade in 1986, and could not expect to supplant the industrial democracies as its major trading area. The industrial nations, which accounted for almost 50 per cent of South African exports and 70 per cent of its imports in 1986, continued to dominate its trade in 1987, in spite of sanctions;[43] sharp declines in South African exports to the US and Western Europe were offset to some extent by a rise in sales to Japan.[44]

Since the 1960s South Africa has courted South American countries in a vague and apparently half-hearted quest for southern hemispheric solidarity with states Foreign Minister Botha praised for being 'very aware of the Communist menace'.[45] A flurry of business and diplomatic activity occurred in the late 1970s, but Pretoria's overtures met with little lasting response except from a few right-wing military regimes, like Chile's. There appears to be no strong economic basis for the sort of expanded trade that has recently occurred between South Africa and Asia.

In conclusion, despite official South African rhetoric suggesting a turning away from the Western powers in favour of dealing directly with the USSR and local states over regional issues, and in spite of its successful efforts to establish important economic, technical and military ties with states like Israel and Taiwan, the industrial democracies remain the essential link in South Africa's external relations. Diplomatically South Africa's leaders depend on the permanent Western members of the UNSC to ward off total sanctions and other punitive measures directed against South Africa in the UN. It is also evident that South Africa, acting alone, lacks the legitimacy and capability to bring about a resolution of the Namibian conflict, or of others in the region. The peace settlement in Rhodesia, the Nkomati Accord and the cease-fire in Angola all required Western intervention and mediation. The progress so far made towards a Namibian settlement is attributable to mediation by the Western powers. In South Africa's internal conflict, too, the Western states' support for orderly change is an important factor in the government's efforts to discredit and weaken those supporting revolutionary change.

Economically South Africa remains heavily dependent on the industrial democracies. Imports of capital equipment are critical to South Africa's economic growth: in 1984 they accounted for 79 per cent of gross fixed investment.[46] While a growing share of such equipment is supplied by the new industrial countries of Asia, South Africa will continue to depend on the industrial West and Japan to meet by far the larger part of its requirements. A South African government study in 1985 concluded that import substitution could effectively replace less than a quarter of the $8 billion of imports by its manufacturing industries that year.[47]

South Africa also depends on the advanced industrial countries for capital investment and for commercial bank credit, both of which have been critical to its industrial growth. By 1985 the cumulative value of direct foreign investment in South Africa totalled $16 billion, 90 per cent of which was accounted for by five states: Britain, the US, West Germany, France and Switzerland. The US sanctions legislation of 1986 prohibits new US corporate investment in the RSA, but imposes no penalties or limitations on existing investments.

The importance of commercial credit to South African business was shown by the panic in its financial community in 1985 when Western commercial banks refused to renew loans to South Africa as they fell due. At that time South Africa's total foreign debt was $24 billion, more than half of which was owed to commercial banks in the US, Europe and Japan. Only in March 1987 did South Africa's Finance Minister reach a debt-rescheduling accord with Western creditors.

There are, indeed, few if any areas of South African official concern where the industrial democracies do not loom larger than any other countries or group of countries. For domestic political reasons the leaders have tried to minimize the growing Western rejection of South Africa's race policies and the significance of Western sanctions and other pressures, and to play up South Africa's ties with other regions as evidence that the country is not isolated. But the leaders cannot ignore, let alone dismiss, the reality of the industrial democracies' vital importance to South Africa's political and economic well-being.

10 Pretoria's Nuclear Diplomacy

PERSPECTIVE

Since August 1977, when the USSR first alerted the US to what appeared to be a nuclear test site under construction in the Kalahari Desert, South Africa has played a subtle but risky game of nuclear diplomacy with the West. The game has not been without cost for South Africa. Yet, unlike most aspects of Pretoria's relations with the West, its nuclear strategy has been active rather than reactive, and to a large degree successful.

For the West the greatest concern has of course been South Africa's nuclear weapons capability and intentions, which – despite more than a decade of intelligence surveillance and low-key diplomatic negotiations – remain shrouded in ignorance and ambiguity. Whether South Africa intended to test a nuclear device in 1977, and whether it actually conducted such a test in 1979, are questions still unresolved among Western scientific and intelligence analysts.

The Western powers, particularly the US, have endeavoured since the mid-1970s to dissuade South Africa from testing a weapon or declaring a weapons capability. Western concern has both global and regional elements. Like Argentina and Pakistan, South Africa is seen as a threshold nuclear weapons state: one of those more likely to break through the fragile non-proliferation barriers. Indeed, South Africa matches in virtually all respects the profile of a likely nuclear weapons state: it is diplomatically isolated, lacking either membership in an alliance or the security umbrella of a great power; its leaders see the regime's survival under external threat; and it has the materials and technology to produce and deliver a nuclear weapon. Declaration of a nuclear weapons capability by the white minority regime might encourage other threshold states to do the same. Moreover it would have a serious impact in the region, and on the region's external relations. It would lead to intense pressure on the industrial democracies for stiffer sanctions against South Africa, and perhaps to efforts on the part of Nigeria or South Africa's neighbours to seek nuclear weapons or guarantees from outside powers.

From the South African perspective, however, the weapons issue is part of a larger nuclear strategy that was also based on commercial export considerations, the need for reactor fuel, and more recently on a drive for recognition as a regional superpower and threshold nuclear state. Since South Africa and Namibia together hold something like a quarter of the non-communist world's uranium deposits, the first stage in South Africa's nuclear development programme was the extraction of ore for export. Its first ore-processing plant, built with US and British assistance, opened in 1952. Exports of uranium oxide to the US alone brought South Africa almost half-a-billion dollars in export earnings during the next 20 years.[1] During the late 1950s and 1960s South Africa purchased its first nuclear research reactor and sent its nuclear scientists and technicians to Britain and the US for training.

These earlier developments – the processing of local uranium ores, access to Western nuclear technology and the acquisition of a research reactor – gave South Africa the necessary technological base for more advanced research on its own. In particular, South Africa was able by 1970 to acquire the means to enrich uranium: the most important step towards achieving an independent nuclear capability.

The decision to develop an indigenous enrichment capability had a plausible commercial basis. In the early 1970s, before the collapse of the world uranium market, South African officials spoke confidently of building a large-scale enrichment plant that would earn $250 million a year from exports of low-enriched uranium for use in nuclear power plants.[2] But uncertain export markets, rising construction costs and the suspension of US nuclear fuel deliveries in 1978 led South Africa to opt for a smaller enrichment facility which could be built more quickly, thereby assuring a supply of fuel for its reactor and its Koeberg power station.

There is little doubt, however, that the possibility of developing a nuclear weapon entered the leaders' calculations from the early stages of South Africa's nuclear development programme. While professing no intention of developing a weapon, South African political and military leaders frequently alluded to their capability to do so. At the inauguration of South Africa's first research reactor in 1965, Prime Minister Verwoerd noted the government's obligation to 'consider' the military aspects of nuclear energy.[3] A few years later a statement by the army's Chief of Staff, General H.J. Martin, that South Africa was prepared to produce nuclear arms, was repudiated by the then defence minister, P.W. Botha.[4]

Moreover, declarations of peaceful intent have themselves often been ambiguous, like Prime Minister Vorster's statement to a *Newsweek* correspondent in 1976: 'We are only interested in the peaceful application of nuclear power. But we can enrich uranium, and we have the capability. And we did not sign the nuclear nonproliferation treaty.'[5] Such statements suggest, at the very least, that at various decision-points along the continuum of nuclear development South Africa's leaders kept the weapons option alive. Indeed, official statements of non-interest in developing a weapon seem disingenuous in the light of strong evidence that South Africa planned to test a nuclear device in 1977 and may have carried out such a test in 1979.

THE KALAHARI CONTRETEMPS

The facts of the so-called Kalahari incident in 1977 are by now too familiar to warrant more than a brief review here.[6] But recent information on South African enrichment problems and capabilities provides a basis for reassessing South Africa's intentions at Kalahari and its nuclear diplomacy.

After being alerted by the USSR, US intelligence specialists reviewed high-resolution satellite photography, which disclosed a hole in the ground and a cluster of buildings around a prominent tower under construction in the remote Kalahari Desert area of the Western Cape.[7] Several US government-connected think-tanks tried but failed to match the site configuration with various non-nuclear activities (such as a missile test-range or a diamond mine). The site design was judged compatible with those of other countries' first nuclear tests of a crude device. Although there were some anomalies, US officials were quoted as being virtually certain that the activities at the site were preparations for a nuclear test.

Intense diplomatic activity followed the discovery. Non-proliferation was of course an issue of high priority in the Carter Administration. Moreover, the US and France were scheduled suppliers of enriched uranium and nuclear power stations, respectively, to South Africa. Both governments, together with Britain and West Germany, made strong *démarches* to the Vorster government. Asked to explain the purpose of the Kalahari site, South African officials denied it had anything to do with nuclear weapons. But the explanations they gave US diplomats were both disingenuous and conflicting. By denying nuclear intentions the Vorster leadership engaged in a sort of mirrors game: asked for firm denials, officials referred to earlier denials which, on close inspection, appeared to have little or no substance.

In spite of such equivocation, President Carter announced in late August that,

> South Africa has informed us that they do not have and do not intend to develop nuclear explosive devices for any purpose, either peaceful or as a weapon; that the Kalahari test site, which has been in question, is not designed for use to test nuclear explosives; and that no nuclear explosive test will be taken in South Africa now or in the future.[8]

Prime Minister Vorster later denied on US television that he had made any promises to Carter, thereby prompting the US to publish a letter from Vorster to Carter stating that South Africa 'does not have nor does it intend to develop a nuclear explosive device for any purpose, peaceful or otherwise . . . and there will be no nuclear testing of any kind in South Africa'.[9] But that letter, which contains the only categorical denial known to have been given, was written on 13 October 1977: more than two months after the initial Western *démarche* to Pretoria.

What were South Africa's intentions? The 'hoax' hypothesis – that the Kalahari site was a dummy, constructed simply to gain nuclear concessions from the US – is the least plausible. South African leaders must have realized that discovery of the site would inevitably bring a storm of international condemnation, as well as embarrassment at being caught out. A hoax with such high costs and uncertain benefits would not be worth undertaking. Moreover, an elaborate hoax was not necessary to gain American attention. Discreetly planted official leaks that a test was under consideration, followed by ambiguous denials, would have been enough.

US officials at the time believed that South Africa was, indeed, preparing for a weapons test. American intelligence is reported to have received later independent confirmation that this was the case.[10] Construction activity continued until at least December 1977, more than four months after the site had been discovered and talks with the US had begun.[11] Vorster thus allowed preparations for a test to go forward even while his government was under intense external pressure, including a British threat to sever diplomatic relations, and while South African officials were issuing patently false statements about the purpose of the site.

How is this behaviour to be explained? And why was the test finally called off? Subsequent analysis has focused on South African enrichment capabilities. Although the Valindaba enrichment facility was said to be 'fully operational' in early 1977, outside experts now believe that it may have encountered technical problems which held production to 3 per cent enriched uranium at that time, so that by mid-1977 it could have produced at most 20 kg of weapons-grade uranium: barely enough for a highly sophisticated weapon, and not enough for the crude designs typical of previous first-test weapons.[12]

One hypothesis, based on this analysis, suggests that test preparations were allowed to go ahead in the expectation that the problems at Valindaba would be quickly solved and that the necessary highly-enriched uranium would be available by mid-1977. Then, as it became clear that the delay would be much longer, the test was called off and the site dismantled.[13] This explanation is consistent with the calculated ambiguity of South African officials about their intentions until Vorster's October 1977 letter to Carter.

Vorster must have weighed the risk of discovery of the test site and concluded that a test was worth that risk. He may well have been led to believe that the chances of detection were small; indeed, discovery of the site appears to have been accidental and by no means inevitable. The disordered and inconsistent reactions of South African officials to the Western *démarche*, however, was probably due less to Vorster's surprise at being discovered than to a widespread ignorance of the test preparations among officials apart from Vorster and one or two close advisers.

At the height of the Kalahari crisis an editorial in the pro-government newspaper, *Beeld*, reflected official testiness on the issue:

> The great powers which have nuclear weapons have adopted an odd attitude. *One would have thought that it would have been tactically more profitable for them to draw closer a potential member of the nuclear club, which South Africa is. Their bullying attitude could result in making us a maverick bull in the nuclear herd*, and that is surely not a sound situation from their point of view. South Africa will go its own way and its own interests will be decisive.[14] [My emphasis.]

When the Carter Administration pressed South Africa to sign the Nuclear Non-Proliferation Treaty.(NPT), Vorster responded in person, saying South Africa would 'consider' signing, but required guarantees of future US deliveries of enriched uranium for its reactors. In negotiations with Carter's special ambassador, South African demands were elaborated. They included resumption of US deliveries of Highly-Enriched Uranium (HEU) for its research reactor; a guaranteed supply of Low-Enriched Uranium (LEU) for the Koeberg power station; relaxation of US export restrictions on non-sensitive technology for the uranium enrichment plant; and American support for reinstating South Africa in its seat on the Board of Governors of the International Atomic Energy Agency (IAEA), the watchdog on nuclear proliferation.[15]

Negotiations broke down in late 1978 because South Africa was unwilling to open its enrichment plant at Valindaba to IAEA inspection as required by the NPT. (South African officials say their refusal reflects a concern to protect what they claim is a unique enrichment process.) By then the US had enacted its own Nuclear Non-Proliferation Act (1978), prohibiting the sale of any enriched fuel to countries not applying IAEA safeguards to *all* their nuclear facilities.

The decision to prepare for a nuclear test at Kalahari was a costly one for South Africa. Its detection caused the US to cancel fuel deliveries for the Koeberg nuclear power station, thereby delaying the station's start-up time. It also reinforced suspicions about South African military intentions, contributing to the UNSC's enactment of a mandatory arms embargo against South Africa in November 1977. But the Kalahari episode, and particularly South Africa's success in maintaining a calculated ambiguity about nuclear test plans, brought anxious Western diplomats to Pretoria to seek an accommodation, while leaving the Western powers a plausible basis for accepting South African assurances that it would not test a nuclear weapon. As one observer noted, the episode demonstrated to South Africa 'the value of the nuclear threat as diplomatic leverage, an option to be foregone *in exchange* for reciprocal favors'.[16]

GROWING NUCLEAR CAPABILITY

The issue re-emerged, however, a year after P.W. Botha took office as prime minister. In September 1979 a US intelligence satellite, the Vela, recorded a double flash of light – a signature unique to nuclear explosions – as it passed over a remote expanse of ocean between South Africa and Antarctica.

As in the Kalahari case, the 'Vela incident' has been extensively analysed.[17] Treatment here will be limited to a brief review of the evidence and its implications for nuclear diplomacy.

In 41 previous cases where the Vela had registered a double pulse, independent sources confirmed the event as a nuclear explosion. But in this instance the usual corroborating evidence was either missing or subject to conflicting interpretation. A panel of scientific experts assembled by the White House, after reviewing the evidence for two months, concluded that the case for a nuclear explosion remained unproven; but it could find no other plausible explanation.[18]

This finding was vigorously challenged within both the scientific and intelligence communities in the US. Several major pieces of evidence suggested that a nuclear test had occurred. *An ionospheric disturbance* for which there was no natural explanation was recorded by a radio telescope in Puerto Rico at the same time and in the same general area as the Vela incident. *A hydro-acoustic signal*, the strongest ever monitored by the US Naval Research Laboratory, originated in the Indian Ocean near South Africa's remote Prince Edward Islands at the same time as the Vela flash. *A study of the detection of seismic disturbances*, prepared by the US Technical Information Service at a cost of several thousand dollars had only one purchaser: South Africa's defence and naval attaché.[19] A *secret South African naval exercise* was reported to have occurred on the night of the Vela incident.[20]

Although the White House panel found problems with much of this evidence, a member of Carter's Office of Science and Technology Policy later acknowledged that the technical data were useless unless they produced an airtight case.[21] In short, an administration that placed so high a priority on non-proliferation would have needed a smoking gun to reach a verdict that South Africa had detonated a nuclear weapon. And among US scientific and intelligence specialists, even those who thought they detected a smoking gun saw it variously in the hands of India, Israel and South Africa, or the latter two in collusion.

South African officials at the time issued brief denials that a test had been conducted. In light of the Botha Administration's worsening relations with Washington by 1979, and the suspension of nuclear negotiations, South Africa apparently saw no reason to engage in detailed discussion of the charges. Indeed, four days after the event the *Rand Daily Mail* quoted P.W. Botha as telling an NP meeting that South Africa had the conventional capability to counter any guerrilla incursion, and further, 'if there are people who are thinking of doing something else, I suggest they think twice about it. *They might find out we have military weapons they do not know about*' [my emphasis].[22]

If the September 1979 event was, as suspected, a South African test, it appears to have followed logically from the Kalahari experience. That is, based on global reactions to the 1977 test preparations, Botha would have realized that detection of a test could have serious consequences, including the possibility of massive sanctions against South Africa. Therefore elaborate precautions would be required so that a policy of plausible denial would stand up. South Africa's Prince Edward Islands, some 1200 miles south of Cape Town and roughly mid-way between South Africa and Antarctica, would offer the remotest practicable site. Moreover a test carried out at night would reduce the chances of inadvertent sighting. Finally, an explosion close to the surface of the sea would prevent fallout from reaching the upper atmosphere, where detection would be almost certain.

As in the Kalahari incident, however, later evidence casts some doubt on South Africa's ability to produce a nuclear weapon by 1979. According to earlier US intelligence estimates, the Valindaba facility might have been able to produce as much as 40 kg of HEU by 1979.[23] This is less than the estimated 48 kg needed to detonate the crude fission devices used in other countries' first tests. But it might have been sufficient for a weapon of highly-advanced design; in other words, only if South Africa had been able to duplicate or acquire more recent techniques in warhead design would it have had enough enriched material for a weapon. This has led some scientists to believe that the 1979 event was either an Israeli test conducted with South African cooperation, or a joint Israeli–South African endeavour, while other analysts say the issue so far remains unresolved.[24]

By 1981, when South Africa announced that its Valindaba facility had produced 45 per cent enriched uranium for the Safari research reactor, the question of South Africa's nuclear weapons *capability* was no longer in doubt. If a facility can enrich to 45 per cent, it can enrich to 90 per cent.

With the advent of the Reagan Administration in 1981, South African diplomats took advantage of the more sympathetic environment in Washington to press their case for an easing of US restrictions on nuclear-related exports. In May the South African embassy sent a secret four-page note to the then Secretary of State, Haig, arguing that signing the NPT would leave South Africa at the mercy of the

USSR and other hostile powers, and urging relaxation of the ban on enriched fuel exports.[25] A few weeks later US uranium brokers, with the knowledge of the State Department, arranged a complicated swap in which France fabricated fuel rods for the Koeberg reactor. This move violated the spirit, though not the letter, of a French commitment to the Carter Administration not to supply enriched fuel to South Africa; but it was consistent with the new US policy, as summarized in testimony by a State Department official: 'We feel that we can achieve our objectives better, non-proliferation objectives, with South Africa by not engaging in unnecessary activities which would produce a deteriorating relationship.'[26] The swap also enabled the US to avoid potentially costly litigation for breach of contract, as a US firm had previously contracted to enrich the uranium for Koeberg.

Despite South African success in acquiring fuel rods from France, the commissioning of the first Koeberg power station was delayed for an additional year by ANC sabotage of the installation in December 1982. But French-delivered fuel enabled South Africa to start up the two Koeberg power stations, one in 1984 and the other a year later, and to keep them operating at least until late 1987, the scheduled completion date for a semi-commercial enrichment plant in South Africa. Once in operation, that plant is expected to supply all the fuel needed for the power stations and the research reactor.

The Reagan Administration also authorized the sale of several major pieces of nuclear-related equipment with dual end-uses. Among them were vibration test equipment, which could be used to test the reliability of nuclear warheads; multi-channel analysers, capable of analysing complex data at a test site; a Cyber-170-750 computer, powerful enough to model a nuclear explosion; and a supply of helium-3, from which tritium, an element used in thermo-nuclear weapons, could be derived.[27]

In January 1984 the chairman of South Africa's state-run Atomic Energy Corporation (AEC) announced that South Africa would conduct its external nuclear affairs – that is, the transfer of nuclear material, equipment and technology – in accord with 'the spirit, principles, and goals' of the NPT.[28] In the same statement the AEC chairman said South Africa was ready to resume talks with the US about nuclear matters. He also indicated his government's willingness to talk with the IAEA about allowing the semi-commercial enrichment plant now nearing completion to be placed under international safeguards. The existing pilot enrichment plant would be excluded, however. Negotiations with the IAEA began in 1985, apparently as a result of US pressure on Pretoria. But the talks collapsed in August 1986 because South Africa demanded the explicit right to withdraw some enriched uranium in the future for possible use in nuclear submarines. South Africa also sought the right to terminate the safeguards agreement without penalty if the IAEA applied sanctions for political reasons, or if South Africa's 'supreme national interests were jeopardized'.[29]

The US continued to seek Pretoria's agreement to signing the NPT. Unlike IAEA safeguards, which would apply only to those installations designated by South Africa, signing the NPT would require that *all* South African nuclear facilities be placed under international safeguards. But in early 1987 senior US diplomats said privately that South Africa, since it no longer needed the US' enriched fuel, was showing little interest in subscribing to the NPT. About all the US could offer South Africa was support for its good standing in the IAEA.[30]

In September 1987, however, President Botha made a surprise announcement that his government was prepared to open talks with the nuclear states about signing the NPT. The timing of Botha's announcement – on the eve of the IAEA's annual conference, where Third World states were expected to press for the expulsion of South Africa – was clearly aimed at giving the US and other IAEA members a basis for voting against the expulsion. Indeed, a few days later, when both the US and Soviet IAEA delegates opposed the move against South Africa, the Third World states' initiative collapsed.[31] If South Africa is serious about signing the NPT, however, that probably means it is ready to shut down the pilot enrichment plant; and that, in turn, would mean giving up the option to produce weapons-grade uranium.[32] Whether it already has a stockpile of weapons is uncertain.

THE QUESTION OF NUCLEAR TARGETS

Whether or not South Africa has nuclear weapons, the development of such a capability is at least consistent with the Botha leadership's well-publicized drive to institute a 'total national strategy' in response to the perceived Moscow-orchestrated 'total onslaught' allegedly being waged against the Republic.[33] It is also consistent with P.W. Botha's perception that South Africa's security situation is analogous

Pretoria's Nuclear Diplomacy 169

to Israel's: a small, technologically advanced state forced to fight alone for its national survival against an array of hostile but weak neighbours armed by the USSR. And among Western scientists, Israel is widely believed to have a nuclear arsenal. Moreover South Africa, like other states with ambitions to be recognized as regional superpowers, could hope to see its claim enhanced if it were believed to possess nuclear arms. Indeed, acquiring a bomb-as-status-symbol would have held particular appeal for Pretoria's leaders because, unlike most threshold states, South Africa already possessed most of the essential ingredients: uranium, a substantial modern industrial sector and indigenous nuclear expertise.

In terms of the possible military use of nuclear weapons, however, South Africa would seem to have little need and few potential targets. A nuclear weapon would be virtually useless against guerrillas, either as defence or deterrent. To the extent that small bands of ANC or SWAPO operatives, or their camps across the border, can be located and identified, South Africa's conventional forces are capable of dealing with them effectively. Neither the ANC nor SWAPO appears capable of moving from sporadic, hit-and-run attacks into the sort of classic guerrilla offensive waged against Rhodesia. The ANC itself foresees no likelihood of such a development. In so far as the threat of nuclear attack might pressure neighbouring states into denying the guerrillas sanctuary, South Africa's conventional and unconventional warfare methods have already accomplished that, except in the case of Angola; and as long as the threat posed by SWAPO can be contained by standard counter-insurgency measures, any South African threat to move that conflict to a nuclear level would be rash indeed.

A nuclear weapon could never be used against the major security threat to the regime: revolt in the black townships, like that of 1984–1986. Although the ghetto communities are in most cases physically separate from South Africa's cities, they are integrated economically into the rest of the country. Nuclear destruction of the black townships would bring economic chaos since the country's railways, mines and factories are dependent on 6 000 000 black workers to keep them operating. Furthermore, most black townships are within a few miles of major cities and white residential areas: far too close to prevent radioactive fallout from crossing the colour line.

To South African military men the worst-case scenario would be an internal black uprising combined with a massive cross-border attack by African forces backed by Soviet and Cuban troops. South

Africa's leaders themselves acknowledge that such a development is extremely unlikely. But they have expressed growing concern over the build-up of heavy armaments in Angola, and the Cuban troop presence there. This appears to be more than a politically-inspired alarm to win larger defence budgets. A well-travelled senior SADF officer noted in private that few of his military colleagues had travelled in African states; and that in the 1950s they took seriously the threats of radical African leaders to mobilize a pan-African army for an all-out assault on apartheid.[34] Currently SADF officials say that, unlikely as a massive invasion may be, it is a worst-case scenario for which the SADF must be prepared. Indeed, during the past few years the focus of South Africa's indigenous arms production has shifted from counter-insurgency weapons to conventional arms. Similarly, major military exercises in recent years have involved defence against a large-scale conventional assault from across the border.[35]

In such a contingency there would of course be a potential role for nuclear weapons. They might be used to 'break up any concentration of conventional forces against South Africa's industrial and population centers', or as tactical weapons in a conventional battle.[36] Or if hostile armies were seen to be massing along the border, a nuclear device might be detonated in a remote area as a warning to would-be invaders. In 1980 a senior South African naval officer stated that South Africa had the capability to 'ward off a combined onslaught by African states, even if this involved *limited* intervention by outside powers' (my emphasis).[37] He then warned that South Africa reserved the right to put its nuclear expertise to practical use.

No hostile forces have invaded South Africa since the Boer War, however. In fact, its only recent involvement in conventional warfare occurred inside Angola. Although South African forces were taking higher-than-usual casualties in support of UNITA in 1987–8, it is extremely unlikely that South Africa would resort to nuclear weapons against Angola in order to prevent the military collapse of UNITA, should that appear imminent. Official South African concern over rising SADF casualties in Angola suggests that there are limits to Pretoria's commitment to the survival of UNITA as a military force. That commitment would almost certainly preclude the use of nuclear weapons inside Angola and the hostile world reaction that would follow.

In conclusion, the only remotely feasible use of a nuclear weapon by South Africa would seem to be a weapon of last resort against an invading army: an extremely unlikely eventuality. This means that nuclear weapons 'seem largely irrelevant to the near- and medium-term military balance in southern Africa and to most of Pretoria's security concerns'.[38]

ASSESSING SOUTH AFRICA'S NUCLEAR DIPLOMACY

South Africa's nuclear diplomacy has involved the pursuit of three objectives, not all of which have been mutually compatible. Access to Western nuclear technology and, until recently, enriched fuel from the West has been a consistent priority. A second goal has been to gain global recognition as a potential nuclear weapons state and, hence, acknowledgement as the regional superpower in southern Africa. Finally, although there is wide disagreement over how far South Africa has moved towards producing and testing a weapon, there is almost no doubt that it has pursued the development of a nuclear weapons capability while trying to maintain some basis for plausible denial of any weapons intent.

During the late 1970s the first and third objectives came into conflict; Vorster sought to resolve this by assuring Carter that South Africa had no plans to produce or test a weapon. But Pretoria's dissembling over the Kalahari site, together with its refusal to sign the NPT, led to a cut-off in American supply of enriched uranium for three critical years, 1978–80, when South Africa was heavily dependent on US fuel to start up its Koeberg power plant. Evidence that South Africa was moving to test a nuclear device also contributed to the decision of the UNSC to impose a mandatory arms embargo against South Africa in late 1977. In the early 1980s, however, South Africa's appeals to the Reagan Administration to help it acquire fuel for its reactors, and not to demand that it sign the NPT as a quid pro quo, met a favourable response.

South Africa also has enjoyed support from both the US and USSR in blocking efforts to expel it from the IAEA, although it has so far failed to win back its seat on the prestigious IAEA board. P.W. Botha's timely statement that South Africa was prepared to discuss signing the NPT helped the two superpowers defeat a vigorous move to expel South Africa in late 1987.

It was clear by 1981, if not before, that South Africa had all the necessary ingredients to produce nuclear weapons. Whether it had them in 1979, and whether it had tested a weapon, remained issues in dispute. While South Africa thus achieved its goal of recognition as a potential nuclear weapons state, this in itself has had little or no impact on its bid for regional superpower status. The concessions wrung from neighbouring states were extracted through armed attacks and economic pressure, and had nothing to do with its nuclear potential. Nor has the possibility of nuclear reprisal led nearby states to agree to diplomatic recognition or military alliance with the Republic. Finally, South Africa's military power, including its nuclear potential, have not induced the Western powers to support Pretoria's long-pursued bid for political and economic hegemony in the region.

Epilogue

A REGIME UNDER SIEGE

The pace of political and social upheaval in South Africa accelerated dramatically during the 1980s. The emergence and recognition of the ANC as a major and legitimate force in South Africa's future; the explosion of black protest that swept the black townships in mid-decade; South African involvement in virtually perpetual conflict across its borders; the sharpening cleavages within South Africa's white and black communities: these were among the more glaring evidence of a fracturing society and a regime under intense pressure.

Yet, despite the dynamic forces in contention, South Africa's internal conflict will not be resolved by the end of the century. The struggle for power is too asymmetrical. The ruling National Party appears to be strong enough and unified enough to retain control over the levers of power for at least the next decade. The coercive resources at its disposal are considerable. Its opponents, black and white, are divided and as yet without the organization or means to extract major concessions, let along dislodge the regime. Barring massive outside intervention, in the form of comprehensive global sanctions or direct military intervention by the great powers, the conflict is likely to remain lop-sided for some time.

But the costs of hanging on to power without moving to negotiate genuine power-sharing with the black majority are rising. ANC support within and outside South Africa is growing, not diminishing. Even conservative Western governments no longer tacitly accept white minority rule as South Africa's internal affair, but instead urge an opening of the political process and negotiation with black leaders. Black labour unions, given legal sanction only a few years ago, have been organizing effectively and testing their muscle. It is inevitable that they will become increasingly involved in the political struggle of their members. Economic sanctions, which were a long time in coming, stand a good chance of being retained, and possibly even expanded, in the absence of moves towards accommodating the black majority. Moreover, as Geoffrey Butler has pointed out (drawing on the Rhodesian experience), the longer the process is delayed, the worse the terms of negotiation will become for the regime, and the more external forces will become entrenched behind different factions.

If these are the circumstances that will prevail in South Africa during the next decade, how will foreign policy be affected? What role can it play in support of the regime? Is it likely to be more or less effective than in the recent past? Indeed, will it change at all? What are the implications for the region, and for the West?

FOREIGN POLICY IMPERATIVES AND CONSTRAINTS

There is little doubt that domestic race policies will continue to be by far the dominant influence on South Africa's foreign relations, as well as the major constraint on its foreign policy-makers. The general outlines of the racial struggle in South Africa are by now so familiar, and the government's policy – whether it be called white supremacy, reform-from-above or neo-apartheid – so at odds with the generally accepted principles of nationalism and self-determination of the past 40 years, that no white minority government in Pretoria can escape the world's opprobrium. The expression of that opprobrium has continued to expand in the form of diplomatic isolation, expulsion from numerous world and regional organizations, arms embargoes, economic sanctions, disinvestment and public criticism by Western leaders.

So far the white leadership has denied blacks free political expression, and has refused to negotiate with them about sharing real political power. Instead it has suppressed black political protest while offering blacks participation in feckless political institutions, like advisory councils or ethnic bodies, designed to exclude them from the organs of real power. As long as this is the policy, it will be difficult even for conservative Western governments to fend off demands for increased pressure against the regime, let alone to remove existing restrictions. Only if the white leadership initiates moves to negotiate genuine power-sharing, and if major black groups accept and respond to those moves, are the isolation and pressure on the regime likely to be relaxed.

In short, the key to improved foreign relations lies not in a benign and astute foreign policy but in the leadership's domestic race policies, which remain the crucial international issue between Pretoria and the rest of the world. Aggressive actions toward the neighbours can, of course, further exacerbate South Africa's already strained international position, as indeed occurred in the mid-1980s. But even a friendly new outward policy would, by itself, be unlikely to affect fundamental attitudes towards the regime on the part of African or Western states.

A second major constraint on foreign policy will be domestic politics: particularly the need to appear tough and resolute in the face of external security threats and economic pressures. In the May 1987 general election, right-wing opposition to Botha's domestic race reforms enabled the Conservative Party to increase its parliamentary seats from 17 to 22, and to become the official Opposition: the first time since 1948 that the ruling NP has faced an official Opposition on its right. The NP, too, gained seats: its total of 123 gave it a more-than-comfortable 74 per cent majority of the white House of Assembly's elected seats. Yet its gains were among the traditionally liberal English-speakers, who abandoned the Progressive Federal Party in droves, and its losses were in its traditional conservative Afrikaans-speaking constituencies. Moreover its winning strategy was to slow the pace of domestic race reform and stress its tough stance against the ANC and against foreign meddling in South African affairs. The Conservative Party won more than a quarter of the popular vote with a platform of reinvigorated apartheid, including geographic partition, and flat refusal 'to negotiate the future of whites with any other nation, of whatever colour'.

The next general election is scheduled for 1989. Botha is seeking a postponement until 1992 to give him more time to carry on with his reform-from-above before facing white voters again. But postponement would require a constitutional amendment approved by all three chambers of Parliament. If that move fails, Botha must either suspend the constitution, thereby precipitating a serious constitutional crisis, or hold the 1989 election on schedule.

However Botha decides to handle the election issue, he will in the meantime try to stem the erosion of Afrikaner support for the NP. This suggests continued caution in promoting domestic race reform, and reduces the likelihood of substantial South African concessions on Namibia, ANC sanctuaries, and other foreign policy issues where the voters want to see a hard line. Indeed, a tough foreign policy appears to be an essential trade-off for assuring continued domestic support of Botha's race reforms.

Thus, as the NP strives to stay in power and to control the process of political and social change during the 1990s, the overriding objectives of foreign policy will be to insulate the country as far as possible from external pressures and attack; to avoid charges of being soft against external enemies; and to win support for its domestic race policy. In trying to win external support, government spokesmen will stress common *interests* between the regime and other states, and will play down the absence of shared *values*.

The NP leadership no longer offers a defence of apartheid. Instead it seeks to persuade the world that apartheid is dead, and that the government's programme of racial reform offers the best hope for a process of peaceful and orderly change that is in the interests of all moderate states in the West as well as Africa. To its African neighbours, most of whom face serious food shortages, rising unemployment and declining growth, South Africa will stress the mutual advantages of increased trade, investment and technical cooperation which could flow in the wake of mutual security accords. The drawbacks and risks of associating with communist states, particularly the USSR and Cuba, will be argued. In the West the minerals dependence card will be played, along with that of stopping Soviet expansionism.

How effective is Pretoria's foreign policy likely to be, given the constraints of a domestic race policy that is abhorrent to most of the world? The leadership may, with good reason, expect little from its traditional diplomacy. It was not diplomatic initiatives but the military's hard-hitting destabilization activities that made possible the Nkomati Accord with Mozambique and Angola's agreement to a cease-fire in 1984; nor were South African diplomats successful in warding off economic sanctions, including those imposed during the relatively sympathetic Reagan Administration.

Those recent experiences, together with the far more prominent role of the military in foreign policy decisions and in the decision-making apparatus since 1978, suggest that a tough, go-it-alone foreign policy will continue to predominate in the 1990s. This will be particularly the case where security or domestic political imperatives are seen to be at stake, as in Namibia, Angola and the activities of SWAPO and the ANC. In such cases the military's hard line seems likely to prevail over counsels of caution, even at the risk of further alienating important states like the US. Following the global reaction to the SADF's attack against three Commonwealth African capitals in the spring of 1986, however, the government appeared to curtail its cross-border strikes. It began to rely instead on small-scale clandestine actions, including assassination and kidnapping of suspected ANC operatives in foreign countries, and low-key economic pressure against neighbours felt to be negligent in rooting out ANC personnel.

The prestige and prominence of the military's role in foreign policy, and particularly its success in clubbing the neighbours into joint security action against the ANC, seem unlikely to fade as the regime faces the external and internal challenges of the next decade. The status of the military is such that even a number of blundering misadventures – the Cabinda raid, the Seychelles invasion and the post-Nkomati assistance to Mozambican guerrillas – caused no heads to roll in the military hierarchy, and failed even to evoke a presidential rebuke. Whether these risky ventures were launched with tacit nods and winks from P.W. Botha or were unsanctioned acts by an SADF confident of its leader's support, there is no doubt that Botha depends heavily on the military and is therefore reluctant to punish its misdeeds for fear of reducing its effectiveness or losing its political support to parties on the right. Magnus Malan, the Minister of Defence, gradually supplanted the Foreign Minister as Botha's spokesman on major foreign policy issues. Thus it was Malan, not Foreign Minister Botha, who proposed a deal with the USSR to end the Angolan war. By 1988 Malan was also being mentioned more frequently as a serious contender for the State Presidency when P.W. Botha, who celebrated his 72nd birthday in 1988, decides to relinquish the reins of Party and government.

To the degree that the regime continues to depend on coercion rather than diplomacy to wring concessions from its neighbours, the SADF will remain capable and willing to carry out a variety of armed actions, from clandestine raids to conventional assaults. Yet South Africa faces a number of changes in its external situation, some of which may pose constraints on future military operations.

THE CHANGING FOREIGN POLICY ENVIRONMENT

On several counts the regime faces a more dangerous situation than it did at the beginning of P.W. Botha's Administration in 1978. South Africa is more isolated from the West politically and economically, and in other ways as well. Relations between the leaders and their Western counterparts range from cool and strained to openly hostile. South Africa can no longer count on continued access to Western investments, credits and technology, all of which are restricted in one way or another.

Economic sanctions are already in place. In some cases it would only take a turn of the screw, not a whole new executive or legislative exercise, to tighten them further. In the US, for example, a simple rider to the 1987 Congressional trade bill eliminated tax credits for American business firms in South Africa. Thus the next major cycle of black protest and police suppression could well trigger a new round of sanctions, as well as a shrinkage of commercial bank credit in the face of political uncertainty.

Since 1986 several of the nearby states, particularly Zimbabwe, Mozambique, Tanzania and Malawi have drawn closer together on economic and security matters. Their security forces have cooperated against Renamo, the Mozambican guerrilla group supported until at least 1985 by the South African military, and they have collaborated in a joint programme to restore and improve transport links through Mozambique. By 1988 more than half-a-dozen Western states were involved in technical and economic assistance to Mozambique's vital Beira transport corridor, and Britain was expanding its military training of the Mozambican army. Thus regional and Western states were involved in programmes to strengthen the Mozambican government, oppose South Africa's former guerrilla clients (Renamo) and back the efforts of local states to reduce their transport dependence on South Africa. All this suggests a further isolation of South Africa from important developments in the region.

Perhaps of most immediate concern to the leadership are the growing costs of the war inside Angola. In 1987–8 South African casualties were the heaviest yet incurred in the fighting there, with no end in sight. SADF losses may appear low by the standards of modern conflict, but the sudden and unexpected rise in battle casualties – deep inside Angola and in support of a guerrilla movement, rather than in defence of the border – led to growing public concern about South Africa's involvement. An editorial in a major Afrikaans newspaper called it South Africa's Vietnam.

The war in Angola thus seems likely to become a more serious issue in South Africa's domestic politics in the years immediately ahead. At the very least it will force the leadership to seek a broader consensus on South Africa's role in supporting UNITA and conducting pre-emptive strikes against SWAPO inside Angola.

Among the unplanned legacies of the destabilization policy is the problem of what to do about the bands of armed dissidents that were sponsored and supported by South Africa to carry out acts of violence against regimes in several nearby countries. Once dependent on

South Africa for weapons and money, and in some cases even for their survival, most of these groups are now capable of surviving on their own. Over time they have, in fact, developed a momentum, a vested interest in organizational survival, that places them well beyond South African control or direction. Renamo's leaders, for example, walked out of South African-sponsored talks with the Mozambican government and refused to return. UNITA's leader, Jonas Savimbi, has made it clear that he will torpedo any accord reached by South Africa and Angola without his participation. In Zimbabwe bands of armed dissidents who, according to both Zimbabwean and Western officials, were originally armed and trained by South Africa, have continued to commit murder and pillage in south-western Zimbabwe long after this ran counter to South Africa's interests in improved relations with the Mugabe government.

By 1988 none of these insurgent groups appeared capable of coming to power through a military victory over government forces. Yet each group appeared able to survive indefinitely, and to continue causing severe social and economic chaos. This military stalemate means that these groups will keep much of the region unsettled for a long time to come. Although destabilization is probably no longer seen by the leadership to serve its best interests in Mozambique and Zimbabwe, Savimbi's UNITA forces in Angola continue to provide an important buffer against SWAPO infiltration and a powerful source of military and economic pressure against the Angolan regime. But if the SADF begins to incur politically intolerable numbers of casualties on behalf of UNITA, or if Angola and South Africa should find a mutually acceptable basis for a Cuban withdrawal and a Namibian settlement, UNITA could become a serious problem, and perhaps a liability, to Pretoria.

In sum, the foreign policy environment faced by South Africa's leaders in the coming decade looks like 'more of the same': that is, a sharpening of unfavourable conditions already present in the late 1980s. There are, however, a number of developments which might occur and which, for better or worse, could break the logjam in Pretoria's foreign relations, or at least move its foreign policy in a different direction.

ALTERNATIVE SCENARIOS

In the unlikely event the government moves to meet the minimal demands of most black leaders – that is, allow free political activity, find a *modus vivendi* with the ANC (perhaps legalizing an internal wing, like that accorded SWAPO in Namibia), consult with legitimate black leaders and agree to share power at the national level – African and Western governments would quickly begin removing sanctions and other restrictions in force against the regime. That might be a step-by-step process, however, to prevent the government from reneging or backing away from its commitments.

In a far more likely scenario the leadership might settle on a formula for race reform that would fall short of the above, but which would appeal to legitimate but conservative black leaders: particularly those who saw themselves as losing ground to the ANC and other more radical black groups. Such an offer might be open, for example, to all groups disavowing violence, thereby excluding the ANC. If the offer won over a group that included well-known figures like the Zulu leader, Gatsha Buthelezi, and a couple of others with large followings among blacks, this would pose difficult problems for the West and for Africa. As with Rhodesia's internal settlement in 1978, conservative voices in the West would urge support for an arrangement that seemed to open the door to a peaceful resolution with moderate black nationalists while, in Kissinger's words, isolating the ideological radicals. The issue would be divisive in the West, and between the West and Africa. Even some nearby African states might be coopted into support.

Although it is difficult to visualize a solution to the Namibia–Angola conflicts which would meet the minimum requirements of all the parties involved, a settlement within the next few years is not out of the question. If the fighting threatens to escalate further and to raise SADF casualties to politically unacceptable levels, and if the internal political parties in Namibia seem no closer to winning broad popular support, the South African leadership might agree to a settlement leading to a SWAPO-dominated government in Namibia and bypassing Savimbi. But its quid pro quo for implementing the UN plan, or anything like it, would be high. It might conceivably include, among other demands, a hard, Soviet- and Western-backed guarantee of a demilitarized southern Angola in place of the buffer currently provided by UNITA forces, indefinite retention of its base at Walvis Bay, an accelerated withdrawal of Cuba's combat brigade, and some sort of political sop to UNITA, with or without Savimbi.

South African policy elsewhere in the region might be moved in more benign directions as sanctions begin to bite. In particular, South

African commerce will to some degree come to depend more on facilities in nearby states to help evade sanctions. Moreover the parlous economic situation in Mozambique, Zambia and other nearby states seems likely to persist and even worsen in the next few years, making them potentially more receptive to South African economic overtures. Whether their economic plight would be enough to induce them to agree to mutual security arrangements and closer official ties with Pretoria remains to be seen. The tension between the economic and technical gains to be had from drawing closer to South Africa and the political costs of doing so will remain a sensitive issue for the region's poorer states.

Since South Africa's foreign relations are conducted in a dynamic and inter-acting global environment, they are of course subject to influence by outside actors. A shift in the superpower relationship, in particular, could have a profound impact in Pretoria. Increasing US–Soviet tensions could lead to a hardening US attitude toward Soviet-backed liberation groups, like SWAPO and the ANC, and to a greater Soviet commitment to their armed struggle. That in turn might result in a softer US policy towards South Africa and a relaxation of restrictions, for example on so-called 'grey area' exports. On the other hand a general lessening of tensions between the superpowers, and mutual agreement that neither has vital strategic interests at stake in southern Africa, could lead them to exert joint pressure for peaceful resolution of the region's conflicts. That situation could put further distance between South Africa and the US.

By 1988 the Soviet leadership appeared to believe that Angola's war against UNITA could not be won, and that the escalation of that conflict might jeopardize higher priority Soviet goals, particularly arms accords with the US. Although the USSR apparently was not yet prepared to reduce the heavy flow of weapons to Angola or to press the dos Santos government to seek an accommodation with UNITA, it was supporting US efforts to reach a negotiated settlement.

In any event, outside influence on the region's affairs is limited. Its conflicts are not externally-generated offshoots of larger conflicts elsewhere, but are rooted in national and regional problems. They have been going on a long time, some for more than two decades, and they turn on questions of legitimacy: hence they are not easily resolved.

South Africa is of course deeply involved in the region's conflicts. In the late 1980s its leaders revived the proposal that South Africa and the other regional states work together to settle the region's problems without the participation of outside states. But South Africa, despite its superior military and economic power, lacks the legitimacy and political authority to play the role it proposes. It is a regional superpower whose influence is not commensurate with its ability to starve or crush its neighbours. Ultimately South Africa, like the other regional states, will have to seek or accept the involvement of outside powers, limited though their influence may be, in the long search for a resolution to the region's conflicts.

Notes and References

1 The Impact of Afrikaner Experience

1. André du Toit, 'No Chosen People: The Myth of the Calvinist Origins of Afrikaner Nationalism and Racial Ideology', *The American Historical Review*, 88, 4 (October 1983), p. 923.
2. Heribert Adam and Hermann Giliomee, *Ethnic Power Mobilized: Can South Africa Change?* (New Haven, Ct: Yale University Press, 1979), Ch. 4.
3. Ibid.
4. John W. Cell, *The Highest Stage of White Supremacy: The Origins of Segregation in South Africa and the American South* (Cambridge: Cambridge University Press, 1982), Ch. 3.
5. Adam and Giliomee, *Ethnic Power Mobilized*, Ch. 4.
6. Hannah Arendt, *The Origins of Totalitarianism* (New York: Meridian Books, 1958), p. 227.
7. D.F. Malan, cited in D. Moodie, *The Rise of Afrikanerdom: Power, Apartheid, and the Afrikaner Civil Religion* (Berkeley, Ca: University of California Press, 1975), p. 248.
8. David Yudelman, *The Emergence of Modern South Africa: State, Capital, and the Incorporation of Organized Labour on the South African Gold Fields, 1902–1939* (Cape Town: David Philip, 1983), p. 184.
9. Gail M. Gearhart, *Black Power in South Africa: The Evolution of an Ideology* (Berkeley, Ca: University of California Press, 1978), p. 31.
10. Moodie, *The Rise of Afrikanerdom*, p. 251.

2 Perceptions of South Africa's International Role

1. Cited in J.E. Spence, *Republic Under Pressure* (Oxford: Oxford University Press, 1965), p. 70.
2. B.M. Schoeman, *Van Malan tot Verwoerd* (Cape Town: Dagbreekpers, 1973), Ch. 9.
3. *House of Assembly Debates*, 1 September 1948, cols 1323–4.
4. Harold M. Glass, *South African Policy toward Basutoland* (Johannesburg: South African Institute of International Affairs (SAIIA), occasional paper, 1966).
5. *South Africa 1983*, Official Yearbook of the RSA (Johannesburg: Chris van Rensburg Publications, 1983), p. 54.
6. Sam C. Nolutshungu, *South Africa in Africa: A Study of Ideology and Foreign Policy* (Manchester: Manchester University Press, 1975), p. 46.
7. Robert S. Jaster, *South Africa's Narrowing Security Options*, Adelphi Paper No. 159 (London: IISS, Spring 1980), pp. 7, 14.
8. *House of Assembly Debates*, 26 April 1972, cols 5783–6.
9. Quoted in *South Africa's Foreign Policy, Defence, and Strategic Value* (London: South African Embassy, Director of Information, 1978), p. 6.

10. See Richard Bissell, 'South Atlantic – New Zone of Strategic Concern?', *The South Africa Foundation News* (August 1981), p. 2.
11. Christopher Coker, *South Africa's Security Dilemmas*, Washington Paper No. 126 (Washington, DC: CSIS, 1987), Ch. 5. Also see Richard Leonard, *South Africa At War* (Craighall: Ad. Donker, 1983), Ch. 5.

3 Decision-Making and the Foreign Policy Process

1. Theodor Hanf, Heribert Weiland and Gerda Vierdag, *South Africa: The Prospects of Peaceful Change* (London: Rex Collings, 1981), p. 175.
2. Deon Geldenhuys, *What Do We Think? A Survey of White Opinion on Foreign Policy Issues* (Braamfontein: SAIIA, November 1982), pp. 6–8.
3. Leonard Thompson and Andrew Prior, *South African Politics* (New Haven, Ct: Yale University Press, 1982), p. 88.
4. Deon Geldenhuys, *The Diplomacy of Isolation: South Africa's Foreign Policy Making* (Johannesburg: Macmillan South Africa, 1984), pp. 47–54.
5. Ibid., p. 51.
6. *Hansard*, 30 January 1976, col. 369.
7. William J. Foltz, 'Political Change in Botha's South Africa', paper presented to the Second Soviet–American Conference on Contemporary Sub-Saharan Africa, Moscow, June 1984, p. 8.
8. *The Star* (Johannesburg), 6 September 1986.
9. Geldenhuys, *The Diplomacy of Isolation*, p. 53.
10. Ibid., pp. 65–6.
11. Robert Schrire, 'Decision-Making and the 1984 Constitution' (unpublished study, University of Cape Town, Spring 1985), p. 18.
12. Geldenhuys, *The Diplomacy of Isolation*, pp. 59–60.
13. H. Adam and H. Giliomee, *Ethnic Power Mobilized: Can South Africa Change?* (New Haven, Ct: Yale University Press, 1979), p. 202.
14. Schrire, 'Decision-Making', p. 9.
15. Geldenhuys, *The Diplomacy of Isolation*, p. 71.
16. Quoted by David Martin and Phyllis Johnson, *The Struggle for Zimbabwe* (London: Faber & Faber, 1981), p. 134.
17. *Sunday Telegraph*, 18 March 1979.
18. Speech of 6 September 1978 in Bloemfontein, cited in *P.W. Botha: A Political Backgrounder* (London: South African Embassy, 1978).
19. Private conversation, March 1986.
20. Private conversation, 1986.
21. B. M. Schoeman, *Van Malan tot Verwoerd* (Cape Town: Dagbreekpers, 1973), Ch. 15.
22. Geldenhuys, p. 97.
23. For a detailed account of the Information initiative, see Geldenhuys, *The Diplomacy of Isolation*, pp. 107–21, and David Harrison, *The White Tribe of Africa: South Africa in Perspective* (Johannesburg: Macmillan South Africa, 1981), Ch. 18.
24. Harrison, *White Tribe*, p. 230.
25. Geldenhuys, *The Diplomacy of Isolation*, p. 110.

26. *House of Assembly Debates*, 20 May 1980, col. 6378.
27. Harrison, *White Tribe*, p. 239.
28. Kenneth Grundy, *The Militarization of South African Politics* (Bloomington: Indiana University Press, 1986), p. 43.
29. Ibid.
30. *Guardian*, 8 August 1979.
31. Geldenhuys, *The Diplomacy of Isolation*, p. 79.
32. Cited, in Grundy, *The Militarization*, p. 53.
33. For detailed accounts of SSC activities, see Geldenhuys, pp. 91–6 and Grundy, *The Militarization*, Ch. 6.
34. Grundy, *The Militarization*, p. 49.
35. Professor Barry Dean, Head of Public Law Department at Cape Town University, 'Control by Cabal', *Leadership* (Cape Town), 5, 4 (1986), p. 60.
36. Private discussion with South African officials.
37. J. E. Du Plessis, former Director-General in the prime minister's office, cited in Geldenhuys, *The Diplomacy of Isolation*, p. 92.
38. *Guardian*, 21 December 1985.
39. Private source.
40. Kenneth Grundy, *The Rise of the South African Security Establishment*, Bradlow Series No. 1 (Braamfontein: SAIIA, 1983), p. 13.
41. *The Economist*, 16 July 1983, and *New York Times*, 11 October 1983.
42. Private diplomatic source.
43. Deon Geldenhuys and John Seiler, *South Africa's Evolving State Security System*, occasional paper (Johannesburg: SAIIA, 1984), p. 12.
44. Private discussions.
45. Private discussion. Also see Geldenhuys, *The Diplomacy of Isolation*, p. 93, and Grundy, *The Militarization*, p. 53.
46. Private discussion. Also see Grundy, *The Militarization*, p. 54.
47. Harrison, *White Tribe*, p. 244.

4 Foreign Policy in Defence of Apartheid

1. Amry Vandenbosch, *South Africa and the World: The Foreign Policy of Apartheid* (Lexington, Ky: University of Kentucky Press, 1970), p. 13.
2. B. M. Schoeman, *Van Malan tot Verwoerd* (Cape Town: Dagbreekpers, 1973), Ch. 15.
3. Ibid.
4. James Barber, *South Africa's Foreign Policy, 1945–1970* (Oxford: Oxford University Press, 1973), p. 241.
5. Described in Deon Geldenhuys, *The Diplomacy of Isolation: South Africa's Foreign Policy Making* (Johannesburg: Macmillan South Africa, 1984), p. 34.
6. Sam C. Nolutshungu, *South Africa in Africa: A Study of Ideology and Foreign Policy* (Manchester: Manchester University Press, 1975), p. 46.
7. David Martin and Phyllis Johnson, *The Struggle for Zimbabwe* (London: Faber & Faber, 1981), p. 134.
8. See Robert S. Jaster, *South Africa's Narrowing Security Options*, Adelphi Paper No. 159 (London: IISS, Spring 1980), pp. 15–16.

5 Deteriorating Security and Policy Reappraisal (1974–8)

1. For detailed discussion of these negotiations, see David Martin and Phyllis Johnson, *The Struggle for Zimbabwe* (London: Faber & Faber, 1981), Chs 8 and 10; and Martin Meredith, *The Past Is Another Country* (London: Pan, 1980), Ch. 9.
2. Private conversation.
3. Deon Geldenhuys, *The Diplomacy of Isolation: South Africa's Foreign Policy Making* (Johannesburg: Macmillan South Africa, 1984), p. 214.
4. Ibid., p. 174.
5. Meredith, *The Past*, pp. 242–3; Martin and Johnson, *The Struggle*, p. 238.
6. Meredith, *The Past*, p. 243.
7. Martin and Johnson, *The Struggle*, p. 250.
8. Private Rhodesian source.
9. Robert S. Jaster, *South Africa's Narrowing Security Options*, Adelphi Paper No. 159 (London: IISS, 1980), p. 31.
10. Private interview.
11. US diplomat in private interview.
12. *The Star* (Johannesburg), 22 March 1969.
13. South Africa, *House of Assembly Debates*, 28 February 1973, col. 1697.
14. *Namibia: The Constitutional Fraud*, Briefing Paper No. 2 (London: International Defence and Aid Fund, July 1981).
15. South Africa, *House of Assembly Debates*, 14 June 1977, col. 10122.
16. Ibid., cols 10127 and 10172.
17. Cited in *Strategic Survey 1978* (London: IISS, 1979), p. 86.
18. Private South African source.
19. Private UN source. For a different view, see Anthony Verrier, *The Road to Zimbabwe 1890–1980* (London: Jonathan Cape, 1986), p. 223.
20. Speech of 2 June 1978, quoted in *P. W. Botha: A Political Backgrounder*, 1978 *op. cit.*
21. Ibid., quoting statement of 30 August 1978.
22. *The Citizen*, 29 September 1978.
23. Michael Wolfers and Jane Bergerol, *Angola in the Front Line* (London: Zed, 1983), p. 11.
24. Robin Hallett, 'The South African Intervention in Angola, 1975–76', *African Affairs*, 77, 308 (July 1978).
25. Jaster, *Narrowing Security Options*, p. 23.
26. Geldenhuys, *The Diplomacy of Isolation*, p. 80.
27. Ibid., p. 79.
28. Wolfers and Bergerol, *Angola*, pp. 12–13.
29. Geldenhuys, *The Diplomacy of Isolation*, p. 79.
30. Wolfers and Bergerol, *Angola*, p. 13.
31. F.W. Heimer, *The Decolonization Conflict in Angola 1974–76* (Geneva: Institut Universitaire de Hautes Etudes Internationales, 1979), p. 70.
32. Geldenhuys, *The Diplomacy of Isolation*, Ch. 4.
33. Ibid., p. 80.
34. For a detailed account of covert US activities in Angola, see John

Stockwell, *In Search of Enemies: A CIA Story* (New York: Norton, 1978).
35. Stockwell, *In Search of Enemies*, p. 208.
36. Ibid., p. 192.
37. See, for example, Mohammed A. El Khawas, 'South Africa and the Angolan Conflict', *African Affairs*, 77, 308 (1978), pp. 35–46.
38. Stockwell, *In Search of Enemies*, pp. 192–3.
39. Heimer, *The Decolonization Conflict*, p. 76, citing Gabriel Garçia Marquez, 'Operaçion Carlota', *Triunfo*, 30, 730/731 (1977).
40. Hallett, 'South African Intervention', p. 369.
41. Wolfers and Bergerol, *Angola*, p. 24.
42. Jaster, *Narrowing Security Options*, p. 24.
43. Stockwell, *In Search of Enemies*, p. 187. An SADF conscript who fought in Angola recalled later that this unit was issued uniforms and equipment with US markings, all of which was turned in before leaving Angola.
44. Hallett, 'South African Intervention', p. 375, citing reports in *The Sunday Times* and *Guardian*.
45. Stockwell, who would almost certainly have known of such a plan, makes no mention of it. Geldenhuys, *The Diplomacy of Isolation* (p. 77), in his interviews with South African officials, found 'no evidence' of such a plan.
46. Hallett, 'South African Intervention', p. 370. Also see Geldenhuys, *The Diplomacy of Isolation*, p. 77. Some analysts have speculated that South African forces were held back until after Angolan independence had been declared on 11 November, so as to keep their intervention secret and avoid compromising UNITA and the FNLA. (See, for example, Heimer, *The Decolonization Conflict*, p. 77.) Since the offensive was resumed within a few days, however, and SADF intervention with all its ramifications would eventually be known, this seems an unlikely reason to have held up the military offensive, particularly when Vorster must have been aware by then that MPLA defences would soon be reinforced by Cuban weapons and personnel.
47. Geldenhuys, *The Diplomacy of Isolation*, citing an official SADF press release. This figure is probably low, particularly given the SADF interest in minimizing the extent of its involvement. Other estimates range up to 6000 which, in view of the limited logistical support effort, seems too high.
48. Wolfers and Bergerol, *Angola*, p. 31.
49. Hallett, 'South African Intervention', p. 365.
50. Wolfers and Bergerol, *Angola*, pp. 30–1; and Heimer, *The Decolonization Conflict*, p. 78 (fn), citing Garcia Marquez.
51. Ibid., p. 79 (fn), Hallett, 'South African Intervention', p. 371. These numbers appear roughly consistent with the ship arrivals reported in Wolfers and Bergerol, *Angola*, pp. 25–31.
52. Private ex-SADF sources.
53. Ibid.
54. Wolfers and Bergerol, *Angola*, p. 43.
55. Hallett, 'South African Intervention', p. 379.
56. *Guardian*, 13 December 1975.

57. Hallett, 'South African Intervention', p. 373.
58. *Rand Daily Mail*, 25 December 1975.
59. Nicholas Ashford, *The Times* (London), 30 December 1975.
60. Hallett, 'South African Intervention', citing Savimbi's own account.
61. Wolfers and Bergerol, *Angola*, p. 44.
62. *Daily Telegraph*, 22 January 1976.
63. Cited in Wolfers and Bergerol, *Angola*, p. 58.
64. Hallett, 'South African Intervention', p. 384.
65. *House of Assembly Debates*, 3 February 1976, cols 851–3.
66. Robert S. Jaster, 'South African Defense Strategy and the Growing Influence of the Military', in William J. Foltz and Henry S. Bienen, *Arms and the African: Military Influences in Africa's International Relations* (New Haven, Ct: Yale University Press, 1985), p. 129.
67. Cited in Geldenhuys, *The Diplomacy of Isolation*, p. 93.
68. Ibid., p. 80.
69. Ibid., p. 79.
70. Ibid., p. 80.
71. Cited in Jaster, *Narrowing Security Options*, p. 25.
72. Private SADF source.
73. Stockwell, *In Search of Enemies*, pp. 188–90.
74. Ibid., p. 186.

6 Growing Militancy and Isolation under P.W. Botha since 1978

1. *P.W. Botha: A Political Backgrounder* (London: South African Embassy, 1978), pp. 2–4.
2. *Strategic Survey 1978* (London: IISS, 1979), p. 82.
3. Kenneth W. Grundy, *The Militarization of South African Politics* (Bloomington: Indiana University Press, 1986), pp. 42–3.
4. Robert S. Jaster, *South Africa in Namibia: The Botha Strategy* (Lanham, Md: University Press of America, and Center for International Affairs, Harvard University, 1985), p. 44.
5. *P.W. Botha*, p. 38.
6. Ibid., p. 40.
7. 'Statement by the Honourable the Prime Minister, Mr. P.W. Botha, to Parliament: 6 March 1979'. For a detailed discussion, see *Strategic Survey 1979* (London: IISS, Spring 1980), pp. 90–1.
8. *Address by the Hon. R.F. Botha to the Swiss–South African Association, 7 March 1979* (Berne: South African Embassy Bulletin 5/1979, 16 March 1979).
9. *The Star* (Johannesburg), 12 April 1979.
10. Private discussions with DFA and SADF officials.
11. *House of Assembly Debates*, 3 April 1979, col. 3919.
12. *Address by the Hon P.W. Botha, Prime Minister, Carlton Centre, Johannesburg: 22 November 1979* (Pretoria Department of Foreign Affairs and Information, 1979).
13. Eschel Rhoodie, *The Real Information Scandal* (Pretoria: Orbis, 1983), pp. 367–71.

Notes and References 189

14. Robert S. Jaster, *South Africa's Narrowing Security Options*, Adelphi Paper No. 159 (London: IISS, Spring 1980), p. 34.
15. Private interview.
16. Ibid.
17. William Branigen, *Washington Post*, 1 December 1979.
18. *Financial Times* (London), 1 December 1979.
19. Western intelligence sources.
20. Ibid.
21. Based on discussions with General Walls and other former Rhodesian officials.
22. Private discussion.
23. Rhoodie, *Information Scandal*, pp. 373–4.
24. Martyn Gregory, 'The 1980 Rhodesian Elections – A First-Hand Account and Analysis', *The World Today*, May 1980, p. 182.
25. Private discussion.
26. *Address by the Hon. P.W. Botha . . . at the Opening Ceremony of the Summit Meeting in Pretoria on 23 July 1980* (Pretoria Department of Foreign Affairs and Information, 1980).
27. For a detailed analysis of these activities, see Deon Geldenhuys, *The Constellation of Southern African States and the Southern African Development Co-ordination Council: Towards a New Regional Stalemate?* (Braamfontein: SAIIA, January 1981), pp. 5–15.
28. Ibid., p. 11.
29. *Address by the Hon. P.W. Botha . . . on the Occasion of a National Party Congress in Durban on 15 August 1979* (Department of Foreign Affairs and Information, 1979).
30. For a detailed analysis of the Twelve Points, see Deon Geldenhuys, *Some Foreign Policy Implications of South Africa's Total National Strategy* (Braamfontein: SAIIA, March 1981), pp. 10–46.
31. *Strategic Survey 1980–1981* (London: IISS, Spring 1981), p. 90.
32. *House of Assembly Debates*, 1 May 1980, col. 5298.
33. Ibid., 21 March 1980, cols 3316–24.
34. Ibid., 1 May 1980, col. 5294.
35. Ibid., 1 May 1980, col. 5296.
36. Geldenhuys, *Constellation of Southern African States*, p. 5.

7 Namibia Policy and the War in Angola

1. *House of Assembly Debates*, 23 April 1979, col. 4738.
2. *Strategic Survey 1979* (London: IISS, Spring 1980), p. 91.
3. 'South Africa's Secret War of Terror', *Guardian*, 29 January 1981; 'Defector Describes SA Raids into Angola', Jonathan Steele, *Guardian*, 2 February 1981; 'Mercenary Missions', Suzanne Cronje, *West Africa*, 9 March 1981; 'Angolan Blacks Join Fight against SWAPO', Stephen Glover, *Daily Telegraph*, 10 March 1981.
4. *Strategic Survey 1980–1981*, p. 90.
5. *Paratus* (official periodical of the SADF), January 1979; Caryle Murphy in *International Herald Tribune*, 25 April 1979; *The Times* (London), 9 February 1981.

6. *Namibia: the Constitutional Fraud*, Briefing Paper No. 2 (London: International Defence and Aid Fund, July 1981).
7. General Meiring, SWAT/F Commander at the time, quoted in *Paratus*, October 1985, p. 6.
8. General Meiring, cited in *The Star* (Johannesburg), 10 January 1987.
9. Ibid., and William Claiborne in *Washington Post*, 3 November 1987.
10. *New York Times*, 11 August 1981, and *The Times* (London), 17 February 1981.
11. Joseph Lelyveld in *New York Times*, 28 August and 14 September 1981; *South African Digest*, 18 September 1981.
12. *The Times* (London), 9 September 1981.
13. *Reuters*, Havana, 28 August 1982.
14. *Washington Post*, 28 July 1982.
15. Philip Frankel, *Pretoria's Praetorians: Civil–Military Relations in South Africa* (Cambridge: Cambridge University Press, 1984), p. 138.
16. *Washington Post*, 5 January 1984.
17. US diplomats in private discussion.
18. Ibid.
19. *Washington Times*, 8 February 1984; *Washington Post*, 17 February 1984.
20. Private conversation.
21. *Paratus*, August 1985, pp. 10–11.
22. Ibid., October 1985, p. 10.
23. For detailed analysis see Robert S. Jaster, *South Africa and Its Neighbours: The Dynamics of Regional Conflict*, Adelphi Paper No. 209 (IISS: London, Summer 1986), pp. 38–41.
24. *Strategic Survey 1986–1987* (London: IISS, Spring 1987), pp. 189–90, and *New York Times*, 17 November 1986.
25. Private discussion.
26. *Covert Action Information Bulletin*, No. 13 (Washington, DC: Covert Action Publications, July–August 1981), p. 38.
27. Private discussions in 1986 and 1987.
28. *Strategic Survey 1985–86* (London: IISS, Spring 1986), pp. 188–9, and private discussions with US diplomats.
29. *Guardian*, 2 October 1985.
30. Allister Sparks in *Washington Post*, 9 October 1985.
31. Private discussion.
32. *The Star* (Johannesburg), 11 November and 9 December 1985, citing interview in *Afrique-Asie*.
33. *Strategic Survey 1986–1987*, p. 189.
34. *The Star* (Johannesburg), 10 January 1987, citing General Meiring, SADF.
35. Lt.-Gen. D. J. Earp, Chief of the SAAF, 'The Role of Air Power in Southern Africa', in *ISSUP Review* (Pretoria: Institute for Strategic Studies, April 1986), p. 34.
36. *South African Digest*, 18 July 1986; Thomas L. Friedman, 'Israelis Reassess Supplying Arms to South Africa', *New York Times*, 29 January 1987.
37. *Financial Mail*, 14 March 1986; *The Star* (Johannesburg), 2 May 1987.
38. *Strategic Survey 1986–1987*, pp. 189–90.

Notes and References

39. *Guardian*, 24 February 1986; Allister Sparks in *Washington Post*, 3 September 1986.
40. David Ottaway and Patrick Tyler in *Washington Post*, 30 March 1986; Richard Hall in *Observer*, 6 April 1986.
41. *New York Times*, 14 November 1987; *The Star* (Johannesburg), 11 November 1987.
42. Ibid.
43. James Brooke in *New York Times*, 16 December 1987.
44. *The Star* (Johannesburg), 6 June 1987.
45. Ibid., 24 November 1987.
46. *Financial Times* (London), 21 July 1982, citing Lopo do Nascimento, Angolan Minister of Planning and External Trade.
47. Private discussion.
48. *Covert Action Information Bulletin*, p. 38.
49. Cited by Michael Clough in *African Index*, 30 June 1981, p. 39.
50. M. Hough, 'SWA/Namibia: Political Settlement or Mobile Warfare?' in *ISSUP Bulletin* (Pretoria: Institute for Strategic Studies, 5 October 1981).
51. Private conversation, 1981.
52. Clough, *African Index*, p. 39.
53. *Financial Times*, 3 February 1982; 'Botha Details Policy on SWA/Namibia' (Press Release, Embassy of South Africa, Washington, DC, 1984).
54. Wolfgang Thomas, 'Challenges of a Namibian Nationhood Strategy', paper presented to the Klein–Windhoek Branch of the Interessengemeinschaft on 3 June 1985, p. 3.
55. Bernard Nossiter, 'U.N. Puzzled by Reply on Namibia', *New York Times*, 13 May 1980.
56. Ibid.
57. For a detailed analysis of the political timing of SADF attacks, see Robert S. Jaster, *South Africa in Namibia: The Botha Strategy*, pp. 60–5.
58. *Financial Mail*, 3 August 1979.
59. Private discussion with South African officials.
60. William Johnson, 'Namibia', in R. Lemarchand (ed.), *American Policy in Southern Africa* (Lanham, MD: University Press of America, 1981), p. 205.
61. *Strategic Survey 1980–81*, pp. 90–1.
62. *The Times* (London), 14 and 15 November 1980.
63. Private discussion with South African officials.
64. Ian Guest in *Guardian*, 15 January 1981.
65. Joseph Lelyveld, 'Namibia Talks on Ceasefire Fail in Geneva', *International Herald Tribune*, 14 January 1981.
66. *The Citizen* (Johannesburg), 16 February 1982.
67. Bernard Simon in *Financial Times*, 15 September 1982; Joseph Lelyveld in *New York Times*, 25 September 1982.
68. Joseph Lelyveld in *New York Times*, 18 January 1983; *Strategic Survey 1983–84* (London: IISS, Spring 1984), p. 112.

69. Joseph Lelyveld in *New York Times*, 30 July 1983; Allister Sparks in *Washington Post*, 23 July 1983.
70. *Africa Confidential*, 11 April 1984.
71. Stanley Uys in *The Star* (Johannesburg), 4 February 1984.
72. Chester A. Crocker, 'South Africa: Strategy for Change', in *Foreign Affairs*, 59 (Winter 1980/1), p. 346.
73. *The Sunday Times* (London), 18 January 1981.
74. Jane Rosen in *Guardian*, 2 April 1981; Bernard Gwertzman in *New York Times*, 2 April 1981.
75. Eric Marsden in *The Times* (London), 15 April 1981.
76. *International Herald Tribune*, 17 May 1981.
77. *The Times* (London), 25 April 1981.
78. Leslie Gelb in *New York Times*, 2 June 1981.
79. Joseph Lelyveld, *New York Times*, 15 July 1987, and private discussion with US diplomats.
80. *International Herald Tribune*, 17 May 1981.
81. *Washington Post*, 3 November 1982.
82. Private discussions, 1986 and 1987.
83. *Rand Daily Mail*, 18 June 1982.
84. *New York Times*, 27 October 1982.
85. *New York Times*, 13 March 1984; *Washington Post*, 14 March 1984.
86. *Weekly Star* (Johannesburg), 28 May 1984; *Washington Post*, 18 May 1984; private talks with participants in the meeting.
87. *Christian Science Monitor*, 8 June 1984; *Weekly Star* (Johannesburg), 28 May 1984.
88. Cited in *Strategic Survey 1984–1985* (London: IISS, Spring 1985) p. 109.
89. *The Star* (Johannesburg), 5 September 1986.
90. Andre du Pisani, 'Namibia: A New Transitional Government', in *South Africa International* (Johannesburg: South Africa Foundation, October 1985); *Strategic Survey 1985–1986*, p. 190.
91. *Financial Mail*, 20 December 1985.
92. *The Star* (Johannesburg), 25 and 27 February 1987, and 1 August 1987.
93. Brendan Seery in *The Star* (Johannesburg) 15 November 1986, and John Battersby in *New York Times*, 29 June 1987.
94. One study, by Professor J.S. Malan, University of the North, cited in *The Star* (Johannesburg), 15 November 1986, showed that the MPC parties had less than 3 per cent support in Ovamboland, Namibia's important and most populous region, which lies along the Angolan border. A majority of those polled supported SWAPO.

8 Regional Destabilization

1. *The Military Balance 1986–1987* (London: IISS, Autumn 1986), pp. 117–18.
2. *The Star* (Johannesburg), 31 October 1983.
3. *Strategic Survey 1981–1982* (London: IISS, Spring 1982), p. 111.
4. *South African Digest*, 27 May 1983 and 21 October 1983; Joseph Lelyveld in *New York Times*, 9 December 1982.

5. Cited by Deon Geldenhuys, 'Crossing the Matola Threshold', in *South Africa International*, January 1983.
6. Alan Cowell in *New York Times*, 22 May 1986; Robin Drew in *The Star* (Johannesburg), 10 September 1984.
7. Deon Geldenhuys, *What Do We Think? A Survey of White Opinion on Foreign Policy Issues* (Braamfontein: SAIIA, November 1982).
8. Text of the Treaty of Friendship and Co-operation between the USSR and the People's Republic of Mozambique signed in Maputo on 31 March 1977 by President Nikolai Podgorny and President Samora Machel.
9. *Guardian*, 23 February 1981.
10. Patrick Laurence in *Guardian*, 2 February 1981, citing an interview in the Sunday *Rapport*.
11. Allister Sparks in *Washington Post*, 12 August 1983; *Rand Daily Mail*, 25 and 26 May 1983. On Swazi–South African land deal, see Joseph Lelyveld in *New York Times*, 17 July 1982.
12. See analysis of the Kabwe meeting by Tom Lodge in *South Africa International* (Johannesburg: South Africa Foundation, November 1985).
13. See *Strategic Survey 1985–1986* (London: IISS, Spring 1986), p. 191; Patrick Laurence in *Guardian*, 21 December 1985.
14. Paul Ellman in *Guardian*, 18 February 1986.
15. See Alan Cowell, *New York Times*, 20 and 21 May 1986; *South African Digest*, 23 May 1986; Pauline Baker, 'What's Behind Pretoria's Brazenness?', *Christian Science Monitor*, 3 June 1986.
16. Private discussion, 1987.
17. Private discussion, 1987.
18. John Battersby, *New York Times*, 26 April 1987.
19. Patrick Laurence, *Christian Science Monitor*, 18 August 1987; Jo-Ann Collinge, *The Star* (Johannesburg), 22 August 1987.
20. *Weekly Star* (Johannesburg), 6 April 1988.
21. Private discussion. Also see Rex Gibson in *The Sunday Times*, London, 30 November 1980, and *Washington Post*, 7 October 1982.
22. Sheila Rule in *New York Times*, 12 October 1987.
23. Private discussion.
24. Joseph Lelyveld, *New York Times*, 12 September 1981; Alan Cowell, *New York Times*, 27 January 1983, *New York Times*, 3 September 1983.
25. Allister Sparks, *Washington Post*, 13 April 1984.
26. See Glenn Frankel, 'S. Africa's Guerrillas', *Washington Post*, 8 October 1984.
27. Resistência Nacional de Moçambique (RNM), *Relatório Referente a Sessão do Trabalho de RNM e do Representativo do Governo Sul Africa Afonso Macacho Maresto Dhlakama*, 25 October 1980, cited by Allen Isaacman in 'The Escalating Conflict in Southern Africa: the Case of Mozambique', unpublished paper presented to IISS Regional Security Conference, Harare, June 1987.
28. See Robert S. Jaster, 'The Security Outlook in Mozambique', *Survival* (London: IISS, November/December 1985), pp. 258–9; Colin Legum, 'The MNR', *Africa Notes* (Washington, DC: CSIS, 15 July 1983).
29. Text of The Accord of Nkomati appears in *Paratus*, April 1984, p. 13.
30. Allister Sparks, *Washington Post*, 7 June 1984.

31. 'Mozambique: What's in it for us?', *The Economist*, 2 June 1984.
32. See *Africa Confidential*, 28 November 1984; 'More Arms After Nkomati', *The Star* (Johannesburg), 17 December 1984; Jaster, 'Security Outlook in Mozambique', pp. 260–1.
33. Joseph Hanlon, *Guardian*, 9 November 1984.
34. *Guardian*, 6 and 28 December 1984; *The Star* (Johannesburg), 17 December 1984.
35. *Cape Times*, 17 March 1985.
36. *Cape Argus*, 2 March 1985.
37. *1984 Diario/Desk Diary*, entry of 16 August 1984.
38. Alan Cowell, *New York Times*, 20 September 1985.
39. *Diario*, 10 September 1984 entry.
40. *Financial Mail*, 11 October 1985.
41. *The Times* (London), 11 March 1985.
42. *Financial Mail*, 4 October 1985.
43. Glenn Frankel, *Washington Post*, 15 May 1986.
44. *The Star* (Johannesburg), 22 November 1986; *New York Times*, 9 October 1986.
45. Godwin Matatu in *Observer*, 12 October 1986; *The Star* (Johannesburg), 15 November 1986, 22 November 1986 and 27 December 1986; *The Independent* (London), 11 October 1986; *Guardian*, 16 October 1986.
46. Karl Maier, *Christian Science Monitor*, 25 March 1987; *The Star* (Johannesburg), 28 February 1987.
47. John Battersby, *New York Times*, 7 August 1987.
48. *Financial Mail*, 9 December 1977.
49. John F. Burns, *New York Times*, 9 July 1980.
50. *Zimbabwe Herald*, 9 May 1981; *Sunday Mail* (Harare), 10 May 1981.
51. *South African Digest*, 11 September 1981; Caryle Murphy in *Washington Post*, 2 November 1981.
52. Private conversation.
53. Allister Sparks in *Washington Post*, 8 January 1982; *South African Digest*, 26 March 1982.
54. *New York Times*, 6 August 1986.
55. Alan Cowell, *New York Times*, 5 August 1986.
56. *The Star* (Johannesburg), 27 December 1986; *New York Times*, 2 January 1987.
57. David Beresford, *Guardian*, 21 January 1986; *Strategic Survey 1985–1986*, pp. 191–2.
58. *The Star* (Johannesburg), Africa News Service, 3 February 1987.
59. Eschel Rhoodie, *The Real Information Scandal* (Pretoria: Orbis, 1983), p. 863; editorial, *Die Vaderland*, 7 February 1983.
60. Joseph Lelyveld, *New York Times*, 5 January 1982.
61. Ibid., 10 May 1982.
62. Ibid., K. Grundy, *The Militarization of South African Politics* (Bloomington: Indiana University Press, 1986), pp. 100–1; Rhoodie, *Information Scandal*, p. 864.
63. Editorial of 7 February 1983.
64. Alan Cowell, *Washington Post*, 22 August 1987; *New York Times*, 27 August 1987.

65. *The Times* (London), 26 July 1982.
66. *New York Times*, 24 and 25 May 1987; private conversation with US diplomats.
67. J.J. van Wyk, *Elite Opinions on South African Foreign Policy*, Occasional Paper No. 1, Research Project on South Africa's Foreign Relations (Pretoria: Rand Afrikaans University, 1984), p. 28.
68. Under Secretary of State Michael Armacost, quoted in *Christian Science Monitor*, 22 December 1986.
69. Joseph Lelyveld, *New York Times*, 11 December 1982.
70. E. A. Wayne, *Christian Science Monitor*, 21 April 1988.

9 Foreign Policy Responses to the West

1. *Rand Daily Mail*, 2 January 1977.
2. *New York Times*, 31 August 1981.
3. Reed Kramer in *Boston Globe*, 28 February 1982.
4. Ibid., 16 March 1982.
5. Seymour Hersh in *New York Times*, 22 July 1986.
6. *Baltimore Sun*, 11 December 1984.
7. Leslie Gelb in *New York Times*, 2 August 1985.
8. Bernard Weinraub in *New York Times*, 29 June 1986, and Ned Temko in *Christian Science Monitor*, 22 December 1986.
9. *Mission to South Africa: The Commonwealth Report* (Harmondsworth: Penguin Books, 1986), p. 12.
10. Ibid., p. 141.
11. Geldenhuys, *The Diplomacy of Isolation*, p. 210.
12. Heribert Adam, 'Outside Influence on South Africa: Afrikanerdom in Disarray', *Journal of Modern African Studies*, 21, 2 (1983), p. 237.
13. Private discussion with senior US diplomats.
14. Private discussion.
15. Ibid.
16. Private discussion with senior US diplomats.
17. Alan Cowell in *New York Times*, 7 May 1986.
18. André du Toit, quoted by Allister Sparks in *Washington Post*, 17 August 1986.
19. *Mission to South Africa*, p. 111; Sparks, *Washington Post*, 17 August 1986.
20. Sheila Rule in *New York Times*, 24 August 1986.
21. Private discussion.
22. Durban speech of 12 August, extracted in *South African Digest*, 15 August 1986, p. 735.
23. Speech to National Party Congress in Orange Free State, reported in *The Citizen*, 3 September 1986.
24. *Pretoria News*, 7 March 1988.
25. Transcript of Arnaud de Borchgrave interview, *Washington Times*, 14 March 1988.
26. Sheila Rule in *New York Times*, 30 November 1986; *Business Day*, 14 May 1987.
27. *Financial Mail*, 15 November 1986; *Business Day*, 3 October 1987.

28. *South African Digest*, 3 October 1986; private discussion with South African bank official.
29. Ibid.
30. Jan Raath in *Observer*, 25 October 1987; John Battersby in *New York Times*, 1 November 1987.
31. Rita A. Houser, 'Israel, South Africa, and the West', *South Africa International*, 11, 2 (October 1980), p. 85.
32. Naomi Chazan, 'The Fallacies of Pragmatism: Israeli Foreign Policy towards South Africa', paper presented to a Symposium of the Afro-American Studies Program, University of Pennsylvania, Philadelphia, 25–27 March 1982, p. 16.
33. Neil A. Lewis in *New York Times*, 3 April 1987.
34. C. Coker, *South Africa's Security Dilemmas*, Washington Paper No. 126 (Washington, DC: CSIS 1987), p. 53.
35. Gary van Staden in *The Star* (Johannesburg), 29 November 1986.
36. Neil Lewis in *New York Times*, 3 April 1987.
37. Thomas L. Friedman in *New York Times*, 19 March 1987.
38. Based on private discussion with former Israeli official.
39. *South African Digest*, 15 February 1980.
40. Judith Miller in *New York Times*, 28 June 1982.
41. Private conversation.
42. John Battersby in *New York Times*, 22 November 1987.
43. *Directorate of Trade Statistics: Yearbook 1987* (Washington, DC: International Monetary Fund, 1987).
44. Michael Parks in *Los Angeles Times*, 18 March 1988.
45. *House of Assembly Debates*, 10 September 1974, col. 2629.
46. *South Africa 1986*, Official Yearbook of the RSA (Cape Town: CTP, 1987), p. 494.
47. *New York Times*, 6 October 1986.

10 Pretoria's Nuclear Diplomacy

1. Ronald Walters, 'Uranium Politics and U.S. Foreign Policy in Southern Africa', *Journal of Southern African Affairs*, July 1979, p. 94.
2. *Financial Mail*, 17 February 1978.
3. Richard Betts, 'A Diplomatic Bomb for South Africa?', *International Security*, 4, 4 (1979), p. 96.
4. Ibid.
5. Ibid., p. 92.
6. See Betts, 'A Diplomatic Bomb?', pp. 105–8; Robert S. Jaster, 'Politics and the "Afrikaner Bomb"', *Orbis*, No. 4, Winter 1984; Ronald W. Walters, 'U.S. Policy and Nuclear Proliferation in South Africa', in *U.S. Military Involvement in Southern Africa* (Boston, Ma: Western Massachusetts Association of Concerned Scholars, South End Press, 1978).
7. *South Africa's Plan and Capability in the Nuclear Field*, Report of the Secretary-General (UN Center for Disarmament, 1981) p. 30.
8. Quoted by James Adams, *The Unnatural Alliance* (New York, London: Quartet, 1984), p. 184.
9. Ibid., p. 185.

10. Ibid.
11. Leonard S. Spector, *The New Nuclear Nations* (New York: The Carnegie Endowment, Vintage Books, 1985), p. 217.
12. Ibid., p. 218. Also Adams, *Unnatural Alliance*, p. 181, citing UN Disarmament Agency Report.
13. Leonard S. Spector, *Going Nuclear* (Cambridge, MA: Ballinger Books, 1987), p. 221.
14. *Beeld*, 24 August 1977.
15. *Financial Times*, 27 and 29 June 1978.
16. Betts, 'A Diplomatic Bomb?', p. 107.
17. See in particular Ronald Walters, 'The September 22, 1979 Mystery Flash: Did South Africa Detonate a Nuclear Bomb?' (Washington, DC: The Washington Office on Africa, 21 May 1985); Eliot Marshall, 'Flash not Missed by Vela still Veiled in Mist', *Science*, 30 November 1979; Adams, *Unnatural Alliance*, Ch. 10.
18. Thomas O'Toole, *Washington Post*, 1 January 1980.
19. Ibid., 14 November 1979.
20. Thomas O'Toole, *Guardian*, 31 January 1980; Adams, *Unnatural Alliance*, pp. 187–8.
21. Eliot Marshall 'Navy Lab Concludes the Vela Saw a Bomb' in *Science*, 29 August 1980, p. 997.
22. *Boston Globe*, 9 December 1984.
23. John F. Burns, *Washington Post*, 30 April 1977.
24. From private discussion. Also see Spector, *Going Nuclear*, pp. 218–19.
25. Jeff Nesmith in Cox News Service release, 5 January 1983.
26. *U.S. Export Policy with Respect to South Africa*, Hearings, Sub-committee on Africa and Sub-committee on International Economic Policy and Trade, Committee on Foreign Affairs, US House of Representatives, US Gov't Printing Office, 2 December 1982.
27. *The Development of South Africa's Nuclear Capability* (New York: UN General Assembly, Special Committee Against Apartheid, 25 October 1983), p. 12.
28. Allister Sparks in *Washington Post*, 10 February 1984.
29. Walter Pincus in *Washington Post*, 1 October 1986.
30. Private discussion.
31. *New York Times*, 22 and 26 September 1987.
32. See interview with Z. De Beers, head of South Africa's Atomic Energy Corporation, in *Business Day*, 12 July 1985, p. 4.
33. See Jaster, 'Politics and the "Afrikaner Bomb"', pp. 157–64.
34. Private conversation.
35. See Robert Jaster, *South Africa and its Neighbours: The Dynamics of Regional Conflict*, Adelphi Paper No. 209 (London: IISS, 1986), pp. 18–20.
36. Kenneth Adelman and Richard Knight, 'Can South Africa Go Nuclear?', *Orbis*, 3 (Fall 1979), pp. 642–3.
37. Quoted in *South African Digest*, 24 October 1980.
38. Michele A. Flournoy, 'The South African Nuclear Threat: A New Variable', in *South Africa in Crisis: Regional and International Responses*, Report No. 28 (New York: International Peace Academy, 1988).

Index

AEC (Atomic Energy Corporation) 167
Afrikaner
  character 3–7
  national identity 8
  nationalism 4
Aktur 108–9
Alvor Accord 69
ANC (African National Congress) 31, 37, 44, 46, 86, 90, 149, 169, 173
  domestic support for 173
  'people's war' 121–2
  relations with sanctuary states 119, 121, 127, 135, 138
  relations with West 145, 146
  sabotage campaign 119, 121–2
  SADF war against 119–24
Anglo-American Corporation 87
Anglo-American proposals *see* Rhodesia
Angola
  and ANC 119
  Cabinda raid 39–40
  Cuban involvement 55, 71, 73, 77, 95, 100–1, 113–14, 115, 117
  declared people's republic (MPLA) 72
  growing conventional warfare 94–101, 102, 178
  guerrilla attacks 45, 69
  peace initiatives 96, 103–4, 152–3
  RSA raid against SWAPO (1978) 80
  SADF attacks (1981–2) 95
  SADF invasion (1975) 11, 22, 27, 35, 68–78
  Soviet military support 94, 96, 99–100
  UNITA insurgency 95, 98–101, 102, 103
  see also Lusaka Accord; Namibia; SADF; SWAPO; SWAT/F; UNITA, US
apartheid, impact on foreign policy 21, 40, 42–4, 46–7, 48, 145, 149, 174, 176
armed forces *see* SADF
arms embargo *see* sanctions
ARMSCOR *see* arms production and procurement
arms production and procurement 47–8, 155–6

Bantustans 61
  and BLS states 10–11, 44
  defence role 69
  government policy towards 10–11, 43, 69
  see also homelands
Bell, Fred 149
black African states 44, 46
  diplomatic and political links to South Africa 26, 46–8, 52–5, 151
  economic relations with South Africa 153–4
  nationalism 44–5
  security pacts with South Africa *see* Nkomati Accord; Swaziland
  see also ANC; BLS states; destabilization policy; Front Line states; *individual African states*; railway diplomacy
BLS states 10–11, 44, 46, 82, 84, 153
  see also ANC; black African states; Botswana; destabilization; Lesotho; railway diplomacy; Swaziland
Boer republics, independent 4
BOSS (Bureau of State Security) 25–6, 34, 35

Index

Botha, Pieter W.
  conflicting objectives, Namibia 118
  'constellation' proposal 11, 30, 151
  defence minister 27, 29, 41, 70, 75, 78, 80, 160
  domestic race reforms 90, 115, 174, 175, 176, 179–80
  election to premier 67
  leadership style 24, 28–31
  prime minister 28–31, 79–81
  relationship with West 30, 81, 89, 114, 143, 147–8, 151–2
  security management system 29, 39
  state president 22, 24, 37, 39
  Twelve-Point Plan 89, 90
  see also destabilization policy
Botha, Roelof ('Pik')
  Ambassador to US 76
  and Contact Group 64
  constellation proposal 82, 86, 88–9
  foreign minister, 1977– 32, 84, 104, 113, 149
  Nkomati Accord 129–30
Botswana 52, 119, 122, 123
  see also ANC; BLS states; destabilization; Front Line states
Broederbond 55
  see also Viljoen, Gerrit
Buthelezi, Gatsha 180

Cabinda raid 138
Calueque Dam, guerrilla attacks 70
Carrington, Lord 86, 87
Carter, (Jimmy) Administration 14, 57, 58, 107, 161, 162, 165, 171
Chona, Mark 53
CIA (Central Intelligence Agency) 71, 72, 76
Clark, William 113
Commonwealth 123, 145–6
  EPG (Eminent Persons Group) 123, 145, 149
Conservative Party (South Africa) 22, 115, 175

constellation of states 11–12, 82–4, 88–9, 151
constitution of 1983 22
constructive engagement 145
  see also US
Contact Group *see* Namibia
Crocker, Chester 112, 114, 134
Cuban involvement in Angola *see* Angola

Democratic Turnhalle Alliance *see* DTA
destabilization policy 12, 31, 119–40, 176–7
détente 11, 27, 51, 52–5, 68
DFA (Department of Foreign Affairs) 27
  diminishing policy role 31–2, 35, 76, 80–1
  policy conflicts with the military 128–31
  see also Information Department; Botha, Roelof (Pik); Louw, Eric
DMI (Directorate of Military Intelligence–SADF) 126
DMZ (Demilitarized Zone, Namibia–Angola) 107
domestic unrest (South Africa) 43, 44, 55, 121, 144, 173–5
dos Santos, José Eduardo 95
DTA (Democratic Turnhalle Alliance) 84, 92, 108–10

ECA (Economic Commission for Africa) 43
Eglin, Colin 22
ELP (Portuguese Liberation Army) 70
EPG (Eminent Persons Group) *see* Commonwealth

FAO (Food & Agriculture Organization) 43
FAPLA (Forças Armadas Populares de Libertação de Angola) 97–8, 99

FNLA (Frente Nacional para a
  Libertação de Angola) 70–1,
  75, 76, 77, 93
Ford (Gerald) Administration 55,
  77
Fourie, Brand 76
Francophone states 46, 71
FRELIMO (Frente de Libertação de
  Moçambique) *see*
  Mozambique
Front Line states 81, 83, 85, 95,
  114, 131
  diplomatic initiatives 52–4, 56–7,
    134–5
  military intervention *see*
    Mozambique
  relations with South Africa *see*
    ANC; destabilization policy;
    individual Front Line states
    (Angola, Botswana,
    Mozambique, Tanzania,
    Zambia, Zimbabwe)

Gorbachev, Mikhail 152
Graaff, Sir De Villiers 22
Graham, Ambassador John,
  Proposals for a Settlement 57
Great Britain 4, 9–10, 13

Haig, Alexander 112, 144, 166–7
HNP (Herstigte Nasionale Party)
  23, 46, 90, 120
Hoare, Colonel 'Mad' Mike 136–7
'homelands' 82, 88, 153
  see also Bantustans

IAEA (International Atomic Energy
  Agency) 164, 167, 168, 171
ILO (International Labour
  Organization) 43
Information Department
  covert activities 32–4, 148–9
  Muldergate affair 25, 32–4
intelligence services *see* BOSS;
  DMI; NIS
Israel 85, 154–6, 157, 165–6

JMC (Joint Monitoring
  Commission) 97

  see also Angola; SADF
Joint Management Centres 38–9
  see also SSC
Jonathan, Leabua 125, 126, 135

Kalahari incident *see* South African
  nuclear programme
Kalangula, Peter 110
Kaunda, Kenneth 11, 26, 31, 52,
  71, 116
Lusaka Manifesto 46–7
Koeberg nuclear power station 160,
  164, 167
  see also South African nuclear
    programme
Kissinger, Henry 55, 56–7

Lancaster House conference 86, 87
Lekhanya, General Metsing 135
Lesotho 119, 121, 122, 124, 125,
  135
  Highland Water Project 153
  see also ANC; BLS states;
    destabilization policy;
    railway diplomacy
LLF (Lesotho Liberation Front)
  125–6
Lloyd, General Charles 38, 94
Lonrho 26–7
Louw, Eric 9
Low, Ambassador Steven, *Proposals
  for a Settlement* 57
Lusaka Accord 96–8
Lusaka Manifesto 46–7

Machel, Samora 51, 120, 132
  Nkomati Accord 127
Malan, D.F. 104
  African defence organization
    proposed 12–13
  Prime Minister 10
Malan, Magnus
  Defence Minister 35, 75, 94, 152,
    177
  SADF chief 35, 64
Malawi 11, 26, 46, 82, 131
Mandela, Nelson 149
Marquand De Villiers, Dr J.T.
  (Lohnro) 26–7

Index

Middle East Defence Organization 13
MIS (Military Intelligence Section) 26, 35
MNR (Mozambican National Resistance, or Renamo) *see* Mozambique
Mobutu, Joseph 71
Mozambique
  and ANC 119, 121, 124
  FRELIMO government 11, 45, 126
  Front Line military support 131, 178
  MNR insurgency 121, 124–32, 140
  Nkomati Accord 127–32
  relations with South Africa 30–1, 39, 119, 120, 121, 126–32
  Soviet support 120
  Western policies toward 139, 140, 178
  see also destabilization; Front Line states; SADCC
MPC (Multi-Party Conference) 111, 116, 118
MPLA (Movimento Popular de Libertação de Angola) 69, 70–1, 72, 76, 77, 103, 152
Mudge, Dirk 109, 110, 111
Mugabe, Robert 87–8, 124, 125, 133, 137–8, 143
Mulder, Connie 32
Muldergate 27, 33–4
Muzorewa, Bishop Abel 54, 84, 85, 86, 87, 124

Namibia
  and constellation initiative 12, 82, 84, 88
  constitutional conference, 1975 51
  Contact Group 62, 63–4, 65, 66–7, 81, 114, 115
  DTA 84
  internal politics 92, 108–11, 116–18
  peace initiatives 62–6, 107, 108, 112–15, 116–18, 180
  relations with West 143, 152
  South African policy 28, 59–68, 80–1, 92–3, 104–8, 115–18
  SWAPO insurgency 59–60, 65, 69, 90, 92–5, 101–2, 103, 139
  Turnhalle Conference 61–3
  UN settlement plan 62–5, 66, 109–10
  see also SADF; SWAPO; SWAT/F; US
National Intelligence Service (NIS) 36, 37, 144
National Party (NP)
  constituency 20
  role in foreign policy 20–4
  split over race reform 115, 118, 175
  white politics as policy constraint 175–6
national security management system 35–41
NATO (North Atlantic Treaty Organization) 8, 9, 12, 14, 74
Nel, Louis 129
Neto, Agostinho 73
Nigeria 73
NIS *see* National Intelligence Service
Nkomati Accord *see* Mozambique
Nkomo, Joshua 54, 55, 87
  ZIPRA guerrillas 52
NP *see* National Party
NPT (Nuclear Non-Proliferation Treaty) 163, 167, 168, 171
nuclear diplomacy *see* South African nuclear programme
Nyerere, Julius 47, 58

OAU 11, 46, 74, 77, 120
Outward Policy 11, 46–7
Ovambo people 60, 69, 92
  101 Battalion protest 102
Owen, David 57

PFP (Progressive Federal Party) 23
Philipp, Major-General Hannes 64–5
Portuguese authorities, Angola 69, 70, 72
  see also Angola

Pretoria Declaration 128
public opinion polls 20, 120, 139

race reform see Botha, P.W.
railway diplomacy 132–5, 148
  see also Lesotho; Mozambique; Zambia; Zimbabwe
Reagan (Ronald) Administration 14, 40, 96, 107, 111–15, 120–1
  and the destabilization policy 134, 135, 139–40, 147–8
  and Namibia negotiations 112–15, 117
  see also constructive engagement, US
Renamo 131, 178, 179
  see also Mozambique
Rhodesia
  Anglo-American proposals 57
  Botha's support for Muzorewa 85–7
  and constellation initiative 82
  issue in South African politics 85
  Kissinger initiative 55–7
  Lancaster House talks 85–7
  South African diplomacy 28, 52–7, 58–9
  South African military intervention 52–3, 86–7
  see also Zimbabwe
Rhoodie, Eschel 32–3, 40
Roberto, Holden 71, 93
Rowland, Roland ('Tiny') 26

SABC (South African Broadcasting Corporation) 20, 134, 140
SACP (South African Communist Party) 5
SADB (Southern African Development Bank) 88, 153
SADCC (Southern African Development Coordination Conference) 83
SADF (South African Defence Force)
  Angolan intervention (1975–6) 31, 35, 68ff
  budget squeeze, 1987–8 102, 105
  bureaucratic rivalry and conflicts 33–4, 35, 129–31
  and destabilization 119–24, 125, 135, 176–7
  escalating war with Angola 94, 99–101, 102–3, 177
  influence on foeign policy 37–41, 65-6, 70, 75, 80–1, 104–5, 129–31, 176–7
  misadventures 39–40, 135–8
  non-white troops 93–4, 102–3
  and Renamo 124–32
  Rhodeisian involvement 52, 86–7
  strategic thinking 104–5
  and SWAPO insurgency 93–7, 101–2
  worst-case scenario 169–70
  see also destabilization; DMI; security threat; SWAPO; SWAT/F; UNITA
sanctions 134–5, 145, 173, 178, 180
  arms embargo 48, 143, 155–6
  South African responses 149–50, 156–7
  and Western policy 143, 144–5
sanctuary states 119, 121
  see also Front Line states
Savimbi, Jonas 71, 72
  and UNITA 98–101, 113, 179
Seychelles, coup attempt 39, 136–7
Sharpeville incident 43
Shultz, George 131
Silvermine 14
Simonstown Accord 13
Sithole, Edson 54
Smith, Ian 51, 52, 54, 55–7, 58–9, 86, 126
  see also Rhodesia
South African nuclear programme
  commercial development 160
  diplomacy 159–72
  Kalahari incident 161–4
  military potential 160–1, 166, 168–71
  nuclear relations with the West 159, 160, 161–4, 165, 166–8, 171–2
  Vela incident 164–6

SSC (State Security Council) 29
  foreign policy role 35–8
  members 36, 38
  military influence 37–9, 135–6
Steyn, Judge M.T. 63, 109
Stockwell, John 71, 76
SWANU (South West Africa
    National Union) 111
SWAPO (South West Africa
    People's Organization) 61, 62,
    69, 90, 169, 179, 180, 181
  Botha's hardline diplomacy 104–
    8
  Contact Group proposals 63–4,
    65, 66–7, 81
  Lusaka meeting (1984) 116–17
  insurgency 59–60, 90, 92, 94
  refusal to join MPC 111
  see also Namibia
SWAT/F (South West African
    Territorial Force) 94
  see also Namibia; SADF
Swaziland
  and ANC 119, 121, 124
  secret pact with South Africa 121
  see also BLS states

Taiwan 154, 156
Tanzania 131
32 Battalion 93
  see also SADF
Toivo ja Toivo, Herman 116
total national strategy 29, 91, 102,
    168
  and total onslaught 6, 29, 61,
    89–90, 91, 102, 108, 168
total onslaught see total national
    strategy
Transkei 43, 82, 88
Treurnicht, Andries 22, 90, 115
Turnhalle Conference 61, 62, 63
  see also Namibia
Twelve-Point Plan 89, 90
  see also total national strategy

UANC (United African National
    Council) 85
Umkhonto we Sizwe (Spear of the
    Nation) 44

UN (United Nations) 11, 106–7,
    108
  on Namibia 59–60, 80
  on race policies 42
  see also sanctions, arms embargo;
    UNSC
UNITA (Uniao Nacional par a
    Independência Total de
    Angola) 70–1, 75, 76, 77, 95,
    113, 124
  and South African military
    intervention 98–101, 102-3,
    178, 179, 180, 181
  US military aid 101, 103
UNSC (United Nations Security
    Council)
  arms embargo 13, 143
  and Namibia 60–1, 62, 143
  Resolution 435 106–7, 111, 112,
    113, 114, 116, 152
  vote to condemn RSA 96
UNTAG (United Nations Transitory
    Advisory Group) 64
US (United States) 117, 179
  Angolan policy 72, 73–4, 76–7,
    100, 103
  cease-fire proposal 96
  Clark Amendment 74–5
  and Front Line states 122, 123,
    127, 132, 134
  Israel selling arms to South
    Africa 155
  Namibia negotiations 62–5, 112–
    15, 116
  nuclear relations see South
    African nuclear programme
  Rhodesia settlement see
    Rhodesia
  sanctions 145, 150
  worsening relations with South
    Africa 81, 139, 140,
    143–5
  see also sanctions; Reagan
USSR (Union of Soviet Socialist
    Republics)
  Angolan involvement 71, 74, 77,
    96, 100, 181
  peace overtures 152
  treaty with Mozambique 120

Valindaba 163, 164, 166
  see also South African nuclear
    programme
van den Bergh, General Hendrik
  26, 34, 35, 75, 80
van der Westhuizen, General P.W.
  110
van Niekerk, Dr Willie 116
Vaz diaries 128–9
Vela incident 164–6
verligte (enlightened) 28, 34
Verwoerd, H.F. 43–4, 45, 46, 160
  Prime Minister (and BLS states)
    10–11
Victoria Falls Conference 54
Viljoen, General C.L. 129, 130
Viljoen, Gerrit 109
Vorster, B.J.
  Angola invasion 22, 68, 75–8
  and BLS states 11
  concessions 147
  détente initiative 11, 30, 68
  leadership style 24–8, 132–3
  Lusaka Manifesto 47
  meeting with Kissinger 55–6
  Muldergate 27, 33, 34–5
  re nuclear capability 161–2, 163–4, 171
  relations with West 58, 143
  Turnhalle Conference 61
  see also *détente*; Outward Policy

Waldheim, Kurt 66, 81
Western powers
  arms embargo *see* sanctions
  importance to South Africa 8–9,
    47, 157–8, 182
  Namibia diplomacy *see* Namibia
  nuclear relations with South
    Africa *see* South African
    nuclear programme
  repudiation by South Africa 150–3, 157
  in South African defence strategy
    8–9, 12–15
  see also Rhodesia; sanctions;
    individual states
white supremacy in Trekboer
  society 4
WHO (World Health
  Organization) 43

Zaire 71
Zambia 26, 52
  and ANC 121, 123, 124
  ZIPRA guerrillas *see* Nkomo
  see also *détente*; Front Line States;
    Kaunda
ZANLA (Zimbabwe African
  National Liberation Army) 45
Zimbabwe 84, 137
  and ANC 119, 122, 124, 125,
    133–4
  détente with South Africa 154
  economic pressures 133–5, 148
  independence, 1980 125, 133
  see also destabilization; Front Line
    states; railway diplomacy
ZIPRA (Zimbabwe People's
  Revolutionary Army) 52

LIBRARY OF DAVIDSON COLLEGE

Books on regular loan may be checked out for four weeks. Books must be presented at the Circulation Desk in order to be renewed.

A fine is charged after date due.

Special books are subject to special regulations at the discretion of the library staff.